Lev Vygotsky

The contemporary debate in psychology and politics over the possibilities for human development has fueled a renewed interest in the early Soviet psychologist Lev Vygotsky. In *Lev Vygotsky: Revolutionary Scientist*, Fred Newman and Lois Holzman argue that Vygotsky was a revolutionary who used – and advanced – Marx's method to make extraordinary discoveries about the nature of learning, development, thinking, speaking and playing.

In this provocative and accessible introduction to Vygotsky and current Vygotskian research, the authors draw upon their own fifteen years' work in creating Vygotsky-inspired therapeutic, educational and cultural environments. That work has produced the discovery that revolutionary activity, typical of early childhood, is the fundamental human characteristic. When revolutionary activity is arrested, not only do development and progress stop, but eventually even adaptation to society becomes impossible.

Lev Vygotsky: Revolutionary Scientist is intended for undergraduate as well as advanced students in psychology, linguistics, education and philosophy.

Fred Newman, who trained in the philosophy of science, teaches at the East Side Institute for Short Term Psychotherapy in New York. **Lois Holzman**, a developmental psychologist, also teaches at the East Side Institute for Short Term Psychotherapy, and at Empire State College, New York.

Critical Psychology
Series editors
John Broughton
Columbia University
David Ingleby
Vakgroep Ontwikkeling en Socialisatie, Utrecht
Valerie Walkerdine
University of Central England at Birmingham

Since the 1960s there has been widespread disaffection with traditional approaches in psychology, and talk of a 'crisis' has been endemic. At the same time, psychology has encountered influential contemporary movements such as feminism, neo-marxism, post-structuralism and post-modernism. In this climate, various forms of 'critical psychology' have developed vigorously.

Unfortunately, such work – drawing as it does on unfamiliar intellectual traditions – is often difficult to assimilate. The aim of the Critical Psychology series is to make this exciting new body of work readily accessible to students and teachers of psychology, as well as presenting the more psychological aspects of this work to a wider social scientific audience. Specially commissioned works from leading critical writers will demonstrate the relevance of their new approaches to a wide range of current social issues.

Lev Vygotsky

Revolutionary scientist

**Fred Newman and
Lois Holzman**

First published in 1993
by Routledge
11 New Fetter Lane, London EC4P 4EE

Simultaneously published in the USA and Canada
by Routledge
29 West 35th Street, New York, NY 10001

Reprinted 1995

Reprinted 2002
by Routledge
27 Church Road, Hove, East Sussex BN3 2FA
29 West 35th Street, New York, NY 10001

Routledge is an imprint of the Taylor & Francis Group

© 1993 Fred Newman and Lois Holzman

Typeset in Palatino by Michael Mepham, Frome, Somerset
Printed and bound in Great Britain by
TJ International Ltd, Padstow, Cornwall

British Library Cataloguing in Publication Data
A catalogue record for this book is available from the
British Library.

Library of Congress Cataloging in Publication Data
Newman, Fred.
     Lev Vygotsky : revolutionary scientist /
     Fred Newman and Lois Holzman.
     p.   cm. – (Critical psychology)
     Includes bibliographical references and index.
     1. Vygotskii, L. S. (Lev Semenovich), 1896–1934.
     2. Psychologists—Soviet Union—History.
     I. Holzman, Lois, 1946– . II. Title. III. Series.
     BF109.V95N49   1993
     150´.92–dc20   92–28810
                                   CIP

ISBN 0–415–06441–4
     0–415–06442–2 (pbk)

If no painting comes to be *the* painting, if no work is ever absolutely completed and done with, still each creation changes, alters, enlightens, deepens, confirms, exalts, recreates, or creates in advance all the others. If creations are not a possession, it is not only that, like all things, they pass away; it is also that they have almost their whole life before them.

Maurice Merleau-Ponty

He not busy being born is busy dying.

Bob Dylan

For Barbara Taylor, a life-long teacher, with the hope that our work will be of value to those who devote their energies to teaching our children.

Contents

Acknowledgements

Thanks to Valerie Walkerdine for giving us the opportunity to write this book, which means for being a colleague – one guided by a shared social vision to build a working relationship marked by intellectual honesty, respect and trust. A distinguished scholar, Valerie has been a colleague and friend for over a decade. Her respect and enthusiasm for our work have meant a lot to us. We greatly appreciate her encouragement and editorial savvy through every stage of this endeavor.

We feel especially fortunate to have had not one but three editors. They were a great team – their intellectual challenges, practical and scholarly advice, and supportive colleagiality were invaluable. Individually, too, they contributed a great deal to this book. Thanks to John Broughton for sticking to his role of curmudgeon on points of style, order and clarity and for pointing out our gaps in presenting psychology's history as a science and ideology. David Ingleby's critical comments led us to clarify and deepen our discussion of the philosophical foundations of Vygotsky's work. For this and for encouraging us to present clearly the significance of our own practice as a Vygotskian zone of proximal development we are grateful. Final responsibility for the ideas presented in this book remains, of course, with the authors.

Thanks also to three dear and wordly-wise friends – Phyllis Goldberg and Dan Friedman, whose research and editorial assistance often times 'completed our thoughts,' and Kate Henselmans, who made certain the manuscript was complete and in order; to the rest of our colleagues and co-workers at the East Side Center for Social Therapy, the East Side Institute for Short Term Psychotherapy, the Castillo Cultural Center and the Barbara Taylor School, for the wonderfully creative and progressive things they make, including the developmental environment which made it possible for us to write this book and to have something to say; and to Empire State College, for its support and for the enthusiastic and serious desire of so many Empire students to learn about Vygotsky.

Introduction

Two years ago, when we first sat down to talk about how we wanted to write a book introducing Lev Vygotsky to college and university students, we faced both an exciting challenge and a dilemma. Writing 'about' Vygotsky, we felt, would be in violation of his life and work, insofar as we understood it. Like the brilliant twentieth-century philosopher Ludwig Wittgenstein, whom he never met but with whom he had much in common (philosophically and methodologically, if not politically), Vygotsky railed against the 'aboutness' that permeated both the form and content of the Western scientific, social-scientific and philosophical traditions they both inherited. Their legacy was a methodology which was dualistic and categorical. For example, it separated 'the world' from 'knowledge about the world' (with 'knowledge about the world' consisting of explanations, descriptions and interpretations); it understood meaning to be essentially 'about' or 'naming' mental objects. No. We did not wish to write about Vygotsky. But what was our alternative to be? How could we present to you Lev Vygotsky – the revolutionary scientist?

When the Vygotsky revival began in the late 1970s, a favorite quotation from his previously unpublished writings was the following:

> I don't want to discover the nature of mind by patching together a lot of quotations. I want to find out how science has to be built, to approach the study of mind having learned the whole of Marx's *method*.

> (Vygotsky, 1978, p. 8)

Similarly, we did not want simply to patch together a lot of quotations from Vygotsky (or rewrites of quotations) – this, we felt, would deny the Vygotskian method.

It is clear to his followers and detractors alike that Vygotsky's 'learning the whole of Marx's *method*' was not done in some library. It couldn't have been; as Vygotsky's biographers Kozulin, Levitan and others make plain, the beginnings of the first socialist state brought enormous practical tasks which Vygotsky and his contemporaries responded to fervently. No, Vygotsky's brilliance as a thinker stemmed from his revolutionary activity – using/ reorganizing whatever there was available: Russian semiotics, linguistics and culture; German philosophy; European and American pedagogy and psychology; Marx and Engels; the intellectual, political, economic and cultural conflicts and contradictions of the new socialist state – to make something entirely new, a (search for) method for the building of a truly human science, one based in Marx's non-dualistic, non-interpretive, anti-about methodology. We wanted to use Marx's and Vygotsky's method.

Later in the passage from which we just quoted, Vygotsky wrote, 'It is necessary to formulate the categories and concepts that are specifically relevant [to the given area of phenomena] – in other words, to create one's own *Capital*.' In writing this book we too sought to create our own *Capital*. In this case (we are eager to say this before our critics do!), what we created was our own Vygotsky. 'Our Vygotsky' is plainly American while distinctly internationalist (he is a Marxist), revolutionary, activistic, developmental, clinical and philosophical. In saying this, we do not wish to be sectarian or chauvinist, only that 'our Vygotsky' grows out of who we are and what we have done.

One of us (Fred Newman) was trained in methodology, philosophy of language, philosophy of history and philosophy of science, where foundational issues such as the nature of the relationship between epistemology and ontology, the history of Western thought and thought about thought, and paradigmism – issues shunned, for the most part, by psychology – are basic. During the mid–1970s, Newman turned to clinical psychology, incorporating critiques of traditional psychotherapy made by the radical therapy and anti-psychiatry movements (e.g. Deleuze and Guattari, 1977; Laing, 1983; and Szasz, 1961) and the methodological concerns of Western philosophy and Marxism, to found the Marxist approach called social therapy.

The other of us (Lois Holzman) was trained as a developmental psychologist and psycholinguist. During the 1970s she was engaged in research that addressed methodological issues, first in the pioneering language acquisition research of Lois Bloom (1970; 1973) at Columbia University and later with Michael Cole at Rockefeller University in the search for an 'ecologically valid' psychology (Cole, Hood and McDermott, 1978). At the Cole lab Holzman began a serious study of Vygotsky that has continued ever since, with a focus on language and cognition, and learning and development. Her collaboration with Newman, which began fifteen years ago, led her to engage the philosophical and ideological underpinnings of psychology and the limitations inherent in efforts to reform traditional psychology.

This book is one of the fruits of our years of collaboration. We have learned from and influenced each other, yet our different ways of seeing have never been lost; indeed, we believe the book is better for them. While you will, no doubt, hear our different voices at times, we hope what prevails is a passable synthesis of psychologist and methodologist.

'Our Vygotsky' is, to use Vygotsky's important psychological-methodological discovery, the tool-and-result of a quite specific practice – the production and distribution of social therapy, a Marxist psychology and the educational and clinical institutions where it can be practiced and developed – which engages the super-alienation, and accompanying emotional pain and cognitive deprivation, of being socialized in the United States of America in the late twentieth century. Our fifteen-year collaboration has been a joint activity with the community in which we work, where our theoretical understanding of what a human science has to be is continuously advanced by the very practical activity of creating environments that make the reinitiation of development possible. As social therapy (the practice) develops (and grows in success and recognition), we gain new-found appreciation for Vygotsky's brilliance and creativity as a revolutionary scientist. We read him with new eyes; we see things we didn't see before. Our understanding of both his methodological breakthroughs and psychological insights about development, learning, language, thought, concept formation, play, etc., is the product of the community, movement, clinical and educational psychology we practice; it constantly evolves. As we continue to create our Vygotsky, to reinitiate community and personal development, social therapy becomes more and more Vygotskian, even as Lev Vygotsky is brought into social therapy. For there is no reason for anyone or anything to stop developing – even after what society calls death.

Chapter 1

Vygotsky and psychology
A debate within a debate

By all accounts, Lev Vygotsky was a brilliant and charismatic thinker, speaker, mentor and builder. He is credited by some with breaking through the stalemate in the debates within Russian and European academic circles about what was the proper object of psychological study, thus influencing the historical course of psychology as a human science from the 1920s up to the present and, in the process, giving birth to what can be properly identified as a Soviet psychology.[1]

Born in 1896 (the same year as Jean Piaget), as an adolescent Vygotsky was passionately interested in philosophy, literature and culture. He was a brilliant student who, as a Jew in anti-Semitic czarist Russia, was limited in the fields of study and professions open to him. Nevertheless, he managed to complete a law degree, write a dissertation on the psychology of art, teach and publish literary works before turning his attention and creativity to fundamental questions of human development and learning.

Although he contracted tuberculosis at the age of 24 and was sickly throughout his short life of thirty-seven years, Vygotsky became the leading Marxist theoretician among the post-revolutionary Soviet psychologists. He formulated one of his primary concerns in this way: 'What new forms of activity were responsible for establishing labor as the fundamental means of relating humans to nature and what are the psychological consequences of these forms of activity?' (1978, p. 19). Even passing familiarity with traditional developmental psychology texts is enough for this question to strike the reader as radical: Vygotsky is talking about activity, not behavior or personality or traits; he claims that human activity (as yet unspecified) produced a specific human activity, namely labor, as the fundamental organization of the relationship between human beings and nature, and that there are psychological consequences of these forms of activity. This question and the premises underlying it are steeped in the Marxian world view, dialectical historical materialism.[2]

Vygotsky's accomplishments are impressive: he played a key role in the restructuring of the Psychological Institute of Moscow; he set up research laboratories in the major cities of the Soviet Union and founded what we call special education. He authored some one hundred and eighty papers, many of which are just now being published. Vygotsky's practical goal during his lifetime was to reformulate psychology according to Marxist methodology in order to develop concrete ways to deal with the massive tasks facing the Soviet Union – a society attempting to move rapidly from feudalism to socialism. He was the acknowledged leader, in the 1920s and '30s, of a group of Soviet scholars who passionately pursued the building of a new psychology in the service of what it was hoped would be a new kind of society. As a contemporary Vygotskian scholar has described it:

> This period, especially after the Civil War in 1922, was one of upheaval, enthusiasm, and energy unimaginable by today's standards. People such as Vygotsky and his followers devoted every hour of their lives to making certain that the new socialist state, the first grand experiment based on Marxist-Leninist principles, would succeed.
>
> (Wertsch, 1985, p. 10)

Tragically, Stalin would all too soon put an end to this brief period of creativity and experimentation during which attempts were made to transform every area of human life – not only politics and economics, but also art and culture, science, the family, education and labor.

The empirical work of Vygotsky and his followers focused on education and remediation, and dealt with illiteracy, cultural differences among the hundreds of ethnic groups that formed the new nation, and the absence of services for those unable to participate fully in the new society. Further, Vygotsky never abandoned his love for art and literature nor his fascination with the clues to subjectivity he believed they held. Although his later works dealt less often with poetry and drama than the earlier ones, his methodological and psychological writings are clearly those of an intensely poetic author. Familiar with the work of the radical and avant-garde filmmakers, dramatists, graphic artists and painters of the immediate post-revolutionary period, he knew some of them personally as well (e.g. the poet Mayakovsky, the filmmaker Eisenstein and the stage director Stanislavsky).

Though they never met face to face, during the 1920s Vygotsky and Piaget were engaged in an intellectual debate about the relationship between language and thought in early child development. For the next thirty years, little was known about Vygotsky's work either in his own country (where it was suppressed under Stalin) or in the rest of the world, and the post-World War II West slowly began to embrace Piagetian theory and research. Then, in 1962, the first English translation of a significant portion of his writings was published (*Thought and Language*). While a few psychologists and linguists read the book with enthusiasm, *Thought and Language* did not have any significant impact on these fields. It was not until sixteen years later, in 1978, when the second English-language volume of Vygotsky's writings, *Mind in Society* (edited by Michael Cole, Vera John-Steiner, Sylvia Scribner and Ellen Souberman), was published that Vygotsky's presence began to be taken seriously.

The vast changes in the world created the conditions for a more receptive audience among Western scholars for the materialist, social-cultural perspective on human development in general and the development of thought and speech in particular.[3] The practicality of Vygotsky's insights and experiments concerning instruction and pedagogy in the elementary school years and for the developmentally delayed and/or disabled was of greater interest.

The fields of psycholinguistics and sociolinguistics had flowered in the late 1960s and early '70s, in large part due to the 'linguistic revolution' precipitated by Chomsky's scientific discoveries about language and grammar in the 1950s. With these new disciplines came a keen interest in the early years of childhood, in the origins and acquisition of language, thought and communication. The philosophy of language, especially the seminal writings on meaning, predication, explanation and speech acts by Wittgenstein and his followers, Austin, Searle and others, began to have an influence on linguistics; their work led to intense research interest in the 'pragmatics of communication,' and, again, a search for the origins of such social skills. Not just words in themselves but 'how to do things with words' became a major focus (Austin, 1962). Side by side with the emergence of cognitive science approaches – which tended to look 'inside the head' for explanations of the remarkable intelligence and achievements of infants and very young children – were attempts to develop alternative paradigms, or models, to capture and express the essential socialness of language and communication. The more socially oriented scientists went beyond offering critiques of the reductionistic, positivistic paradigm which dominated developmental research and tried to develop new models. Many returned to studying the rich historical tradition of models and paradigms outside of and, in some cases, oppositional to the mainstream of psychology, with its focus on the individual as the proper unit of analysis; they found much that was useful in these older works, and applied their insights to contemporary social and scientific issues.[4] Within this rich intellectual environment, Vygotsky's work was a gold mine.

What also made Vygotsky more appealing in the 1970s and '80s than in the early '60s were the socio-political changes occurring in the institution of human science research. In the United States, for example, no longer were 'applied' areas of the social sciences (e.g. child development, learning and instruction, reading and literacy) regarded so plainly as of lower status than the 'pure' areas. With the failure of President Lyndon Johnson's 'War on Poverty,' the federal government was making severe cutbacks in research funds and insisting on a more pragmatic justification for the money it did allocate for research. Many of the once 'pure' social scientists in psychology, anthropology, sociology and linguistics were forced to turn their attention to applied areas in order to continue their careers. Many were also truly concerned about the severe social problems of the day, especially the impact of poverty and racism on educational failure and the role of communication in cognitive and social development and underdevelopment. There was a quiet optimism among some scholars that a more socially based and socially relevant psychology could contribute to alleviating, if not eliminating, social ills and injustice.[5]

The decade 1978–88 was a period of intense research activity. The group of psychologists, linguists, anthropologists and educators working and training others in the Vygotskian tradition grew and became international, to the point where in the late 1980s the existence of a Vygotsky 'revival' was noted (Holzman, 1989; Kozulin, 1986a). In the Soviet Union and many other countries, there was an upsurge in the publication of Vygotsky's writings (suppressed in the Soviet Union for fifty years) and works about Vygotsky and Vygotskian research – in 1988–91 alone, no fewer than seven new books appeared.[6] Increasingly, we find references to Vygotsky's relevance to practitioners in early childhood, special education and adult literacy in newsletters and publications of associations for professionals and paraprofessionals in these fields, such as the American Montessori Society and the American Federation of Teachers.[7] Textbooks in developmental psychology that formerly had devoted a couple of sentences (at most) to Vygotsky now treat him as a 'school' nearly on a par with Piaget, Freud, Skinner and social learning theorists, and the recently established US National Teacher Examination includes questions on Vygotsky.[8] To all intents and purposes Lev Vygotsky, the radical Marxist psychologist, has entered the mainstream of psychology.

THE DEBATE ABOUT PSYCHOLOGY

To the naive mind, revolution and history seem incompatible. It believes that historical development continues as long as it follows a straight line. When a change comes, a break in the historical fabric, a leap – then this naive mind sees only catastrophe, a fall, a rupture; for the naive mind history ends until back again straight and narrow. The scientific mind, on the contrary, views revolution as the locomotive of history forging ahead at full speed; it regards the revolutionary epoch as a tangible, living embodiment of history. A revolution solves only those tasks which have been raised by history: this proposition holds true equally for revolution in general and for aspects of social and cultural life.

(Vygotsky, quoted in Levitan, 1982, inside front cover)

The sheer weight of years of hard, creative work by committed Vygotskian scholars, coupled with the astonishing events that took place in the Soviet Union and Eastern Europe in late 1989 – and which continue as we write this – have transformed what was a revival of interest and research activity into a full-fledged psychological, philosophical and political debate. What is the relevance of Vygotsky's work to psychology today? With the demise of communism, why should we be interested in the works of a Marxist? Which of his contributions can help us deal with contemporary social issues? Was he primarily a psychologist, a methodologist, a literary critic? Was he really a Marxist: did he merely pay lip service to Marxian conceptions; was Marxism just one of several intellectual traditions that Vygotsky – according to some, a classical eclectic – incorporated into his very original thinking; or did the new world view that was Marxism permeate his entire life's work? Was he a hard-line Stalinist? What debt did he owe to Lenin? Why was his work suppressed in the Soviet Union for half a century – because he refused to censor Western (bourgeois) thinkers from his writings; or because his work, particularly what he accomplished in the years immediately after the Bolshevik Revolution of 1917, was too radical for the bureaucratic and totalitarian Stalin? What are we to make of the recent flurry of interest in Vygotsky? Stripped of his Marxism, is he distorted to 'fit in' with Western psychological theory, as really a Piagetian or Deweyian or Meadian, or even an information processing psychologist, after all? How are we to understand his passion for poetry, theater, film? As the 'real' Vygotsky? As the idealism and spiritualism of a Russian Jewish intellectual youth? Or as a critical component of his contributions to a new theory and practice of human development? These questions and others contribute to the current (relatively) healthy intellectual-political climate in which fundamental issues about the relationships between psychology and politics, social science and social change, and reform and revolution are not only being raised, but increasingly appear in some manner, shape or form in the mass media.[9]

While we will touch upon all these topics to varying degrees, our main focus will be the role of Vygotsky and his followers in the contemporary debate about the very nature of psychology as a scientific enterprise. Of course, this is not a new debate. In its short history, psychology has had ongoing lively and heated discussion on such questions as: What is its proper subject matter? How does one engage in studying it? What paradigm, or model, will dominate – an existing one, such as the natural science paradigm, or something entirely new?[10] Does a dominant and agreed upon psychological paradigm exist or is the psychological community still in the process of developing it? Some of the more radical voices in this century-long debate include the phenomenological psychologists, the critical theorists of the Frankfurt School, and adherents of humanistic psychology, hermeneutics, the anti-psychiatry and anti-psychology movements, and dialectical psychology and feminist psychology.[11] The Vygotskians bring still another dimension (and debates about it) to this broader debate.

PSYCHOLOGIST AND/OR METHODOLOGIST

Vygotsky as psychologist and/or Vygotsky as methodologist is a useful shorthand for characterizing the role of Vygotsky in the debate within the debate. The two descriptions raise the question of the vantage point from which one sees psychology in general and Vygotsky's contributions in particular. Perhaps even more importantly, the connective 'and/or' suggests Vygotsky's radical unwillingness to make a sharp distinction between the substantive content of psychology – what it is about – and its more formalistic (for some, meta-psychological) method – how it is done.

Treating Vygotsky as primarily a psychologist assumes that psychology's nature is relatively clear, its subject matter and paradigm established. On this account, Vygotsky has made major contributions to the development of psychology and, while he has perhaps made some important methodological contributions, his work fits comfortably inside the dominant paradigm and can advance, deepen and reform psychological practice as it currently exists. Further, according to this view, his scientific significance will ultimately be a function of the ability of contemporary researchers to apply his specific findings about human development to contemporary social issues. Many modern Vygotskian researchers understand Vygotsky in just this way. (We will discuss their work in subsequent chapters.)

An alternative view (which we share with a number of philosophers, historians and psychologists) – taking Vygotsky as a methodologist who did psychological research in the interest of discovering what psychology is – characteristically begins from the vantage point that a psychological paradigm has not yet evolved and that there is still an active debate concerning the very nature and activity of psychology itself. From this point of view, Vygotsky's work was and remains foundational: he was engaged in investigating the nature of paradigms in general and psychological paradigms in particular as an essential part of developing a qualitatively new science. As Bakhurst put it, 'For Vygotsky, the identity of psychology as a science depended on the degree to which it could contribute to the transformation of the object it investigates.

Its tasks were not simply to mirror reality but to *harness* reality'
(1986, pp. 122–3).

Certainly Vygotsky made contributions to our understanding
of human development, in particular the nature of learning and the
relationship of language to thought. But on this view (which is also
ours) he remained true to the scientific task of investigating the
very nature of psychological science even as he made a host of
practical-critical discoveries within the science of psychology.

Significantly, Vygotsky was a Marxist methodologist. Neither
he nor Marx ultimately succeeded in creating a full-blown
paradigm (or, if you prefer, an anti-paradigm)[12] for psychology,
economics or history, but both advanced the ongoing debate regarding the very nature of paradigms in the specific context of their
efforts to discover/create a genuine comprehension of human
progress and human science.

What was Marx's methodology? The textbook version
presented in the philosophy, political science and even some
psychology literature speaks of the Marxian dialectic as 'the unity
of opposites' and of Marx as a materialist, i.e. one who takes the
material world, or matter, as basic and ideas, or mind, as derivative.
But Marx's writings are far more complex and scientifically radical
than this. We will need to consider ever so briefly some of Marx's
methodological thinking to make clearer the debate within the
debate.

INTERPRETATION-FREE SCIENCE

> Life is not determined by consciousness, but consciousness by
> life. In the first method of approach, the starting point is con-
> sciousness taken as the living individual; in the second method,
> which conforms to real life, it is the real living individuals
> themselves, and consciousness is considered solely as their con-
> sciousness.
>
> (Marx and Engels, 1973, p. 47)

Marx, especially in his early philosophical-methodological writings, put forth the fundamentals of dialectical historical
materialism, the methodology he was developing as a challenge
not only to the specific dominant philosophical traditions of the
nineteenth century, but to philosophy in general. For philosophy
is interpretive. As a radical materialist, Marx insisted that the

starting point of science and of history is life-as-lived, not interpretations or abstractions extrapolated from life. The following paragraph is one of the most succinct formulations of his methodology:

> This method of approach is not devoid of premises. It starts out from the real premises and does not abandon them for a moment. Its premises are men, not in any fantastic isolation and rigidity, but in their actual, empirically perceptible process of development under definite conditions. As soon as this active life-process is described, history ceases to be a collection of dead facts as it is with the empiricists (themselves still abstract), or an imagined activity of imagined subjects, as with the idealists.
>
> (Marx and Engels, 1973, pp. 47–8)

Note that Marx insists that a premise is a real state of affairs, not an intellectually abstracted axiom from which implications are drawn – this, in itself, is monumentally radical. Virtually all of Western philosophy and methodology, from Plato to Descartes and Kant, is challenged in this statement. Marx exposed the dualistic and ahistorical nature of philosophy's foundation as propositions and interpretive assumptions, where premises are understood as separate from what follows from them. Particularly well trained in the Cartesian and rationalist tradition, Marx understood, for example, that Descartes had first to translate the historical actuality I-am-sitting-here-and-thinking into the propositional premise 'I think' in order to derive 'I am.' While in philosophy propositional and/or linguistic forms may be what follow from sitting there and thinking, this is not so in history. What follows in history is whatever actually develops from that complicated but describable social arrangement of sitting there and thinking.

What does Marx mean by history? Not surprisingly, not what bourgeois historians mean – they define history societally (usually referring to 'the past' divided from 'the present' and 'future,' or to 'what happened' relative to a particular spatio-temporal moment). History, to Marx, is the living, sensuous, continuous, indivisible totality of human existence, the complex yet describable 'process of development under definite conditions.' His methodology is historical and not merely dialectical insofar as: 'This conception of history... does not explain practice from the idea but explains the formation of ideas from material practice' (Marx and Engels, 1973,

p. 58). Marx developed this historical, non-propositional, radically monistic (i.e. non-dualistic) scientific method in his political-economic analysis of capitalism; Vygotsky advanced it into the area of psychology.

In one of his earliest methodological statements, written in 1845–6, Marx addressed the dichotomy between objective and subjective:

> The chief defect of all hitherto existing materialism (that of Feuerbach included) is that the thing, reality, sensuousness, is conceived only in the form of the object or of contemplation, but not as sensuous human activity, practice, subjectively. Hence, in contradistinction to materialism, the *active* side was developed abstractly by idealism – which, of course, does not know real, sensuous activity as such. Feuerbach wants sensuous objects, really distinct from the thought objects, but he does not conceive human activity itself as *objective* activity. Hence, in *Das Wesen des Christenthums*, he regards the theoretical attitude as the only genuinely human attitude, while practice is conceived and fixed only in its dirty-judaical manifestation. Hence he does not grasp the significance of 'revolutionary,' of 'practical-critical,' activity.
>
> (Marx and Engels, 1973, p. 121)

While the concept of activity was not, of course, unique to Marx,[13] the specification of activity as revolutionary, practical-critical activity did originate with him. Revolutionary activity is overthrowing/transforming the existing state of affairs, i.e. changing the totality of what there is. For the Marxian dialectic is not the abstract textbook 'unity of opposites,' but the actual practice of method whereby the totality of what there is (the unity of history) both determines and is qualitatively transformed by human activity. Activity theory, the psychological perspective with which Vygotsky is associated, partially originated with Marx's radically monistic and revolutionary conception of activity. Yet while most contemporary activity theorists acknowledge Marx as, if not the only founder, then one of the founders of activity theory, on our view most do not even remotely understand the revolutionary character of Marx's practical-critical conception of practical-critical activity.

The attempt to categorize Vygotsky, to 'dualize' him as either a psychologist or a methodologist, contradicts, ironically, not only Vygotsky's life-as-lived, but his self-conscious intellectual revolt against dualism.[14] Over hundreds of years, Western thought had amassed an almost endless list of philosophical and methodological dualisms or bifurcations: mind, body; form, matter; past, present; particular, universal; individual, society; individual, group; empiricism, idealism; permanence, change; conscious, unconscious; premise, implications of premise. Vygotsky, like Marx before him, inherited these dualisms; within the newly emerging social science of psychology, they were pervasive and pernicious. In fact, during Vygotsky's early years the question of whether it was even possible to study the mind, consciousness or thought scientifically was the subject of considerable debate, owing to the dualistic conceptualization of the objective and the subjective. Vygotsky addressed himself to this debate: to those who believed the mind was subjective, that subjectivity was not worthy of or accessible to scientific study and therefore could not be scientifically studied; and to others who believed the mind was objective, not subjective, and therefore could be studied using scientific (i.e. objective, experimental) methods. Another, and related, dualism Vygotsky worked all his life to synthesize was that of the individual and society: if the individual and society are separate, as was the prevalent belief, then how does a human being ever develop?

Along with the specific dualisms and the generally dualistic methodology Vygotsky inherited were the varied and often metaphysical attempts of philosophers to synthesize these dualisms – to bring together a philosophically divided universe.[15] In the late eighteenth century Kant had created a paradigm which brought these varied empiricistic and rationalistic syntheses together. His *Critique of pure reason*, a study of the *a priori*, is in many respects the foundational or philosophical world view on which much of modern psychology was (and still is) based. What Kant did was to create a synthesis of knowing – the objects of knowledge, what there is to know (what philosophers call ontology) – and the mind – the activity of knowing, how we know (what philosophers call epistemology) by analyzing the necessary conditions of knowing. According to Kant, human beings are capable of understanding the world as it is because the human mind is constructed to make sense of the world. In the well known methodological-epistemological dictum articulated at the very outset of his first *Critique*, Kant made two critical philosophical points. He observed that while all knowledge may begin with experience it does not follow that all knowledge is reducible to experience, nor is knowledge caused by experience. His beginning insight concerning the process of human knowing was that experience is the occasion for knowing. This was a proto-constructionist conception because for Kant knowledge is built. For others, such as Hume, the British philosopher who most directly formulated the questions that Kant was trying to answer, knowledge is deconstructed or reduced. The proto-constructivist conception was used by Kant himself – ultimately a rationalist – to evolve a reified, deductivist structure of thought. A logical look at experience itself reveals, he said, the existence of fundamental *a priori* (not derived from experience) categories of thought or pure reason, categories of the mind, that include space, time, object, relation, quantity and quality and that are preconditions for experience itself. Thus was mind defined as a maker of judgments. Most subsequent studies of human cognition follow in one of his footsteps, focusing most times on the mind as the reified *a priori* categories he deduced and less often on the proto-constructionist insight which gave rise to the deduction of the categories.[16]

While the monumental Kantian attempt to synthesize idealism (rationalism) and empiricism dominated much philosophical and psychological thinking in the nineteenth and early twentieth centuries and, as such, necessarily influenced Vygotsky, it was Marx's dialectical historical materialism – a qualitative rejection of Kant's philosophically overdetermined world view – which shaped him. Yet even during Vygotsky's short life, Marx himself was being conservatively and abstractly deformed into twentieth-century Marxism. The radical activistic, materialist, anti-interpretive philosophy and methodology of Marx – characterized by the denial of dualism – was, ironically, revised by Engels, Bernstein, Kautsky and others into a 'Kantianized,' 'Germanized,' idealistically dualized Marxism. Vygotsky, engaged in the scientific revolutionary activity of investigating/developing a new human psychology, was thus forced to take on both the rationalistic Kantian world view which has philosophically dominated Western psychology in this century of its infancy and the Kantianized (revisionist) Marxism which has philosophically dominated Marxism in this century of its own infancy. This search for a new psychology turned out to be a search for a new activity that synthesized human science and human progress and was free of dualistically determined interpretations.

Vygotsky's thinking was therefore not simply radical in the context of the dominant psychology and meta-psychology of his times, but radical within the tradition of Marxism as well. After all, he engaged consciousness and psychology head on, which Marx hadn't – thereby advancing Marxist methodology itself.

With Vygotsky, as with Marx, it is extremely tempting to take the substantive discoveries as most important since they are both pragmatically useful and compelling. But to do so, we think, is to minimize and, in fact, to distort Vygotsky's (and Marx's) contribution. However rich the content of their discoveries, the value of their work lies in their method – in which results of method and method itself are inseparable. If this is so, then it follows that to benefit fully from Vygotsky's work contemporary psychologists would have to continue in a scientifically revolutionary tradition. In other words, it is not Vygotskian to simply apply Vygotsky.

Lev Vygotsky was a Marxist methodologist and a psychologist. That he was both raises fundamental questions about Marxism, methodology, and psychology. In his own writings, Vygotsky constantly went back and forth between an examination of method and discussions of practical implications (to the delight of some of his followers and the frustration of others). So, too, our discussion will weave back and forth between explication and examination of method and discussion of specific implications/applications, both Vygotsky's own and contemporary research that is representative of the Vygotsky revival. It follows from our view of Vygotsky as a revolutionary methodologist that in order truly to understand his work and to be true to its spirit, i.e. the search for method, we must examine how his methodology has been used. Thus, our methodology for this book, guided by our belief that Vygotsky's writings are nothing less than a foreword to any future psychology, is to focus on his key methodological discoveries to explore how they have been manifest, or have failed to be manifest, in the works of contemporary, self-identified Vygotskians and neo-Vygotskians.

We begin in Chapter 2 with a detailed narrative of the origins and methodological-practical work of the US laboratory founded in the 1970s by a leading American Vygotskian, Michael Cole. We have chosen to take a close-up look at the Cole laboratory because it was one of the most comprehensive attempts to create a Vygotskian learning environment. In the fifteen-year evolution of the research done there, it is possible to see the use and, we would argue, the misuse of Vygotsky's method. Chapter 3 unravels the complex relationship between the dominant Western philosophical traditions and the newly emerging Marxian tradition. This chapter provides the methodological basis for our claims concerning Vygotsky's advances on fundamental Marxian concepts and their significance for a truly human science. We aim to show how Vygotsky's discovery of tool-and-result methodology – his radical break with dualism – is precisely the epistemological advance on Marx's discovery of the socio-historical fundamentality of practice, of revolutionary, practical-critical activity, that makes a Marxian psychology possible. Chapters 4, 5 and 6 use this analysis to understand further (or, in our preferred language, practically-critically activate) two of Vygotsky's most recognized contributions: the zone of proximal development (ZPD) and speaking-and-thinking. Throughout these chapters, we intersperse discussions of contemporary Vygotskian researchers' understanding and use of Vygotsky's work and subject it to revolutionary methodological scrutiny. Finally, Chapters 7 and 8 discuss the implications of Vygotsky's revolutionary methodology for the organizing of educational, clinical and cultural ZPDs and for the building of community.

Chapter 2

The laboratory as methodology

In 1962 Michael Cole, a US psychologist with a background in learning theory and mathematical psychology, spent a year in Moscow with the Soviet psychologist Alexander Luria. Originally Vygotsky's student and later his colleague, Luria outlived Vygotsky by more than forty years and became one of the most famous Soviet psychologists after Pavlov. Best known as a founder of neuropsychology – his specialties were brain dysfunction, aphasia and speech disorders – Luria's work spanned a tremendous variety of techniques and areas of human cognitive activity. In Cole's account of his fifteen-year apprenticeship and growing relationship with Luria, he reflects on his own former narrowness and naïveté – he had found Luria's interests incomprehensible:

> What did his cross-cultural work have to do with his work in the Institute of Neurosurgery? Why was he no longer doing conditioning experiments? Why, in his book about S. V. Sherashevsky, the man with an unusual memory, did he spend so much time discussing his personality when his memory was at issue?
>
> (Cole, 1979, p. 195)

Equally perplexing to Cole in the early '60s was Luria's intense interest in the work of Vygotsky.

> Nor could I make much of Vygotsky. He had been Luria's teacher, and Luria made it clear that he considered him a genius. But both Vygotsky's prose and the style of his thought defeated my attempts to understand Luria's admiration for him. I had read Vygotsky's *Thought and Language* as a graduate student, but except for some observations on concept learning in children, which at the time I knew nothing about, I could see little in his

work to generate enthusiasm. Still, I was polite. I read what I could and listened. Alexander Romanovich [Luria] did not push the topic unduly. He knew he could only plant seeds of understanding and hope they would germinate. He also knew that the more seeds he sowed, the more likely that one would grow. He waited a long time.

(Cole, 1979, p. 194)

Sixteen years, to be exact. Cole reports that from the beginning Luria urged him to publish some of Vygotsky's unpublished manuscripts; in 1978, along with three other editors (Scribner, John-Steiner and Souberman), he did so. It is a tribute to Luria's persistence and Cole's development that, from these uninspired beginnings, the work of Vygotsky, hailed as not only ahead of his time, but 'ahead of our time' (Minick, 1987, p. 34), has been revived to change the face of Western psychology. Cole, more than any other individual, is responsible for making Soviet psychology scientifically legitimate in the West.

Over the years Cole turned from the narrow confines of 1950s-style experimental psychology and became a leading researcher in cross-cultural psychology and 'social cognition.' He established one of the most innovative social science research laboratories in the United States – the Laboratory of Comparative Human Cognition at Rockefeller University in New York City. It was during the early years of this lab that Cole oversaw the publication of Vygotsky's *Mind in Society*. Recognizing that one could not develop a new science without building an environment where such a new science, or new methodology, would be nourished, Cole designed the lab as a challenge to the traditional institutional organization and structure of academia. It was a context for a multi-racial, multi-disciplinary grouping of social scientists, all with a social perspective, to work together to advance a humane vision in psychology. More African-American, Puerto Rican, Chicano and women social scientists trained there than anywhere in the country. Scholars from Great Britain, Western and Eastern Europe, and Africa visited and joined the team for anywhere from a week to several months. There was almost no work that was out of bounds; obscure, radical and alternative writings and research were studied. The lab integrated methodological approaches from other disciplines such as ethnography, anthropology and ethnomethodology, as well as from earlier critical approaches in psychology, most notably ecological psychology (Barker, 1968; Bronfenbrenner, 1977), Black psychology, cognitive science and systems theory. But Vygotsky and Luria played a central role. Cole and his colleagues (like many psychologists at the time) were interested in how ordinary people – poor and working-class people – behave, think and act, regarding them as legitimate subjects in their own right and not in comparison with their 'superiors' or 'the norm.' Accordingly, these psychologists went outside the laboratory and into the life spaces where people live – into their homes, schools and day care centers, into stores and into taxis, and on the streets. During the late 1970s and into the 1980s, the Laboratory of Comparative Human Cognition (which relocated to the University of California at San Diego in 1979) was one of the few US sites where Vygotskian research was practiced. Its newsletter, the *Quarterly Newsletter of the Laboratory of Comparative Human Cognition* (earlier known as the *Quarterly Newsletter of the Institute of Comparative Human Development*), was a forum for dialogue on Vygotskian research-in-progress all over the world. The Cole lab played a central role in the formative years of the Vygotsky revival and still is a major voice in the international dialogue on what psychology – a human science – is to be. We will review its history in some detail to examine how Vygotsky's key methodological discoveries have and have not been manifest in the lab's research.

ECOLOGICAL VALIDITY: METHODOLOGICAL CHALLENGE TO THE DOMINANT PARADIGM

The key issue at the lab in its earliest days was the methodological-philosophical question of validity. Drawing upon earlier discussions of validity in psychology (e.g. Brunswik, 1943; Lewin, 1943), Cole and his colleagues asked: if the theory and findings of experimental cognitive psychology are generated solely in laboratory settings under strict conditions which 'isolate' variables and constrain people's activities so that the object under study can be examined 'purely', how can we, with any degree of validity, generalize to everyday life? Is this kind of traditional laboratory psychology ecologically valid? The members of the lab, who thought it was not, did more than issue a passive critique of traditional psychology; they attempted to develop a methodology for an ecologically valid psychology. This effort was certainly Vygotskian; the concern to discover something significant about learning and development and the effort to create the methodology necessary to make such discoveries possible were inseparable. Central to the lab's early work was Vygotsky's insistence on the primacy of the search for method, specifically on the necessity of discovering the proper unit of study. In a series of monographs and articles, Cole, Hood (now Holzman) and McDermott argued that the proper unit of analysis for an ecologically valid psychology (a non-laboratory psychology of person–environment interaction, i.e. the life space/activity in which people exist) was not the individual, but the 'person–environment interface' or the 'scene' (Cole, Hood and McDermott, 1978, 1979; Hood, McDermott and Cole, 1980; see also Lewin, 1943).

Such an approach necessitated a fundamentally new model of research. There could be no mere reformulation of existing psychological principles, because such principles yield an ecologically invalid psychology! They are grounded in a psychology of the individual, in Kantian *a priori* synthetic assumptive premises and categories and in reductionistic research practices the social sciences inherited from the natural sciences. As articulated in *Ecological niche-picking*,

> But we will argue that if experimental practices preclude the operation of principles essential to the organization of behavior in non-laboratory environments, theories and data derived from the laboratory will at best be a faulty basis for predictions about the behavior of individuals once they leave the laboratory . . . We are making such arguments because our own self-conscious attempts to contrast a particular set of laboratory and non-laboratory settings where individuals engage in remembering, thinking and attending activities suggest that important principles operating outside the laboratory are missing from current experimental procedures, and consequently, from current cognitive theories. Insofar as our observations are correct, they provide the basis for our suggestion that ecological invalidity is an axiom (albeit an implicit axiom-in-practice) of current cognitive psychology.
>
> (Cole, Hood and McDermott, 1978, pp. 2–3)

In contrast, an ecologically valid psychology would offer findings that could be used to reason effectively about the differences and similarities in the behavior of different persons as they move through the various institutional complexes that

make up the contemporary world. We are a long way from reaching such a goal, but this is no reason to limit ourselves to a theoretical paradigm that makes it systematically impossible.
(Cole, Hood and McDermott, 1979)

The Vygotskian-inspired argument continued. The laboratory, the most popular site for psychological research, is not merely a location or setting, but a methodology:

> On the one hand, everyday life and the psychologist's labora- tory can be contrasted as different types of social scenes (niches), the latter being generally better specified as consisting of an experimenter (sometimes out of sight, but known to be present), one or more subjects, special rules for guiding their interaction (including cash payment or a course grade), a place, and usually some carefully designed materials for probing and organizing the behavior of the subject(s). On the other hand, there is a laboratory/everyday life contrast in the methodological as- sumptions that underlie what could be considered a useful description of any scene and how such a description can be used to model aspects of the real world. What marks the laboratory perspective at this level of contrast is an assumption that what is of interest in any scene can be defined *a priori* by the experimenter's theoretical interests and the careful design and control of key variables.

(1979, p. 119)

Distinguishing these levels of contrast between laboratory and everyday life is critical, it was argued, because most naturalistic or observational research conducted in everyday life settings outside the university walls is guided as much by the laboratory's method- ological assumptions as is research conducted in the laboratory itself! Conversely, much of what happens in laboratory research is the same as what happens in social activity that occurs anywhere, but in the laboratory it is systematically ignored because the methodological assumptions of the laboratory disallow it! While Vygotsky did not make this critique of the laboratory as a meth- odology (he could not, since it was not a full-blown paradigm but only in its infancy in his day), his characterization of the psycho- logy of his time as 'fossilized' is reminiscent of such a critique. Here he is criticizing the standard practice of discarding the data from initial sessions, when the response is being established. Uniformity was sought, so that it was never possible to grasp the process in flight; instead researchers routinely discard the critical time when the reaction appears, and its functional links are established and adjusted.

(Vygotsky, 1978, p. 68)

For Vygotsky, 'The fossilized form is the end of the thread that ties the present to the past' (1978, p. 64). Cole, Hood and McDermott saw the fossilized form as the end of the thread that ties the infinite scenes of human activity together.

The research into ecological validity most directly relevant to Vygotsky's analysis of learning and development (discussed extensively in Chapter 4) dealt with school-age children in and out of school settings. To Vygotsky, it was imperative to understand the relationship between learning and development in order to come up with educational practices which maximize the learning and development of all children. This was also a central goal of the lab's initial research. Cole, Hood and McDermott conducted a two-year study of seventeen children between the ages of 8 and 10 who attended a small private school in New York City. The school's population was heterogeneous in terms of social class, ethnicity and performance levels. The children were extensively audio- and video-taped in a variety of settings: in their classrooms and special subject areas of the school, such as art class and shop; in after-school cooking and nature clubs specially set up for them at Rockefeller University; on trips; and taking a standard IQ test individually.

The initial goal was to 'find' in these everyday life environments evidence for the kinds of cognitive processes said to occur in laboratory settings. But they simply could not be found. The activities of thinking, perceiving, problem-solving and remembering that, according to laboratory-informed science, are supposed to go on inside the individual's head are, in point of fact, patently social. They occur in the 'person–environment interface' (Cole, Hood and McDermott, 1978), in the 'life space' (Lewin, 1943), in 'mind-in-society' (Vygotsky, 1978), between and among people and the institutions that mediate our relationships to ourselves, each other and the world.

For example, problem-solving in the cooking club often looked like this: the club leaders/researchers had inadvertently equipped the club's kitchen with a two-cup measuring cup, which confused the children no end. Both their confusion and problem-solving are mutually, socially produced and organized. On one occasion, as a child is pouring flour into the two-cup measuring cup, one of her partners points to the top of the cup and tells her that that's where one cup is. The pourer corrects her: 'One cup, one cup, one cup.' 'That *is* one cup,' the partner responds, pointing to the cup. A third partner resolves the argument by pointing out that 'You do it up to where it *says* one cup.' Not only does the physical environment contain cues that are simultaneously salient and misleading (e.g. the conflict between the cup as physical object and as metric quantity), but the problem and its solution are socially constructed.

The failure to find evidence for individual, isolated, mentalistic cognitive processes of the kind sought out by diagnostic tests as the dominant mode of real life problem-solving was taken as evidence that experimental, laboratory method cognitive psychology has serious validity problems. It also led to a deeper appreciation of Vygotsky's claim that learning and development are social, and that not only experimental psychology but the majority of educational and instructional settings distort this fact about human activity.

Concern with institutional educational failure and interest in the 'learning biographies' of individual children were the motivation for investigating and detailing this process and its consequences in the case of 'learning disability.' One child, Adam, was officially described as learning disabled (LD).

> As soon as we went to tell his story, we were immersed once again in the problems of how to do an ecologically valid description. His head did not seem to work very well on isolated cognitive tasks, either on standardized tests given by the school reading specialist or on the more theoretically sensitive tasks we gave him. Did we really want to describe what went on in his head? Just what was the phenomenon under investigation anyway? Where is LD to be found? Is it to be 'found' at all?
>
> (McDermott, 1987, p. 7)

Such questions were not meant to deny that some people learn differently from and/or more slowly than others, but that without social arrangements for making such differences meaningful in the complex social-cultural-political ways they are, there is no such thing as 'learning disability.' What followed was a search for the means to specify how Adam's disability was socially produced and organized and the conditions under which both his disability and ability were 'displayed.' Detailed analyses of video-tapes revealed the ongoing work the children did to organize contexts for the sequencing of psychological activities. It also provided evidence for how psychological processes are actively maintained as a function of ever-changing socio-environmental circumstances, which are themselves changed by the active maintenance of psychological processes.

One study in particular, involving Adam, is helpful in illustrating the use of Vygotskian principles. Hood, McDermott and Cole (1980) present data from an 'IQ bee' (a collective IQ test) conducted at the final meeting of the club run for the children. Two of Vygotsky's major contributions – the dynamic and developmental view of psychological processes, and the social embeddedness of higher psychological functions – informed the analysis and conclusions. The children were divided into two teams for the competition and took turns answering the questions. There were prizes for everyone but the winners got first choice.

As it happened, Adam was the third child on his team to get a turn. Since items on IQ tests get progressively more difficult, by the time he was presented with a question it was the sixth in the series and a difficult one. For example, in the subtest 'general information,' the first question asked was, 'From what animal do we get bacon?' The children found that one easy. The last question, which went to Adam, was, 'How many pounds are in a ton?' Adam guessed 100; three other children tried 1,000, 200 and 12; Adam tried again with 1,200. Finally the club leader told them the correct answer.

While four children gave incorrect answers, only Adam's error was attended to. What were the conditions which led to this 'display' of Adam's disability, and what were the consequences of it? How were both 'subject' and 'environment' dynamically involved in the organization of particular behavior displays? The analysis details the work done by everyone involved in the club both to display and to keep hidden Adam's disability. This includes: the children laughing at how easy the easy questions are; making comments like 'Adam had his turn, but remember he can't guess'; 'Will you pass it to me, Adam?'; Adam whining, 'By the time it gets to be my turn, they're gonna be so hard'; Adam refusing to pass up his turn; the club leader giving Adam only four digits to remember instead of six on the 'digit-span' subtest, and everyone cheering his success on this item. These constitute elements of Adam's task environment:

> Just what is Adam's task environment? How could we ever be sure of what Adam is working on at any given point in the IQ bee? It is not the case that a task is simply presented to an ever-waiting organism, well-organized to pounce on the question asked. Rather, we can see Adam squirming about, attending carefully to the remarks of his peers, organizing an environment in which everybody feels uncomfortable about his plight, and reorganizing both the social and intellectual task put before him by the rest of the group.
>
> (Hood, McDermott and Cole, 1980, p. 111)

In specifying how intellectual performances are socially produced, the authors concluded that 'the face-to-face social world is the most powerful environment' for their performance. Furthermore, they said that, 'contrary to the methodological assumptions of contemporary cognitive psychology, social interaction provides a systematically reactive and therefore informative environment for psychological events' (Hood, McDermott and Cole, 1980, p. 112). Utilizing Vygotsky's discovery of the zone of proximal development – the means by which higher psychological functions are produced socially – the authors pointed out how the 'social world' can also systematically withhold support at certain times.

> Not only must we understand any appearance of a particular skill as well sequenced and aligned with particular environmental happenings (rather than as an internalized state simply making its way to the outside); we must also understand the nonappearance of a particular skill at times when it could be useful as equally well orchestrated. Both performance and nonperformance can be understood in terms of the particular configuration of supports given a child at different times.
>
> (p. 113)

They concluded with questions concerning how it was that Adam's days are so difficult; even when he has a 'good day' it is against considerable odds, stemming from the complex interaction between 'his' difficulty in doing certain psychological tasks and how the environment appears to be designed to make such tasks even more difficult than an analysis of the task in isolation would suggest.

Looking back on these early studies at the Cole lab, the methodological discovery that people learn about themselves and others primarily by the work they do in constructing environments to act on the world seems most important and, not surprisingly, most Vygotskian. Of course it applied not only to Adam and his fellow students but also to the researchers – as they constructed the research environment necessary to intervene on contemporary cognitive psychology and the institution of special education.

Nevertheless, this attempt to develop an ecologically valid methodology ultimately failed on its own terms – it was not ecologically valid, nor was it Vygotskian in this sense. Cole, Hood and McDermott's (1978) distinction between laboratory and everyday life identified the laboratory as not merely a site but a methodology that predetermined and seriously distorted any analysis of human activity. But, setting up 'real' or everyday life situations – said to be a break with experimental (laboratory) methodology – turns out to be continuous with laboratory methodology. Observing and analyzing children's activity/behavior – more precisely, 'the person–environment interface' – in a researcher-created real life situation may well make it possible for the researchers to see different things (e.g., how human beings collectively organize their environments, the socially constructed display of learning disability rather than a learning disabled child). But the scientific enterprise is still fundamentally an experimental one; the 'seeing' it produces is still a societal behavior, albeit an ecologically valid one. It is not a revolutionary activity because while it may entail seeing new things, it does not transform what seeing is. Neither is it sensitive to the discrepancy between the analytic and instrumentalist nature of the scientific enterprise and the behavior, activity and experience of the participants. The set-up situation is, after all, an environment or tool for analysis rather than being itself the analysis. From the vantage point of the children, it was not an experiment. It was a scene of life's seamless, continuous performance.

Our critique here in no way denies the contribution of this early Vygotskian research enterprise. We are addressing what we take to be the central question raised by Vygotsky's work and life-as-lived – what revolutionary psychologists are to do.

Traditional science – including radical, ecologically valid science – sets up experimental situations that replicate real life and uses them to describe what is, in the Marxian sense, alienated reality. The Vygotskian enterprise, as we see it, is to create zones of proximal development – environments where people can perform life – and in so doing transform alienated reality. The difference could not be greater.

As the years went by, Cole's efforts turned to integrating concepts of the cultural-historical school of psychology, including Vygotsky, with concepts and methods of cultural psychology, an approach developed primarily in the United States (Cole, 1990a; 1990b). Research at Cole's lab became increasingly focused on exploiting one of Vygotsky's most significant 'purely psychological' discoveries – the zone of proximal development – in studies of the organization of educational settings. The pragmatics of American education and educational research – with more children being failed by schooling, the enormous growth of the learning disabled population and the advent of the computer as classroom – no doubt influenced Cole's directions. Since 1981 he and his current associates have been involved in creating 'activity systems' that are designed to promote development.

One such activity system is the 5th Dimension, a 'specially designed cultural medium for promoting the all around intellectual and social development of 6–12 year old children while introducing them to computers and computer networking' (Cole, 1990b, p. 13). Two features of the 5th Dimension are cited by Cole as significant: children learn to make choices that satisfy their own goals within the constraints of this 'bounded alternative world with its own social norms, tasks and conventions' (p. 13); and the power relations between children and adults are changed by virtue of the presence of the Wizard, a computer-generated figure who plays a key role in the 5th Dimension as the adjudicator of all disputes.

There are others who, like Cole, worked to fit Vygotsky's insights into existing psychological paradigms or quasi-paradigms. Among them are his colleagues D. Newman and Griffin, whose research fits Vygotsky into the cognitive science paradigm (D. Newman, Griffin and Cole, 1984; 1989), and Tharp and Gallimore, who fit Vygotsky into an interactionist paradigm in their attempt at 'uniting behavioral science and neo-Vygotskianism' (Tharp and Gallimore, 1988, p. 8).[1] But Vygotsky's search for a new method –

and, thereby, a new psychology – revived in the early days of the Rockefeller lab, had become part of the international public domain. While some moved west (literally and metaphorically) with Cole and company, other Vygotskians pursued a more revolutionary route – or at least kept the revolutionary path open.

Those who see in Vygotsky a revolutionary methodology and argue against assimilating him into mainstream psychology include the Soviets Davydov and Radzikhovskii (1985). Arguing that Vygotsky's work has rarely been evaluated on the basis of its own internal logic, they offer an analysis of his methodology which, they maintain, shows that the 'internal bond of methodology and psychology constitutes the very foundation of all of his work' (p. 37). They suggest that Vygotsky the psychologist did not use all the possibilities presented by Vygotsky the methodologist.

Kozulin, a Soviet psychologist who emigrated to the United States in 1979, observes a more synthesized Vygotsky and sees no such conflict (Kozulin, 1986, 1990). Indeed, in his view, Vygotsky did not even take psychology to be the object of study, but rather took it to be a tool with which to investigate culture and consciousness.

Bakhurst (1988), an Oxford-trained philosopher who studied the socio-philosophical-political climate in which Vygotsky worked as part of an investigation of the Soviet philosopher Ilyenkov, sees Vygotsky as a major figure in the historical dialogue over fundamental issues of methodology, paradigms and world views:

To a certain extent Vygotsky found the Marxist tradition a congenial medium in which to work. His critique of psychology is in many respects a critique of precisely the kind of framework psychology inherited from the 18th century, the Cartesian and post-Cartesian framework. The Marxist intellectual climate of the Soviet Union in the '20s was a congenial medium for someone who was seeking to break with those 18th century categories, someone who was trying to diagnose the crisis in contemporary psychology as a crisis which was tied up with the legacy of the 18th century. Hence, insofar as the project of building a Marxist psychology was a project which would overcome this crisis, a project which would be of enormous practical significance, which would contribute to the building of the kind of society in which the injustices of the old regime would be overcome, and which would itself facilitate a richer flowering of human psychological capacities – then that's what it is for Vygotsky to be a Marxist, at both the theoretical and the practical level.

(Bakhurst, quoted in Holzman, 1990, p. 19)

Expanding this view to the issue of what impact Vygotsky might have on social change today, Wertsch, the leading US researcher and writer on Vygotsky and cognitive development, comments:

. . . what I see as potentially very important is the lesson that it [Vygotsky's work] might be able to teach Americans . . . namely, that there are very legitimate well-grounded alternative world views or modes of thinking . . . in an era when the Berlin Wall comes down, the Soviet Union is falling apart, South Africa's changed, all the things in Eastern Europe that are going on, psychologists in the traditional American mode have practically nothing to say about any of this stuff! The reason we can't is not because we're neutral – although that's the claim – but because we presuppose our own world view as the ideal one . . . all the while hiding the fact that [psychology] is grounded in American individualistic ideology. Exposing this and 'proving' it scientifically is what I see as the powerful lesson that is potential in Vygotsky.

(Wertsch, quoted in Holzman, 1990, pp. 21–2)

To learn 'the powerful lesson' (both psychological and methodological) of Vygotsky, we must have some understanding of the scientific methodological debate that has dominated this century and which remains unresolved as we move rapidly toward the next. It is to this debate that we turn in the next chapter.

Chapter 3

Practice

Vygotsky's tool-and-result methodology and psychology

> The search for method becomes one of the most important problems of the entire enterprise of understanding the uniquely human forms of psychological activity. In this case, the method is simultaneously prerequisite and product, the tool and the result of the study.
>
> (Vygotsky, 1978, p. 65)

In their most scientifically and philosophically lucid moments, Marx and Vygotsky, his follower, reject much more than an ill-formed psychological paradigm. Their intellectual challenge is to the entirety of Western thought, including thought about thought. Marx's writings both assume and imply the invalidity of Aristotelian and scholastic philosophies that came before him, and world views that developed in his time, e.g. rationalism, empiricism, positivism and vulgar materialism (the latter being the simplification and distortion of Marxism that takes the material world as basic and therefore causative). Marx subjected the broad and varied families of concepts associated with these historically interconnected world views to intense scrutiny, using the method he developed – dialectical historical materialism – to challenge the fundamental epistemic (how we know) and ontic (what there is) categories of Western cognition.

Most notably, Marx took on Kant's *Critique of Pure Reason* (out of which, as we have already noted, much of modern psychology grew). He exposed it as being no less metaphysical than any other 'philosophy' – German or otherwise. Indeed, Marx challenged the enterprise of philosophy itself, which was dominated in his youth by Hegel and the 'young Hegelians.' This was especially true in his early writings, where Marx put forth the premises and process of the revolutionary methodology he was developing (Marx, 1964; 1971; Marx and Engels, 1973).

'But isn't Marx's method of dialectical historical materialism simply another world view, another paradigm, another philosophy?' every critic of Marx since 1848 has asked. 'Isn't a challenge to philosophy, no matter how radical, still a philosophy?' The Marxian-Vygotskian answer to this apparent contradiction is radically methodological; it challenges how we challenge and introduces a qualitatively different (practice of) method.

For Marx and Vygotsky the object of study and the method of study are practical. By this they did not mean 'useful'; they were speaking of practical-critical activity, i.e. revolutionary activity (Marx, 1973, p. 121). The world historical environment ('scene') is both spatially and temporally seamless and qualitative, not quantitative; it can only be comprehended by a scientific practice free of interpretive assumptions, or premises. But this by no means implies that it is without premises. Such a scientific practice is, Marx explained, filled with the real premises that are 'men, not in any fantastic isolation and rigidity, but in their actual, empirically perceptible process of development under definite conditions' (Marx and Engels, 1973, p. 47). This Marxian method, the method of practice (if not yet the practice of method), not only redefines what science (or any other world view) is to be; it redefines what method is to be.[1]

PRAGMATICS

While the question of method has concerned philosophers since Plato, it was not until the emergence of modern science in the sixteenth and seventeenth centuries that it took center stage in philosophical investigation. Bacon (1960) took method to be the key to knowledge as he attempted to subject the tools of observation associated with the newly developing modern science to philosophical scrutiny. Since Bacon's time, most traditional views on methodology treat or define method as fundamentally separate from experimental content and results, i.e. from that for which it is the method. Indeed, it is considered unscientific to do otherwise. Method is understood and used as something to be applied, a functional means to an end, basically pragmatic or instrumental in character. In sharp contrast, Marx and Vygotsky understand method as something to be practiced – not applied. It is neither a means to an end nor a tool for achieving results. Rather it is, in Vygotsky's formulation, a 'tool and result.' On this view, as Vygotsky tells us, the method is 'simultaneously prerequisite and product' (1978, p. 65).

But what does this provocative formulation of Vygotsky's mean? Indeed, to what are we to appeal in determining what it means? In the language of the early Cole laboratory, what sense of 'validity' (not to mention ecology) is (to be) understood in the search for ecological validity? After all, validity, like truth, proof, method, inference, explanation, concept and paradigm, is, so we are told, but one member of a broad family of concepts that are the ontological and epistemological core of Western cognition itself and/or our understanding of Western cognition. Can we use these concepts to determine what *tool-and-result* means? If we cannot, then what else do we have at our disposal?

Pragmatism, which has emerged as the dominant methodology of the twentieth century, has spent a good deal of energy seeking answers to these questions. Developed in the United States, pragmatism is particularly associated with Peirce and C. I. Lewis (who were oriented toward the philosophy of science) and with Mead, Dewey and William James (all oriented toward psychology and sociology). Pragmatism rejected the dichotomous terms of the two major philosophical traditions of the late nineteenth and early twentieth centuries. One was empiricism, which took the world and mechanical biological processes to be dominant. The other was rationalism and/or idealism; taking the human mind to be dominant, they ascribed to it enormous power in determining the universe. The pragmatists made a genuine break with the dichotomy of mind and matter by focusing their investigation on the connection between thinking and doing. The term pragmatism was coined by Peirce (1957) – from the Greek *pragma* – act or deed – to emphasize the fact that words acquire their meanings from actions. According to Peirce, meanings are derived from deeds, not intuitions. In fact, there is no meaning separate from the socially constituted conception of its practical impact; a word or idea is meaningless if we cannot conceive of any practical effect relative to that word or idea. For James, the commercializer of pragmatism ('you must bring out of each word its cash-value': 1916), pragmatism has no content, but is pure method. Oriented toward results and consequences – it is fundamentally instrumentalist – pragmatism does not specify any particular results. Ultimately, the

ITEM CHARGED

LIB#: *1000191039*
GRP: STUDENT

Due: 8/10/2011 08:00 PM

Title: Lev Vygotsky : revolutionary scientist /
Fred Newman and Lois Holzman.
Auth: Newman, Fred.
Call #: 150.92 NEWMAN 1993
Enum
Chron
Copy:
Item *0044637O*

meanings of theories are to be found in their capacity to solve problems.

The pragmatists' world view has become the principal paradigm of late twentieth-century capitalist science; their answer to the fundamental problems of methodology, particularly of validity, has become dominant in a world where decisions are based by and large on instrumentalist reasoning. This is the case not only philosophically but practically.

Quine offers a sophisticated formulation of pragmatism's philosophy/methodology in his seminal 1950s work, 'Two Dogmas of Empiricism.' He employs a 'core–periphery' image, in which world view is depicted as a web-like network, with logical and other fundamental ontic and epistemic concepts occupying a core (central) position and immediate sensory experiences (or reports thereof) occupying the most peripheral locations. In between are the complicated practical/theoretical links which connect the two. The model is meant to illustrate several critical features of pragmatism: (1) the relativity of world views; (2) the relativity within world views (anything might be changed); (3) the interdependence of the varied elements of a world view; and (4) the pragmatic value of preserving the core (or elements closest to it) as opposed to the periphery. For Quine, perhaps the most eloquent of the pragmatist methodologists, decisions as to what alterations should be made to a current conceptual framework or world view in the face of new developments (both large and small) and/or the decision to retain or reject a world view altogether are entirely based on the pragmatic criterion of 'efficaciousness.' In an oft-quoted statement Quine succinctly sums up his own methodological world view:

As an empiricist I continue to think of the conceptual scheme of science as a tool, ultimately, for predicting future experience in the light of past experience. Physical objects are conceptually imported into the situation as convenient intermediaries – not by definition in terms of experience, but simply as irreducible posits comparable, epistemologically, to the gods of Homer. For my part I do, qua lay physicist, believe in physical objects and not in Homer's gods; and I consider it a scientific error to believe otherwise. But in point of epistemological footing the physical objects and the gods differ only in degree and not in kind. Both sorts of entities enter into our conception only as cultural posits. The myth of physical objects is epistemologically superior to most in that it has proved more efficacious than other myths as a device for working a manageable structure into the flux of experience.

(1961, p. 44)

On Quine's pragmatic account, then, the conceptual scheme of science (which is, most would agree, the hegemonic twentieth-century world view) is itself a tool, a tool applied to the 'flux of experience,' a tool deemed 'superior' by appeal to a pragmatic criterion (efficaciousness). It is, to employ an overused word, a tool that 'works' – but not, make careful note, a tool-and-result.

SETTING UP THE DEBATE

What is a tool, anyway? And what is a conceptual framework, schema or world view? And whatever shall we employ and how shall we employ it in an effort to answer these kinds of questions? What method do we use in finding answers to these most fundamental questions of methodology? From our brief discussion thus far, it should be clear that Quine, Marx and Vygotsky, each in their own ways, appreciated the utter failure of nineteenth- and twentieth-century empiricism to answer such questions and attempted to develop alternatives. For while empirics – systematic observations – are obviously critical in the process of determining what is, empiricism's self-serving assertion that empirics alone can determine what is has failed to pass many valid tests, including, ironically, the test of empirics – the claim that all things can be tested by empirics cannot itself be tested empirically!

The first half of the twentieth century brought one last ditch effort by philosophers/methodologists to synthesize nineteenth-century empiricism and idealism in the pseudo-scientific criterion of verifiability put forth by the logical positivists of the Vienna Circle.[2] Both pragmatism and practice – the only seriously viable alternatives to empiricism – also took shape. Yet revolutionary practice, the methodology created by Marx, was being deformed even in its infancy by revisionist philosophers and politicians who would turn it from a method for transforming all of social reality into a theory for guiding economic development. Pragmatism and the capitalist system with which it is associated have fared better, if not well, during these ninety years. Thus, as we move toward the twenty-first century, a methodological confrontation between the well-funded (albeit deformed) method of pragmatism and its poor relative, the (also deformed) method of practice, unfolds. Even as worse-for-wear capitalism now stands victorious over revisionist Stalinist communism in the domain of practical politics here in the prologue to the twenty-first century, the most basic practical-critical scientific issues of world view and method remain essentially unresolved, with practice and pragmatics the only important players left standing in the world historic contest.

This debate between pragmatism and practice, between method as a tool for result (the pragmatic method) and method as tool-and-result (the method of practice), cuts across the nationalistic, everyday politics of contemporary international society. It does not fit into any neat categories, certainly not the recently deceased dichotomy between capitalism and revisionist communism. The debate is not societal – it is historical. There is good reason to believe that its outcome will determine and be determined by whether or not our species will follow a progressive or regressive direction in the years ahead.[3]

What is the difference between tool for result and tool-and-result? At the risk of seeming ridiculously simplistic, we suggest that the difference may turn on the distinction between the words 'for' and 'and.'

PRACTICE

We begin our discussion of the method of practice, seemingly indirectly, by investigating tool. Even in its simple dictionary denotative use (definition), the term 'tool' is exceedingly complex. In contemporary industrial society there are at least two different kinds of tools. There are tools that are mass produced (hammers, screwdrivers, power saws, etc.), and there are tools designed and produced typically by tool- and die-makers or toolmakers, i.e. tools specifically and uniquely designed and developed to assist in the development of other products (including, often, other tools). Because the distinction between these two kinds of tool is of such methodological importance, we want to make clear what it is and what it is not. The distinction we are making is not between mass-produced and hand-produced tools, nor between tools when used for the purpose intended by the maker (hammering a nail with a hammer) and tools when used for another purpose (hitting someone over the head with a hammer), nor between tools that remain unchanged in doing a job and tools that are transformed thereby.

Not everything that is needed or wanted by humankind can be made by simply using (applying) the tools that have already been mass manufactured in modern society. Often we must create a tool which is specifically designed to create what we ultimately wish to produce. The tools of the hardware store and the tools of the tool- and die-maker are qualitatively different in a tool for result/tool- and-result sort of way. Hardware store tools, such as hammers, come to be identified and recognized as usable for a certain end, i.e. they become reified and identified with a certain function and, as such, insofar as the manufactured hammer as a social extension (a tool) of human activity comes to define its human user (as all tool use does), it does so in a predetermining sense. Marxists of all persuasions (and many others) accept that tool use impacts on categories of cognition. Tools for results are analogous to (as well as producers of) cognitive equipment (e.g. concepts, ideas, beliefs, attitudes, emotions, intentions, thought and language) that are complete (fully manufactured) and usable for a particular purpose.

The toolmaker's tool is different in a most important way. While purposeful, it is not categorically distinguishable from the result achieved by its use. Explicitly created for the purpose of helping to make a specific product, it has no reified prefabricated social identity independent of that activity. Indeed, empirically speaking, such tools are typically no more recognizable as tools than the product (often a quasi-tool or small part of a larger product) itself is recognizable as product. They are inseparable. It is the produc- tive activity which defines both – the tool *and* the product (the result).

Unlike the hammer (the hardware store, manufactured, tool for result tool), this kind of tool – the toolmaker's tool-and-result – has no completed or generalized identity. Indeed, it typically has no name; it appears in no dictionary or grammar book. Such tools (or, semantically speaking, such a sense of the word 'tool') define their human users quite differently from the way hardware store tools, whether of the physical, symbolic or psychological variety, do. The inner cognitive, attitudinal, creative, linguistic tools developed from the toolmaker type of social tools are incomplete, unapplied, unnamed and, perhaps, unnameable. Expressed more positively, they are inseparable from results in that their essential character (their defining feature) is the activity of their development rather than their function. For their function is inseparable from the activity of their development. They are defined in and by the process of their production. This is not to say that such tools-and-results are without functions. It is, rather, to say that the attempt to define tools-and-results by their function (as is the case with tools for results) fundamentally distorts what they are (and, of course, in the process, what definition is).

This issue of tools – and the distinction we are taking such pains to put forth – is of great importance to understanding Vygotsky's work and the understandings and applications of his work by others. Every Vygotskian of both the revolutionary and reformist variety notes how important the concept of tool is for Vygotsky. But which tool (meaning of tool) do they employ?

In his prologue to the English edition of Volume 1 of *The Collected Works of L.S. Vygotsky* (1987) Bruner, who had written an introduction to Vygotsky's *Thought and Language* in 1962, addresses the matter of tools:

> In the new lectures it is quite evident once again that instrumental action is at the core of Vygotsky's thinking – action that uses both physical and symbolic tools to achieve its ends. The lectures give an account of how, in the end, man uses nature and the toolkit of culture to gain control of the world and of himself. But there is something new in his treatment of this theme – or perhaps it is my new recognition of something that was there before. For now there is a new emphasis on the manner in which, through using tools, man changes himself and his culture. Vygotsky's reading of Darwin is strikingly close to that of modern primatology . . . which also rests on the argument that human evolution is altered by man-made tools whose use then creates a technical-social way of life. Once that change occurs, 'natural' selection becomes dominated by cultural criteria and favors those able to adapt to the tool-using, culture-using way of life. By Vygotsky's argument, tools, whether practical or symbolic, are initially 'external': used outwardly on nature or in communicating with others. But tools affect their users: language, used first as a communicative tool, finally shapes the minds of those who adapt to its use. It is one of the themes of Vygotskian psychology and his six lectures are dedicated to its explication in the context of human development. His chosen epigraph from Francis Bacon, used in *Thought and Language*,

could not be more apposite: neither hand or mind alone suffice; the tools and devices they employ finally shape them.

(1987, p. 3)

In our opinion, Bruner is correct in speculating that it is his own 'new recognition of something that was there before', rather than there being 'something new' in Vygotsky's treatment of the self- and species-transforming effect of the use of tools, which in fact is basic, although not unique, to Marxism – as Vygotsky was well aware. While Marx himself did not develop a new psychology that made use of this recognition, Vygotsky went a substantial way toward doing so. Fundamental to his work was the specification to psychology of the Marxist socio-methodological principle of self- and species-transformation through the use of tools. Tool-and-result psycho-methodology, or toolmaking, is precisely that specification.

Vygotsky's tool-and-result method is purposeful in the Marxian sense, not, contrary to Bruner's formulation, in the instrumentalist sense. Vygotsky's rejection of the causal and/or functional methodological notion of tool or instrument *for* a purpose or result in favor of the dialectical notion of tool-and-result in the study of human psychology is new and revolutionary.[4] Apparently, Bruner does not see this. Only the denial, whether intended or not, of Vygotsky as a Marxist revolutionary scientist (in contrast to the view of him as a psychologist who quotes Marx) by Bruner and so many others could lead them to miss what Vygotsky brings to his research and, therefore, to miss his advancement of Marxism as a methodology and humanistic science – the method and science of psychology as revolutionary practice.

For both Marx and Vygotsky, revolution was the driving force of history. Marx observes:

. . . all forms and products of consciousness cannot be dissolved by mental criticism . . . but only by the practical overthrow of the actual social relations which gave rise to this idealistic humbug; that not criticism but revolution is the driving force of history.

(Marx and Engels, 1973, p. 58)

Vygotsky, in the passage quoted earlier (p. 9), makes the following clear statement of what he takes the scientific revolutionary activity to be:

The scientific mind . . . views revolution as the locomotive of history forging ahead at full speed; it regards the revolutionary epoch as a tangible, living embodiment of history. A revolution solves only those tasks which have been raised by history: this proposition holds true equally for revolution in general and for aspects of social and cultural life.

(Quoted in Levitan, 1982, inside front cover)

Marx, by no means a psychologist, was concerned with the sociology of history and the science of revolution. One of his most significant discoveries – that the nature of human activity is practical-critical – he took to be a socio-historical fact, not a psychological fact. His concern was the making of revolution. It remained for Vygotsky, in his quest to develop a Marxist psychology – a revolutionary practice that would transform human beings in a post-revolutionary period – to discover the methodological-psychological tool-and-result approach which identifies practical-critical revolutionary activity as what people do. Both the pragmatist Quine and his follower Kuhn, whose positing of 'paradigm shifts' as the central 'structure of scientific revolutions' has become the major explanatory principle in the history of science (Kuhn, 1962), regard changing an entire world view as a 'rare' revolutionary act. The revolutionaries Marx and Vygotsky consider it the practical-critical activity of everyday life.

In our view, the implications of thus standing Quine and the pragmatists on their heads are profound. A synthesis of Marx's discovery of practical-critical, revolutionary activity and Vygotsky's tool-and-result methodology yields a new understanding of the psychology of human beings consistent with Marxian and Vygotskian principles. It remains for us and other revolutionary Vygotskians to sketch out and develop this new mode of understanding.

Practical-critical activity transforms the totality of what there is; it is this revolutionary activity that is essentially and specifically human. Such activity 'overthrows' the overdetermining empiricist, idealist and vulgar materialist pseudo-notion of particular 'activity' *for* a particular end – which in reality, i.e., society, is behavior. The distinction between changing particulars and changing totalities is vital to understanding tool-and-result methodology and, therefore, revolutionary activity.

CHANGING TOTALITIES IN EVERYDAY LIFE

> The coincidence of the changing of circumstances and of human activity or self-changing can be conceived and rationally understood only as revolutionary practice.
>
> (Marx, 1973, p. 121)

In the seventeenth century Leibniz first made plain that, from a naturalistic or spatio-temporal point of view, changing a single 'thing' (spatio-temporal point) entails changing everything (the totality). Indeed, the common sense notion of a particular action or event altering a single other or even several other states of affairs – but not the totality – is illusory; it is an abstraction beyond any type of verification.

This causal, 'a *for* b' paradigm (derived from and inextricably linked to tool for result methodology) has been outgrown in the physical sciences, yet persists within so-called common sense and the so-called social sciences. Why? The answer is exceedingly complex and to spell out the circumstances and process of its overthrow is beyond the scope of this chapter – indeed, of this book. Yet the overriding reason seems clear and simple. In modern times, an understanding of physical phenomena no longer demands that a moral-ideological and/or economic-political account be implicit or explicit in the explanation, as was the case in pre-feudal and feudal times when Aristotelian and scholastic physical science made just such a demand. This demand was overcome by the rising bourgeoisie's need for knowledge that was quantifiable, measurable and right here on earth, and by the radical discoveries of Copernicus, Galileo and others. It was then that the natural sciences were mathematicized, technologized and, thereby, fully liberated from the feudal constraints of teleology and God. To this day, however, the social sciences are fettered by 'deistic' dogma; they remain in the service of the dominant ideology. On the one hand that ideology and the class for which it speaks require accountability and responsibility (the law must know, for example, what was done – in particular – and who – in particular – did it). On the other hand, the ruling ideology eschews revolutionary activity (the concept and, especially, the practice). That is why Marx's insistence that revolutionary practice is the 'peep stone' required to comprehend the ordinary practical-critical activity of people changing circumstances which are changing them, and Vygotsky's tool-and-result psychological practice, are still regarded as esoteric. In fact they are the nineteenth- and twentieth-century analogs to Galileo's revolutionary *Two New Sciences*.[5]

But do we human beings engage in revolutionary activity? What does the practical-critical activity of everyday life look like? Doing something in particular, a, to bring about a certain particular end, b, is real enough behavior relative to our societal definitions and identity, but is, historically speaking, illusory. We are employing here the critical distinction (not a dichotomy) between society and history as human life spaces. As human beings, we all live simultaneously in *history* (the open-ended, seamless totality of existence) and in *society* (the name given to a specific spatio-temporal institutional arrangement 'within' history); we all live in history/society.[6] All societies necessarily adapt their members to this dual location and dual identity, but they vary widely in the degree to which they require adaptation just to themselves or to history as well. Modern liberal-religious industrial societies, the ultra-pragmatic United States in particular, adapt their members to society to such an extent that most people do not even know that they are in history – or that history is something to which one can adapt. This deprivation of historical identity leaves us vulnerable to both reactionary political change (fascism) and psychopathology (e.g. depression) (Holzman and Polk, 1988; F. Newman, 1987). In speaking of the US experience, Newman says:

> Our sensibility, such as it is, is mediated by an incredible barrage of words and images carefully shaped in such a way as to not simply create a certain picture, but to explicitly create a certain sense of alienation from the sources and objects of that picture. That is, to destroy our sense of history. There is ample evidence to suggest that as a people, we have not simply been alienated from the historical process of work and production but we have been alienated from the historical process of our own historical development. We have been denied the *possibility* of history as well as the *actuality* of history.
>
> (1987, p. 20)

Life is lived from one day's 6 o'clock news to the next – governed by what we might well call radical chauvinism![7]

Adapting to history means engaging in the revolutionary activity of changing totalities; adapting to society, in the case of the societies in which we currently live, means carrying out certain acts, behaviors and roles appropriate to and having exchange value within the narrow confines of this particular time and place (moment) in world history. Thus, our day-to-day societally determined and commodified 'activities' are not activity at all in the Marxian, historical sense. Just like economic commodities under the socio-economic-ideological system known as capitalism, they are simultaneously real (societally) and illusory (historically).

Why is this so? Because the process of commodification totally misrepresents and radically distorts by alienation the actual historical process of production. As Marx points out, commodification occurs under the domination of the process of producing for exchange (which means, in the final analysis, for profit), not for use. Virtually all of the things that get produced under capitalism – cars, houses, food, books, diplomas, ideas, feelings – are not produced because they are useful (although they may be useful) but in order to be distributed and sold on the market. This activity of producing what we use in a manner which has less to do with our own needs as human beings and more to do with the need of some to make a profit has the effect of separating, in a profound way, the activity of production from the product of production. This social phenomenon is what Marx (1967) termed 'alienation.'

Such causal and societal, a for b, commodified 'activity' is best understood as *fetishization* (Marx, 1967, pp. 71–83). Marx took pains to understand commodities not just economically but also ideologically and/or subjectively. To Marx, commodities are fetishized, i.e. their very existence and character have the property of being structurally disengaged from the process by which they were created, while appearing, in society, otherwise. In this, they are much like gods – created by us to be incomprehensible to us.[8] Just as the fetishized commodity appears, within society, to have an existence and a motion independent of the social process of production that gave rise to it, so societal a for b 'activity' (behavior) is god-like and overdetermined, i.e. seeming to be lawfully (causally, functionally) connected independent of active human agency and, even more, unchangeable. For example, this book you are reading is, while useful (we hope!), a commodity; it was produced for exchange; it has the characteristic of being fetishized, i.e. it exists and is related to independently of the social process of production that gave rise to it (which includes the complex conjuncture of many processes of production, including but not limited to the process of production of human language, written language, printing presses, mass-produced books, educational institutions, publishing institutions and the discipline of psychology). So, too, societal a for b 'activity,' or behavior – the things we do every day – appear to exist (and do so, societally) and are related to in a way that separates them from the process of their production – in particular, from the actual human activity that produced them. (We created these words using language created by people – historically speaking; the book was printed on presses built and operated by workers, etc.).

The seemingly lawful connections of a for b 'activity' (behavior) independent of historical, active human agency is one of the primary ways that an essentially religious world view – including notions of predeterminism, overdeterminism and, indeed, vulgar determinism – have been incorporated into capitalist ideology and bourgeois scientific methodology as causality or functionalism. Kant went so far as to glorify causality as one of the *a priori* synthetic categories (conditions) necessary for the human experience itself. During the two centuries since Kant, traditional physical science has pretty much abandoned the notion of cause. Nevertheless, a for b, means–end instrumentalism, or functionalism, remains within 'common sense' syntax and embedded in the pre-scientific study of what is traditionally called psychology.

While causality – as both an explanatory principle and a topic to be investigated – permeates all of psychology, it is perhaps most pernicious and distorting in developmental psychology. No less renowned a developmentalist than Piaget is little more (or less) than a supplier of evidence for the 'psychological reality' of Kant's *a priori* categories of experience. For Piaget development consisted of the means by which the child, acting upon the world (in societal reality, behaving in the world), moves her/himself through stages in the acquisition and use of the basic human epistemological tools by which it is possible to understand 'our' world. These tools are Kant's categories of experience – the concept of the object, relation, temporality and causality. According to Piaget, the concept of causality develops slowly; he made great use of what he saw as the child's lack of correct (adult) usage of causal terms such as 'because' and 'so,' the primitive 'why' questions young children ask and the animistic answers they give when asked 'why' to provide evidence for both Kant's contention that the mind is structured to see causality and for his own stage theory of intellectual development. This he did without ever questioning the particular causal connections a specific culture has produced nor, what is methodologically even more problematic, the socio-cultural-historical notion of causality itself![9]

Thus, while the natural science community has shaped a methodology suitable *to* its own development in the process and practice *of* its own development, psychology grafted an eighteenth- and nineteenth-century methodology onto itself and, to this day, has not fully discovered the human methodology necessary for a uniquely human psychology. In our view, Vygotsky and Marx made significant contributions to such an effort. To complete our sketch of their work on this project, we would do well to summarize the complex relationship between: (1) revolutionary (practical-critical) activity; (2) a and b (tool-and-result) as opposed to a for b (tool for result) methodology; and (3) changing particulars vs changing totalities.

REVOLUTIONARY, PRACTICAL-CRITICAL ACTIVITY

Revolutionary practice or activity (not to be equated with the particular revolutionary activity of making a revolution)[10] is ordinary day-to-day, hour-to-hour, human (historical) activity: it is a particular action, a, changing the totality of circumstances (historical 'scenes') of human existence B, C, D,... and combinations of circumstances {B, C, D,... }, etc. The distinctly human quality of our species is its capacity to practice revolutionary activity, a capacity, as we have said, that is, unfortunately, only sometimes self-consciously manifest. Instead, our ordinary activity (so-called) is non-revolutionary; in fact, *it is not activity at all*. Rather, it is either societally determined behavior or the motion of natural (physical, chemical) phenomena; it is, thereby, neither uniquely nor specifically human. What we are calling human activity, in all its infinitely complex variations, is always changing that which is changing, which is changing that which is changing ... It is changing the historical totality (or, more accurately, the many totalities) that determines the changer. Indeed, this radically non-dualistic dialectic-in-practice is what changing – i.e. activity – is.

As a species, we are distinguished from other species, as far as we can tell, by the fact that we are never fundamentally changed, as human beings, except insofar as (by our revolutionary activity) we fundamentally change other things. What our species changes are the circumstances of our continued historical existence.

What, then, is the relationship between changing particulars vs changing totalities and tools? Recall that the toolmaker's tool-and-result is that tool specifically created to assist in the development of something that we wish to create. Tools of this sort are paradigmatically 'prerequisite and product' in that the creation of the product is not limited by the pre-existent, societally determined manufactured tools (linguistic, cognitive or store bought) available for its conceptualization and its actualization.[11] Indeed, it could not be so limited, for the tool, not yet made, is a precondition for the product. It is not linearly in advance of the product, either conceptually or materially. Tool *and* product of tool are therefore, of necessity, a produced unity. The toolmaker and the poet (by contrast with the users of manufactured tools and/or ordinary language) do not begin with tool for product and move to product; rather, the toolmaker and the poet create the unity (totality) tool-and-product, since tool is materially defined by product as much as product is defined by tool. (The product makes the tool every bit as much as the tool makes the product.) The toolmaker must create the totality tool-and-result just as the poet must create meanings as she/he creates the poem. Unlike the user of hardware store tools who is defined and predetermined by the particular behavior of using those tools which are made *for* a particular (and also predetermined) function, the toolmaker is neither defined nor predetermined. As the producer of the totality tool-and-result, the toolmaker is a changer of historical totalities. She/he is engaged in revolutionary (human-historical) activity.

THOUGHT AND LANGUAGE

We have taken pains to explain the significance of Marx's notion of revolutionary activity as being central to an understanding of Vygotsky as a revolutionary scientist and of Vygotsky's foundational discoveries in psychology and methodology (in particular, tool-and-result methodology). Yet no less a thinker than Marx himself was vulnerable to the dominance of tool for result methodology and causal and/or functional models. In an oft-quoted section of *Capital*, Marx exposes a functionalist bias:

> We presuppose labor in a form that stamps it as exclusively human. A spider conducts operations that resemble those of a weaver, and a bee puts to shame many an architect in the

construction of her cells. But what distinguishes the worst architect from the best of bees is this, that the architect raises his
structure in imagination before he erects it in reality. At the end
of every labor process, we get a result that already existed in the
imagination of the laborer at its commencement. He also realizes
a purpose of his own that gives the law to his modus operandi,
and to which he must subordinate his will.

(1967, p. 178)

The above statement delineates what Marx took to be the essential characteristic of human labor as opposed to animal labor.
(Many have used it – erroneously and opportunistically, we think
– to justify their own denial of revolutionary activity and as the
basis for claiming that Marx took labor to be the essentially human
activity.)[12] But Marx's tool for result, functionalist description is
both philosophically (analytically) and empirically (descriptively)
inaccurate. If the structure is 'raised in imagination' before it is
'erected in reality,' i.e. if the process is linear, then what and where
is the dialectic of this human process? If, as Marx teaches us, 'life
precedes consciousness' (not the other way around), then how is
imagination to precede its actualization or materialization? To be
sure, one might imagine Marx arguing that the imagining activity
associated with any labor process could derive from a prior process
and/or set of material circumstances. But this simply puts off our
question; it does not answer it. For we should still wish to know if
the process or set of circumstances that 'yielded' the prior labor
process had an imagining associated with it. And if not, from what
did it come? This reification of imaginings and the reintroduction
of purpose as a psychological construct allows the old philosophi-
cal-theological argument of first cause back into play even as the
early methodological Marx had ruthlessly eliminated it.

As is so often true with Marx, the corrective to this mistake is to
be found in his own writings, portions of which we have already
quoted. We point out this misleading inaccuracy on his part because it is useful in illustrating how we understand Vygotsky's
revolutionary scientific understanding of thought, language and
meaning as revolutionary activities.

In the beginning the human species (anthropologically and
psychologically) is neither word nor imagining, neither thought
nor language – we are, Marx has said, without propositional or
mentalistic premises.[13] In the beginning is the revolutionary

activity of reorganizing the totality or totalities of human circum-
stance. The unique quality of human labor is not to be found in the
realization of preconceived purpose but in the meaningfulness (the
practical-criticalness, the revolutionariness) of human activity. The
bee may very well have something in mind before it moves ahead,
and the human worker, particularly with advances in the use of
computers in the labor process (but even before), may have nothing
in mind. But the bee knows and cares nothing of meaning. Meaning
has no meaning in the life of the bee! No doubt, there is communication among (and perhaps even between) the bees and spiders,
but there is no meaning. Animals communicate (some make
honey) but they don't make meaning. For us, meaning is to be
located precisely in the human capacity to alter the historical
totality even as we are determined (in our societal particularity) by
it. The activity of making meaning is a fundamental expression of
revolutionary activity. It is the toolmaker (our species) making
tools-and-results using the predetermining tools of the hardware
store variety (including nature and language) and the predetermined tools of mind developed by them to create something – a
totality – not determined by them. It is the meaning in the emerging
activity, not the preconceived imagining followed by its realization, which is transformative, revolutionary and *essentially*
human.[14]

Vygotsky provides valuable insight into meaning-making as
revolutionary activity in early childhood in his discussion of concept development. He identifies the pseudo-concept as a 'critical
moment in the development of the child's concepts, a moment
which simultaneously separates and connects complexive and
conceptual thinking' (1987, p. 142). In discussing the value of
experiments which investigated pseudo-concepts, Vygotsky reveals the process of meaning-making (concept formation) as the
activity of utilizing what we just called the predetermining tools of
the hardware store (language) and the predetermined tools of
mind developed by them to create something not determined by
them.

According to Vygotsky, concepts develop in a dialectical manner, not 'freely or spontaneously along lines demarcated by the
child himself'; however, the adult cannot simply 'transfer his own
mode of thinking to the child' (1987, pp. 142–3). Rather, there is an
internal contradiction in pseudo-concepts in that they look just like
adult word meanings yet they are constructed in an entirely

different manner from adult word meanings. A child's language (word meanings, concepts, generalizations) is produced using word meanings predetermined by the adult language, but the child's language is not the adult language: 'the speech of those who surround the child predetermines the path that the development of the child's generalizations will take. [But] it links up with the child's own activity' (p. 143). This activity produces the pseudo-concept, something new, something not determined by the tools used to produce it. The child's language learning activity is, then, one of making meaning. To use Wittgenstein's rich description (1953), it is the activity of playing language games.

While there is no evidence that Vygotsky had such a formulation in mind, his arguments for the dialectical character of pseudo-concepts and the significance of experiments which reveal this process are strikingly supportive of precisely this understanding:

The experiment . . . allows us to discover how the child's own activity is manifested in learning adult language. The experiment indicates what the child's language would be like and the nature of the generalizations that would direct his thinking if its development were not directed by an adult language that effectively predetermines the range of concrete objects to which a given word meaning can be extended.

One could argue that our use of phrases such as 'would be like' and 'would direct' . . . in this context provides the basis for an argument against rather than for the use of the experiment since the child is not in fact free to develop the meanings he receives from adult speech. We would respond to this argument by noting that the experiment teaches more than what would happen if the child were free from the directing influence of adult speech, more than what would happen if he developed his generalizations freely and independently. The experiment uncovers the real activity of the child in forming generalizations, activity that is generally masked in casual observation. The influence of the speech of those around the child does not obliterate this activity. It merely conceals it, causing it to take an extremely complex form. The child's thinking does not change the basic laws of its activity simply because it is directed by stable and constant word meanings. These laws are merely expressed in unique form under the concrete conditions in which the actual development of the child's thinking occurs.

(1987, p. 143)

How did Vygotsky discover that what makes thinking and speaking uniquely human is *the revolutionary activity of making meaning*? We think it was his practical-critical understanding of Marx's radical non-propositional historical monism, whose premises are 'men . . . in their actual, empirically perceptible process of development under definite conditions.'

Vygotsky speaks further about the inseparability of the human capacity to make meaning (to engage in revolutionary activity) from speaking and thinking. He makes plain that thinking and speaking are not linearly, causally, teleologically, purposefully or functionally related; they are dialectically unified by meaning. Unlike functionalist or causal/linear theorists (such as Piaget, for example), Vygotsky (speaking and thinking dialectically) says that meaning

> belongs not only to the domain of thought but to the domain of speech... A word without meaning no longer belongs to the domain of speech. One cannot say of word meaning what we said earlier of the elements of the word taken separately. Is word meaning speech or is it thought? It is both at one and the same time; it is a *unit of verbal thinking*. It is obvious, then, that our method must be that of semantic analysis. Our method must rely on the analysis of the meaningful aspect of speech; it must be a method for studying verbal meaning.

(1987, p. 47)

The study of thinking/speaking as activity exposes the meaning-making essence of humankind and, thereby, the revolution-making essence of our species. Thinking and speaking do not make us human. Rather, thinking and speaking are uniquely human in that their dialectical unity derives from the ability of the species to make meaning, which is nothing more nor less than the ability to make revolution, to make tools(-and-results). Verbal behavior (the computer-like use of language as a tool for result by tool for result-determined thinking) may dominate societally fixed intercourse, precisely as exchange value in general dominates within an economically commodified society. But the sometimes manifest ability to use such tools for result to create meaning and thereby reorganize thinking/speaking and much else (potentially everything else) is the essentially human, essentially revolutionary activity. In its absence, there would be no thinking/speaking at all. As Wittgenstein took great pains to teach us, the essence of language is not that *it* refers but that *people* refer (and do much else) using it (1953). What is fundamental is the activity. Unsegmented and timeless history in which we all live makes possible the uniquely human activity of transforming all of history at any historical moment.

Those who seek to study human activity by somehow eliminating the experimenter are indistinguishable from those who would study birds as if they could not fly. One can do so but only at the cost of no longer studying birds. As the Vygotskian-informed Rockefeller researchers noted, the 'proper unit of analysis for an ecologically valid psychology' is not the individual, but the 'person–environment interface' or 'the scene.' Yet while 'the scene' takes into account the socialness of the human being, it does so in a way that hardly distinguishes the human being from the bee or spider. While Cole, Hood and McDermott were splendidly sensitive to the overdetermining categories and language of society and sometimes they were even concerned with the 'history' of these and other social institutions and the genetic analysis of people functioning within them, they were seemingly oblivious to the activist (as in revolutionary activist) nature of human beings in history and, therefore, to an historical method for psychology. Hence, while their approach is social, and perhaps even radically so, it is not historical. The object of study in an historical psychology is the revolutionary activity of our species.

Vygotsky's overriding scientific concern was to study people as people, not as something other than people. He shared with Freud the drive to discover the uniquely human. For Freud it was the unconscious mind and the societal need to repress it. For Vygotsky, like Marx, it was the fundamentality of revolutionary activity and the societal need to express it. (Those radically opposed world views make a Marx/Freud 'synthesis' impossible.)[15] Marxian psychology is Vygotskian, for both Marx and Vygotsky treat revolutionary activity as human activity. Those social and functional approaches that fail to treat revolutionary activity as their object of study fail, thereby, to study human beings as human beings.

While many who have studied thought and language have sought to explicate the complex and dynamic relationship between the rule-governed component of thought/language and the creative component of thought/language, few have done so as revolutionary activity theorists. Vygotsky is one of them. Another is Wittgenstein. While he might not have treated revolutionary activity as fundamental (indeed, it is not clear that Vygotsky does so self-consciously), in his later work Wittgenstein took activity as that which forbids the deadly dualistic separation of thought and language and of language and what, presumably, language is about. In doing so, he was engaging in the study of meaning-making as ordinary revolutionary activity.

As life-in-history/life-in-society is the ongoing dialectical environment (scene) of human existence, so, then, is revolutionary activity/verbal behavior the ongoing speaking/thinking environment (scene) of human learning and development. A Marxian developmental, clinical, social and educational psychology must be located within the history/society scene and directed towards the study of the revolutionary activity/verbal behavior scene.

The tool-and-result study of speaking/thinking (which on Vygotsky's account is, after all, 'semantic analysis') would do well to incorporate a Wittgensteinian approach to semantic analysis – most particularly, to employ Wittgenstein's notion of 'language games':

> I shall in the future again and again draw your attention to what I shall call language games. These are ways of using signs simpler than those in which we use the signs of our highly complicated everyday language. Language games are the forms of language with which a child begins to make use of words. The study of language games is the study of primitive forms of language or primitive languages. If we want to study the problems of truth or falsehood, of the agreement and disagreement of propositions with reality, of the nature of assertions, assumptions and questions, we shall with great advantage look at primitive forms of language in which these forms of thinking appear without the confusing background of highly complicated processes of thought. When we look at such simple forms of language the mental mist which seems to enshroud our

ordinary use of language disappears. We see activities, reactions, which are clear-cut and transparent.

(1965, p. 17)

Language games help us see clearly the activity of language and thought, i.e. the revolutionary process by which language and thought are produced, by which meaning is made. The 'confusing background' mentioned by Wittgenstein is societally fixed semantics and syntax which do more to hide speaking/thinking as activity than to expose it. Revolutionary activity is, on this account, itself a game which, in Wittgenstein's words, bears only a 'family resemblance' to other games. It is the revolutionary game of making new meanings that shows the social activity of language/thought through the 'mist' of societal and metaphysical meaninglessness.

Chapter 4

The zone of proximal development

A psychological unit or a revolutionary unity?

We turn in this chapter and the next two to Vygotsky's pychological findings and how contemporary Vygotskians have utilized them. We seek to examine Vygotsky's tool-and-result methodology in his and others' specific psychological research and discoveries about development and learning, and language and thought. In this chapter we focus on what is considered Vygotsky's most important psychological-methodological discovery, the zone of proximal development (ZPD).

THE ZPD-IN-USE: THE RELATIONSHIP BETWEEN LEARNING AND DEVELOPMENT

Vygotsky's consideration of the relationship between teaching/learning or instruction and development is extremely rich and complex.[1] It is where we see him most clearly creating the ZPD, a critical tool-and-result of his own Marxist tool-and-result psychological method. In these discussions of learning and development, topics appear, disappear and reappear; Vygotsky seems to contradict himself many times; there are inconsistencies and jumps to topics seemingly unrelated to what came before. For example, Koffka, a leading gestalt psychologist of the day, is both criticized for his dualistic understanding of development and credited with making a breakthrough in its theoretical understanding. Some of Vygotsky's most interesting insights are presented in the context of this overall discussion: he addresses discipline, learning to write, grammar, meaning, consciousness, scientific concept learning and everyday concept learning and foreign language learning in what reads to us like a passionate intellectual struggle to advance beyond the existing state of theory and break the chains of linear, cause–effect, tool for result methodology.

In investigating the relationship between learning and development, Vygotsky made the common sense (but no less significant) observation that if we determine the child's level of development from observations of what she/he can do independently (of others), then we are in fact considering only that which has already matured. This, he argued, is wholly inadequate:

> The state of development is never defined only by what has matured. If the gardener decides only to evaluate the mature or harvested fruits of the apple tree, he cannot determine the state of his orchard. Maturing trees must also be taken into consideration. The psychologist must not limit his analysis to functions that have matured. He must consider those that are in the process of maturing. If he is to fully evaluate the state of the child's development, the psychologist must consider not only the actual level of development but *the zone of proximal development*.
>
> (1987, pp. 208–9)

Central, then, to the discovery-in-use of the ZPD was Vygotsky's concern with the character of the relationship between 'matured' and 'maturing' processes and, what seems plainly related (it surely did so to Vygotsky), the relationship between what the child can do independently and in collaboration with others. While recognizing, as some of his contemporaries also did, that a child can accomplish more with collaboration, help or support than she/he can alone, Vygotsky noted that the child's potential – even with help – is not unlimited. The ZPD is critical to this understanding as well. For example, the view that imitation is a purely mechanical process and that therefore the child is capable of imitating virtually anything was, according to Vygotsky, incorrect. The child – and the rest of us, for that matter – can only imitate what is in the range of our developmental level (the ZPD): 'If I am not able to play chess, I will not be able to play a match even if a chess master shows me how' (1987, p. 209). Studies of early language acquisition conducted in the 1970s gave further empirical weight to Vygotsky's argument. It was found that individual children not only vary in the amount they imitate the language they hear, but they are selective in what they imitate, i.e. children do not imitate what they know well nor what is far beyond their linguistic level. They imitate what they are in the process of learning (Bloom, Hood and Lightbown, 1974).

Mistaken paradigms

In reviewing the educational theory and practice of his day, Vygotsky saw three major perspectives on the relationship between development and instruction. (In many ways, these views are still dominant.) First is the *separatist* perspective – that development and instruction are separate and independent processes. According to this view development obeys internal, natural laws (laws of maturation), and instruction externally utilizes the potentials of development. We see this perspective expressed in research designs, educational practices and diagnostic and evaluation procedures that attempt to isolate that which is a function of 'pure' development from that which is a function of instruction. In rejecting this view Vygotsky (1987) noted wryly, 'The fact that not a single investigator has succeeded in this task is generally attributed to limitations in research method. The attempt is made to compensate for these inadequacies of method through the power of abstraction' (p. 194).

A variation of this separatist perspective puts forth a thoroughly one-sided dependency relationship: instruction, though separate from development, depends on development, while development is unaffected by instruction. Commenting on this variation of the separation of learning and development, Vygotsky makes the apt comparison to the relationship between production and consumption: 'Instruction consumes the products of development. It uses them and applies them to life' (1987, p. 195). While Vygotsky recognized a kernel of truth in this view, he was firm in his insistence that whatever developmental prerequisite for learning there might be, it is of secondary importance and obscures the true relationship between development and instruction. He writes:

> The attempt to represent it as the central issue, or, indeed, as the whole issue, leads to several misunderstandings and mistakes. Specifically, it has been assumed that instruction reaps the fruit of the child's maturation while it has no significance for development. The child's memory, attention, and thinking develop to the level where the child can be instructed in writing and arithmetic. In response to the question of whether instructing

the child in writing or arithmetic affects his memory, attention, or thinking, however, traditional psychology suggests that these processes always change when they are exercised whatever form that exercise may take. The course of development itself, however, does not change as a consequence of instruction. Nothing new emerges in the child's mental development when we teach him to write. The child we have when we finish is identical to the one we had when we began, with the sole exception that he is literate.

(1987, pp. 195–6)

According to Vygotsky, Piaget pushed this separatist perspective – which was dominant in their time – to its logical limit. Piaget's mode of investigation, the clinical interview, was based on the assumption that one could and should examine the child's capacity for thinking in areas in which she/he is absolutely devoid of knowledge. For if we ask children about things they know, we will be discovering something about what they have been instructed in, and not about their 'pure' thinking. The separation here between development and learning and thinking and knowing is very sharply drawn indeed. Although Piaget is often credited with having rejected IQ and other quantitative tests in favor of his 'clinical method,' the Piagetian separation of 'pure development' from learning has dominated twentieth-century educational psychology, as manifest in concrete and biased practices such as IQ testing.[2]

The second perspective on development and instruction is the *identity* perspective – that they are essentially the same. Vygotsky attributed the origins of this view to William James' educational psychology. James believed that habits are the basis for both development and instruction. It is by forming associations between stimuli and responses that both learning and development occur. Following James, Thorndike 'advanced' this theory by equating mental development with the gradual accumulation of conditioned reflexes.

Vygotsky's objections to the identity perspective are applicable in certain ways to the separatist view as well. Not only are both views inaccurate, he said, but they also close down any discussion of the actual relationship between development and learning. Speaking of the limitations of both perspectives, Vygotsky noted,

Rather than untying the knot which represents the relationship between instruction and development, the first theory cuts it. This theory recognizes no relationship between the two processes. The second theory eliminates or avoids this knot entirely. Since they are one and the same thing, the issue of the relationship between instruction and development or the nature of this relationship cannot arise.

(1987, p. 196)

What of a synthesis of the separatist and identity positions? This is precisely the position of the third group of theories. To Vygotsky, it was as methodologically flawed as the other two.

There is a *third* group of theories that have been particularly influential in European child psychology. These theories attempt to rise above the extremes inherent in the two perspectives outlined above, they attempt to sail between the Scylla and Charybdis. The result, however, is typical of theories that attempt to occupy a middle ground between two extreme perspectives. This third group of theories fails to gain a position *above* the other two and assumes a position between them.

(1987, p. 197)

Locating itself in the theoretical no-man's land between two mutually exclusive positions, this group of theories embodies an inherent 'liberal' duality. For example, Koffka proposed that development itself has a dual character – there is development as maturation and development as instruction. Each influences the other to some degree, but Koffka does not specify how. While this is a slight advance on the previous extreme positions, far from 'untying the knot' and making it possible to explore the deeper relationship between development and instruction, Koffka's theory tightens the knot further:

Koffka's position not only fails to resolve the issue but confuses it. It lifts itself upward to the level of the principle which underlies the mistake that is common to both the first two groups of theories, to the level of the principle that produced their shared misstatement of the problem.

(1987, p. 197)

Nevertheless, Vygotsky saw ways in which Koffka's position might be useful in advancing an understanding of the actual relationship between development and learning. For one thing, Koffka at least recognized that some instruction produces structural changes, i.e. leads to development (e.g. learning a new way of thinking). Being a structural process, instruction restructures development itself. 'Instruction is not limited to trailing after development or moving stride for stride along with it. It can move ahead of development, pushing it further and eliciting new formations' (1987, p. 198).

A new view

Where did the radical Vygotsky take this? What was his own view on the relationship between development and learning? Vygotsky saw learning and development as neither a single process nor as independent processes. Rather, the unity learning-and-development has complex interrelationships, which are the subject of his inquiry (1987, p. 201). How does instruction elicit development? The answer lies in the zone of proximal development. *'Instruction is useful when it moves ahead of development.* When it does, it *impels or wakens a whole series of functions that are in a stage of maturation lying in the zone of proximal development'* (1987, p. 212). Moreover, 'Instruction would be completely unnecessary if it merely utilized what had already matured in the developmental process, if it were not itself a source of development' (1987, p. 212).

According to Vygotsky, one of the developmental outcomes of learning leading development in the ZPD is that the child becomes able (as does the adult) to engage in developmental activity volitionally and with conscious awareness rather than merely spontaneously. Vygotsky discusses this finding at length in the context of investigating the relationship between the learning of spontaneous and scientific concepts. It is a serious challenge to the traditional understanding of 'motivation' as being internal and a prerequisite for, rather than an outcome of, learning. Volition and self-consciousness typically are seen as having a critical relationship to motivation. As educators and parents, we are constantly reminded (scolded) that children must be motivated in order to learn. However, according to Vygotsky (and we agree), children must learn in order to be motivated. In other words, learning leads development.

Vygotsky's analysis of the developmental history of the relationship between spontaneous and scientific concepts is an excellent example of learning leading development and of his claim that an outcome of learning leading development in the ZPD is the growing ability to engage in activity volitionally and with conscious awareness. On our view, both his approach and findings are evidence for the social nature of volition and conscious awareness.

Vygotsky never formally defines spontaneous and scientific concepts. Remember that, for Vygotsky, nothing is a thing-in-itself; in this sense, nothing is defined. What something is is determined by what it does and by its interrelatedness to other systems, processes and concepts. Nevertheless, it is possible to characterize the two kinds of concept. Scientific concepts typically are learned in school settings as part of a system of knowledge; they have explicit verbal definitions; their learning is made conscious; they are taught in the context of academic subjects such as social studies, language instruction and mathematics. Some examples of scientific concepts are: exploitation, causality, history, Archimedes' law. Spontaneous (sometimes called 'everyday') concepts are those the child learns in the course of her/his daily life. Their learning is not usually made conscious; the child uses such concepts with ease and without any awareness that there is such a thing as a 'concept.' Some examples of spontaneous concepts are: brother, numbers, the past. Thus, the two kinds of concept have a different relationship to the child's experience, and each manifests features both opposite from and identical to the other (1987, p. 177).[3]

Vygotsky summarizes the experimental work done by his colleague, Shif, with school-age children, who were asked to make complete sentences by adding to clauses which expressed causal relations (with the word 'because') and to clauses which expressed adversative relations (with the word 'although'). Some were clauses about spontaneous concepts, such as: 'The man fell off his bicycle because...' and 'Olya still reads poorly although...' Others were expressions of scientific concepts, such as: 'Planned economy is possible in the USSR because...' The findings are, on the face of it, counter-intuitive: the children did better at completing sentences with scientific concepts than they did at completing those with spontaneous concepts. Among the second-grade children, the difference was most striking with expressions of causal relations; these children were presumably not at all familiar with adversative relations, either as spontaneous concepts in their everyday life or as scientific concepts learned in school, and so they did equally poorly on both. The fourth-grade children did equally well on scientific and spontaneous concepts with causal relations, but better on scientific than spontaneous concepts with adversative relations.

Vygotsky interpreted these results in the following manner:

> ...there is a higher level of conscious awareness of scientific than everyday concepts, and there is a progressive development of scientific thinking which is followed by a rapid increase in levels of performance with everyday concepts. This indicates that the accumulation of knowledge leads directly to an increase in the level of scientific thinking and that this, in turn, influences the development of spontaneous thinking. This demonstrates the leading role of instruction in the development of the school child.
>
> (1987, p. 168)

Vygotsky attributes the greater level of conscious awareness of scientific concepts to the fact that they are produced in 'systematic cooperation' between teacher and child:

> The maturation of the child's higher mental functions occurs in this cooperative process, that is, it occurs through the adult's assistance and participation. In the domain of interest to us, this is expressed in the growth of the *relativeness* of causal thinking and in the development of a certain degree of *voluntary control* in scientific thinking. This element of voluntary control is a product of the instructional process itself.
>
> (1987, p. 169)

Scientific concepts and spontaneous concepts differ in their relationship to objects. Scientific concepts imply relations of generality among concepts (Vygotsky, 1987, p. 224);

> Concepts stand in a different relationship to the object when they exist outside a system than when they enter one. The relationship of the word 'flower' to the object is completely different for the child who does not yet know the words rose, violet, or lily than it is for the child who does.
>
> (p. 234)

Empirical connections, those between objects themselves (e.g. roses and violets), are what exist prior to types of flowers being in a systematic conceptual relation to the category of flower. Vygotsky argues that it is through the formation of such a system that conscious awareness develops, and from conscious awareness that voluntary control develops. His investigation was premised on the materiality of these mental processes; they are activities, simultaneously process and product, tool-and-result. His concern was to understand how the functional structure of consciousness changes through development and how its development reorganizes overall development. He differentiated conscious awareness and lack of conscious awareness from both consciousness and the Freudian unconscious, insightfully pointing out that, according to Freud, the unconscious is a comparatively late development that is derived from consciousness. Conscious awareness is a qualitatively different activity from consciousness. For example, if you are tying a knot you can be conscious of your action, i.e. you can focus your attention on your action, that of tying the knot, without having conscious awareness that you are or how you are tying the knot ('Right now I am tying a knot' or 'Now I am placing the left string over the right one'). 'Conscious awareness is an act of consciousness whose object is the activity of consciousness itself' (1987, p. 190).

Vygotsky goes on to explore how scientific concepts develop and, in turn, come to have a strong influence on the further development of spontaneous concepts. He never loses sight of his starting point: the development of conscious awareness, the role of meaningful speech in its development, and the type of investigation one would have to engage in to discover something useful and valid. He takes to task the psychologists of his day, including Piaget, for whom he had the most respect. According to Piaget, conscious awareness develops with the loss of egocentrism; concepts do not have their own process of development, he thought, but are simply acquired ready-made through the processes of 'understanding' and learning. Since for Piaget learning does not impact on development, he understood scientific concepts as coming chronologically and developmentally later – shadowing spontaneous concepts. In his own research of a similar nature to Vygotsky's, Piaget accounts for his finding that young children are unable to complete sentences with causal relations correctly (as the adult language user does) by claiming that they do not understand causality (Piaget, 1955; 1968).[4]

Of course, Vygotsky rejects this non-explanation. Concept formation is a social-cultural-historical activity which 'contains the key to the whole history of the child's mental development'

(Vygotsky, 1987, p. 167). The development of spontaneous and scientific concepts takes different routes.

> The birth of the spontaneous concept is usually associated with the child's immediate encounter with things, things that are often explained by adults but are nonetheless real things. Only through a long developmental process does the child attain conscious awareness of the object, of the concept itself, and the capacity to operate abstractly with the concept.
>
> (p. 219)

The relation between the objects and the concepts proceeds from the object to the concept, with the child not having (and not needing to have) any consciousness that she/he has a concept or is thinking. In contrast, scientific concepts typically begin without any direct encounter with real objects but through instruction, most usually in school settings through collaboration between teacher and children about the concepts. Relationships between concepts form and mediate the concept's relationship to the object. How does the development of these two types of concept proceed?

> Both types of concept are located in one and the same child and at more or less the same level of development. In the thinking of the child, one cannot separate the concepts that he acquires in school from those he acquires at home. Nonetheless, these concepts have entirely different histories. One concept reaches the level it has attained while having undergone a certain portion of its development from above. The other reaches this level having completed the lower portion of its developmental path.
>
> (1987, p. 219)

While they move in opposite directions, spontaneous and scientific concepts are 'internally and profoundly connected with one another' (p. 219). The development of one is both necessary for the development of the other and also leads to its own further development. Their relationship through development transforms not only each of their 'separate' paths, but the totality of the child's mental processes.

Vygotsky ends his discussion by pointing out future research directions, the limitations of his own work, and what he sees as its significance: what it tells us about language and speech. The child's acquisition of a new word is not the culmination but the beginning of the development of a concept. Word meaning is an active process – 'the basic and decisive process in the development of the child's thinking and speech' (1987, p. 241). Building upon this discovery, Hood, Fiess and Aron noted that

> the relationship between spontaneous and scientific concepts is a dialectical one, where the psychological tool [-and-result] of language is both the redefiner and redefinition of the concept. The paradox is that in using language we are not only 'doing language,' we are reorganizing the activities we are engaged in – one of them being the language activity itself.
>
> (1982, p. 247)

On our view, the ZPD was Vygotsky's extraordinary discovery of the proper unit of study for understanding uniquely human activity, most especially learning and development and their relationship and, thereby, virtually all 'mental' activities. His understanding of methodology led him to search for a social-historical unity (rather than a traditional psychological unit), one grounded in the material existence of women and men 'in their actual, empirically perceptible process of development under definite conditions' (Marx and Engels, 1973, pp. 47–8) – that is, one grounded in history. In discovering/creating the ZPD, he thoughtfully practiced tool-and-result methodology: he discovered the uniquely human 'psychological' unit of study, which, it turns out, is not a psychological unit at all but a social-historical unity; he discovered the unity {learning-and-development}.[5] For the ZPD is nothing less than the psychological unity (as opposed to a unit or paradigm) of history (not psychology) and, therefore, the location of revolutionary activity.

To Vygotsky the mind (a psychological activity/an historical unity) is comprehensible historically because it is historical. It is literally created or produced through the participation in and internalization of social-cultural-historical forms of activity:

> Every function in the child's cultural development appears twice: first on the social level and later, on the individual level; first *between* people (*interpsychological*), and then *inside* the child (*intrapsychological*). This applies equally to all voluntary attention, to logical memory, and to the formation of concepts. All the higher mental functions originate as actual relations between people.
>
> (Vygotsky, 1978, p. 57)

This statement, one of the most quoted by contemporary Vygotskians, is also one of the most controversial, for it is the heart (and the historical soul) of the ZPD. And it is the ZPD which, more than any of Vygotsky's discoveries, has captured the interest of Western psychologists over the past decade. No doubt this is because it lends itself so well to contemporary interests in social cognition and classroom interaction, because it gets to the essence of learning and development, and because it is an expression of the synthesized individual-in-society.

How contemporary researchers understand what Vygotsky means by inter- and intrapsychological levels and the ZPD (and, therefore, to a large extent, his major works) is, not surprisingly, intimately connected to how they 'use' it. Their varying understandings/uses of the ZPD locate current research on a 'pragmatism–practice, Vygotsky as psychologist–Vygotsky as methodologist' continuum. At one end is work which is fundamentally instrumental; it uses the ZPD as a store-bought tool for result to be applied within some traditional psychological framework. At the other end of the continuum is work which takes the ZPD itself to be the proper historical unit of study. There is, of course, Vygotskian research which lies between these two extremes. It is instructive to review examples of contemporary Vygotskian research at different points along this right to left (pragmatism to practice) continuum.

USING AND MISUSING THE ZPD

Psychologists and linguists interested in communicative and cognitive development in the first years of life and during the school years have found in the ZPD a useful (hardware store) tool. So, too, have educators concerned to create new instructional practices which might facilitate learning for the millions of children currently being failed by the dominant educational theory and practice. For it is clear to all but the most extreme Neoplatonists that learning occurs in 'a social context'; along with others we ourselves follow the radical Vygotsky in taking learning to be essentially social. Moreover, it is widely acknowledged that traditional developmental and educational psychology fail to give anything but lip service to 'the social aspects' of cognitive development. The ZPD, generally understood as where and/or how the transformation from the interpsychological to the intrapsychological plane takes place, certainly seems, to the more open-minded, an attractive solution.

In the late 1970s and early '80s Wertsch conducted a series of studies that, in addition to being significant in their own right, introduced a theoretical construct and a method for investigating learning in the ZPD. Wertsch (1985) was interested in the production and internalization of certain problem solving skills through mother–child 'joint activity.' He coined this term because, he explained:

> For my purposes, one of the most important tenets of the theory of activity is its recognition that a new unit of analysis is needed to carry out the Vygotskian enterprise. Instead of focusing on the study of psychological entities such as skills, concepts, information-processing units, reflexes, or mental functions, it assumes that we must begin with a unit of *activity*.
>
> (p. 199)

The method he introduced, following Vygotsky's mandate that one must study 'a given thing's development in all its phases and changes,' was *microgenetic analysis* of time-limited (usually 30 minutes or so) mother–child interactions with children from 2 to 4 years of age. For example, in a task situation set up by the experimenters, mothers were instructed to work with their children to copy a model puzzle. One puzzle (the model) was set up in completed form; the other puzzle (the copy) was laid out with the pieces apart from the frame. The task was for the mother and child to copy the model, ending up with a puzzle identical to the model. The interaction was video-taped and later analyzed for the mechanisms by which the mothers were successful in helping their children accomplish the task and the developmental course of shifting the task activities from mother to child.

Two aspects of the situation were of theoretical importance. First, how does each participant understand the activity they are engaged in? We surely cannot assume that a mother and a 2½-year-old child share the same goal or understanding of what they are doing together during this particular 30 minutes of 'joint activity.' What does the mother do when she realizes that her child does not share her understanding of what they are doing together? How does she get the child to recognize – and accept – her definition of the task environment, her goal (what Wertsch calls the 'situation definition')? Second, how is the teaching of the task accomplished?

What is the process by which the mother teaches her child how to do the task? How do the two of them accomplish the task together and how does this joint activity lead to internalization of both the goal-oriented activity (e.g. when there is a model puzzle and a copy puzzle, one thing you can do is put the puzzle together by copying the model) and the specific skills necessary to accomplish it (e.g. looking at the model, picking up the pieces, putting them in the copy frame)?

Wertsch's observations revealed that the mothers utilized consistent strategies. For example, they continuously adjusted their talk and gestures and the interrelationship between talk and gesture. In one case, one 2½-year-old referred to the puzzle pieces that were wheels of a truck as 'crackers'; he would pick them up from the pile of pieces and put them down, paying no attention to the model. His mother acknowledged that they looked like crackers but weren't and told him they were supposed to 'make this truck,' pointing to the model. She did not succeed in getting the child to accept her definition of the task at that moment. Much later in the session she introduced the word 'circle' to describe the crackers-wheels, asking him if what he was holding was a circle; the child acknowledged that it was. According to Wertsch, the child 'bought in' on his mother's referential perspective or categorization. Agreeing that the referents (the wheel pieces) were circles allowed the mother and child to continue their joint cognitive activity and reach a higher level of intersubjectivity (1985, p. 174).

Wertsch's concentration on the role of verbal and non-verbal communication ('semiotic mechanisms,' he calls them) stems from his interpretation of the importance Vygotsky placed on signs (indicators of meaning, like words) as psychological tools. (We would want to ask, what kind of psychological tools – tools for results or tools-and-results?) His studies examine in detail the function and development of particular semiotic mechanisms mothers use in situations of joint cognitive activity.

Wertsch also presents an excellent summary of research in this area, including studies of people for whom putting a puzzle together is likewise a common culturally appropriate activity (e.g. older American children, children with language disorders), and those for whom it is not (e.g. rural Brazilian mothers and children). Comparisons of these different populations revealed interesting similarities and differences among them. For our purposes, however, the most significant conclusion concerns the more fundamental issue of the relationship between thought and action and the role of the ZPD in facilitating that relationship. Wertsch says,

> While forms of interpsychological functioning differ significantly, there seems to be at least one common tendency in how children in these studies come to master the situation definition [the mother's/experimenter's definition] of the task: they first participate in the execution of the goal-directed task on the interpsychological plane, and only subsequently do they recognize and master the strategic significance of their behaviors. Rather than understanding the task and then doing it, the children seem to have done the task (as a participant in interpsychological functioning) and then understood it.
>
> (1985, p. 166)

This finding of the dialectical relationship between thought, action and what we call meaning-making (the activity relation between goal-directedness and specific behaviors) appears to be wholly consistent with Vygotsky's claim that learning leads development in (because of) the ZPD. Curiously, Wertsch does not make this connection. The parameters of his discussions of the creation of intersubjectivity through joint activity do not extend beyond semiotic and discourse concepts.

Readers will recall that Vygotsky made clear that the ZPD's 'practical' significance was twofold: it is the only accurate measure of development and it is the crucial variable to take into account in creating pedagogy. Several researchers have taken him to heart on both counts, using the ZPD to develop assessment tools, devise curricula and teaching methods, and evaluate classroom practices.

For example, Brown and her colleagues are best known for their work challenging the IQ test as an accurate measure of cognitive ability (A.L. Brown and French, 1979; A.L. Brown and Ferrara, 1985; Campione, Brown, Ferrara and Bryant, 1984). They devised a series of experiments that utilized the concept of the ZPD to create tests of interpsychological functioning (e.g. by seeing how children use adult 'prompts' in testing and experimental situations), concluding that such tests revealed a great deal about students' cognitive level that was not revealed (or revealable) in tests of intrapsychological functioning such as standard IQ tests. In several experimental studies, they found that traditional measures of IQ failed to predict learning speed or degree of transfer from one task to another, but that utilizing interpsychological assessment allowed them to see a variety of learning profiles which otherwise are masked by intrapsychological assessment (A.L. Brown and Ferrara, 1985). Another ongoing research project is that of McNamee and her colleagues, who have 'applied' the ZPD in devising basic activities to develop literacy in preschoolers and language-learning disabled children (McNamee, McLane, Cooper and Kerwin, 1985; McNamee, 1990; Harris-Schmidt and McNamee, 1986).

Other researchers have examined common elementary school classroom practices which appear to be explainable by an intrapsychological understanding of learning – for example, the traditional recitation method whereby the teacher asks questions and individual children answer them. The ZPD calls into question the intrapsychological (privatized) explanation of learning thus 'displayed'; the learning in its totality cannot be accounted for by such an explanation.

Much of the research utilizing the ZPD as a means for understanding the importance of adult–child interaction in the learning process is fit into a cognitive developmental research paradigm, such as the one developed in the mid–1970s by Wood, Bruner and Ross (1976). They introduced the term 'scaffolding' to describe the process by which an adult assists a child in carrying out a task beyond her/his capacity. Although Wood, Bruner and Ross did not refer to Vygotsky's work, subsequent research often draws parallels between scaffolding and the ZPD, with the ZPD understood as the construct that motivates attention to the process by which 'control' of the task is transferred from the adult to the child or the expert to the novice (see also, Clay and Cazdan, 1990; Greenfield, 1984; Rogoff and Gardner, 1984). This research is surely at the 'pragmatism, Vygotsky as psychologist' end of the continuum. Rather than Vygotsky's radically monistic methodology being employed to call into question the fundamental mentalism and dualism of cognitive psychology, the ZPD, his tool-and-result, is made into a 'more social' tool for result, thus reinforcing the mentalism and dualism.

In addition to observational studies of classroom interaction, interventional research that introduces collaborative methods of instruction has been conducted (D. Newman, Griffin and Cole, 1984; Tudge, 1990). Findings indicate that creating a classroom environment that allows the social nature of learning to be expressed leads to increased learning. Furthermore, some studies noted difficulty in overcoming teachers' resistance to change (e.g. D. Newman, Griffin and Cole, 1989). Such resistance is understandable, given the socialization and professionalization teachers go through – producing a static, privatized and mechanistic understanding of knowing that defines themselves as the knowers and their students as potential receptacles of knowledge with varying levels of developmental receptivity. Like the mother–child interaction research discussed above, this work attempts to uncover the mechanisms by which the internalization of higher psychological processes occurs in joint activity. In other words, how does an individual learn? How does responsibility for carrying out a task shift to the individual child from the adult, another peer or the group?

This research question, it should be noted, is different from the one that concerned at least some of us at the Laboratory of Comparative Human Cognition in its early years (see Chapter 2). You will recall that, for the lab at that time, fundamental methodological questions were in the forefront and the fundamentally social nature of human activity, including learning and development, was empirically established. The concern there was with the fact that higher psychological processes, while eventually internalized, never lose their socialness; moreover, everyday life situations are marked by the continual collective creation of task environments for cognitive activities to occur. The unit of analysis was the 'person–environment interface.' What we see in many recent studies (two of which are discussed below) is a shift back to the individual as the unit of analysis, with activity transformed into 'scene' or 'context.' The unity of the historical/psychological ZPD is turned into a spatio-temporal situation or environment. Ecological invalidity is, perhaps, engaged. But there is a total adaptation to *historical* invalidity.

Newman, Griffin and Cole (1989) address how children's cognitive processes change as they interact in educational settings with teachers and other students. Their discussion is based on research in a third–fourth-grade classroom. The ZPD is combined with Leont'ev's concept of appropriation[6] to create the foundation for what the authors call the 'construction zone' – where and how cognitive structures originate.

They point out that the concept of the ZPD contrasts sharply with traditional notions of how cognitive change takes place;

consequently, it leads to different educational practices, particularly in how learning tasks are presented and instructions sequenced.
Traditional views minimize or misunderstand the role of social
interaction and see the learning of a given task as facilitated by the
appropriate breakdown of the whole task into components based
on characteristics of the task-in-itself, e.g. according to a temporal
('first you do this and next you do that') or a hierarchical (from the
simple to the complex) sequence. However, with the ZPD as one's
conceptual framework (in the Quinean sense, no doubt; see Chapter 3), the breakdown of components of a given learning task is
achieved in the social interaction. The student and teacher are
involved in doing the task from the beginning: the task is socially
distributed. 'There is a sequence involved in the ZPD, but it is a
sequence of different divisions of labor. The task – in the sense of
the whole task as negotiated between the teacher and child –
remains the same' (D. Newman, Griffin and Cole, 1989, p. 153).

Since Newman, Griffin and Cole (pragmatists all) do not move
beyond the 'task at hand,' we do not know what cognitive change
is because we never learn what its relationship to learning and
development is. Much of their work has been concerned with the
use of computer instruction to contribute to a ZPD, and they make
strong recommendations concerning how computers should be
utilized:

> ...the design of intelligent tutoring systems should not attempt
> to replace the teacher but rather it should set the machine up as
> a tool that mediates between the teacher and the child . . . Our
> recommendation . . . requires that the designer of the machine
> be sensitive to the socially organized settings in which the
> machine might function in the classroom. It would not stand
> alone. It would be integrated into a setting in which it had a
> functional role.
>
> (1989, p. 149)

Another project which emphasizes the role of the ZPD in learning is the pedagogy developed by Tharp and Gallimore (1988).
Their analysis and recommendations are based primarily on the
Kamehameha Elementary Education Program (KEEP), a Hawaiian
educational project in existence since 1970. Understanding the ZPD
as the difference between assisted and unassisted performance,
Tharp and Gallimore see the creation of ZPDs in instructional
settings as critical to good teaching: 'Teaching consists in assisting

performance through the ZPD. Teaching can be said to occur when assistance is offered at points in the ZPD at which performance requires assistance' (p. 31). However, they warn that focusing exclusively on the psychological aspects of adult–child interaction distorts the realities of human life; their neo-Vygotskian approach considers the social context of interaction as well:

> Taking the context seriously means treating the ZPD as more than a psychological phenomenon. For a ZPD to be created, there must be a joint activity that creates a context for teacher and student interaction. Once the zone is open, the 'expert' can use any of the means of performance assistance described in Chapter 3. But our analysis cannot end there, because the qualities of the assistance rendered in the zone are determined by the nature of the joint activity.
>
> (p. 71)

According to the authors' neo-Vygotskian approach, one cannot understand the social context of assisted performance without the concept of *activity settings* – contexts in which collaborative interaction, intersubjectivity and assisted performance occur (p. 72). The thesis of their project is that activity settings in traditional schools are not really activity settings at all – they do not contain the above conditions. For example, there is rarely joint or collaborative productive activity, either between administration and teachers or between teachers and students. Thus, designing schools in which teaching can go on (i.e. in which assisted performance occurs at all levels) requires the creation of true activity settings. Their institutional model, of which KEEP is an exceptionally fine example, consists of 'a reorganization of overall goal' from the traditional hierarchical model – where an individual, A, directs and assesses individual(s) B, who in turn directs and assesses individual(s) C – to one based on assistance of performance at all levels; the purpose of A assisting B is to develop B's ability to assist C, and so on. They summarize: 'Every member of the school community should be engaged in the joint productive activity of activity settings whose purpose is an ever-increasing competence to assist performance' (p. 92). This model, they say, promotes a 'culture of learning.'

This statement is at once inspiring and troublesomely ambiguous. What is meant by 'the joint productive activity of activity settings'? Does it mean the joint productive activity of producing activity settings? Or does it mean the joint productive activity that occurs in, or is characteristic of, activity settings? If the authors meant the former, then why didn't they say so clearly? If they meant the latter, then the question of where activity settings come from – how they are produced – remains.

Back to the future, i.e. Vygotsky

For Vygotsky, this was the question of central concern, for it is in the production of activity (settings) that learning and development occur – as a Marxist, he understood that the activity of producing was inseparable from the product. Vygotsky's revolutionary monistic discovery of the radically synthesized individual-in-society-(in-history) – the sociological expression of the ZPD, transforming the very institutions that determine one's learning and development – has been lost in a good deal of contemporary neo-Vygotskian work. The activistic revolutionary Marxian concept of activity has been 'passified,' turned into a setting, which is nothing more than the 1990s term for what in the 1970s was called the scene or the context.

As we stated in Chapter 3, such an approach seems to us to miss what is uniquely human, not to mention uniquely Vygotskian. Taking into account the social nature of human beings – how we are influenced, determined, shaped by and interact with the complex network of social institutions – in the absence of addressing the uniquely human capacity for transforming these very institutions (revolutionary activity) does not in the least distinguish us from the bee or the spider. It is essentially an ethnographic approach, an analysis of human beings in society, from the perspective of and overdetermined by society. For it ignores the truly activistic nature of human beings in history; its object of study is not the revolutionary activity of our species in history, but societally overdetermined behavior. Scenes may be more easily discernible than continuousness – certainly for spectators. But life, unlike a film, is not a series of scenes – even scenes created by the very actors who walk into them. Even if life is filled with scenes, life itself is not a scene. Life, if you will, is seamless, continuous performance.

From our point of view, with the turning of activity into activity settings the relationship between learning and development – and the real significance of the ZPD – is lost. Remember, Vygotsky's

discovery was that any learning worthy of the name leads development. His investigation of and experimentation with
instructional settings was never directed toward learning as a
thing-in-itself – to him, there was no such worthwhile thing! What
exists is the unity {learning-and-development}. It is relative to this
unity that the ZPD has meaning. Yet the studies just reviewed are
either not concerned with this relationship between learning and
development or appear to misunderstand it. We saw that Newman, Griffin and Cole (1989) focus on 'cognitive change,' which
appears as some amalgam of learning and/or development, and
that Tharp and Gallimore (1988), while calling themselves
(neo-)Vygotskians, explicitly put forth some of the very positions
Vygotsky took great pains to critique. It is interesting to see what
Tharp and Gallimore themselves have to say about the ZPD:

> Developmental processes, arising from assisted performance in
> the ZPD, can be observed not only in the ontogenesis of the
> individual but also in the microgenesis of discrete skills as they
> develop through the life course.

(p. 31)

And,

> For any domain of skill, a ZPD can be created . . . Boys in
> Micronesia, where sailing a canoe is a fundamental skill, will
> have a ZPD for the skills of navigation, created in interaction
> with the sailing masters.

(p. 31)

And,

> It is conventional and correct to assess a child's developmental
> level by the child's ability to solve problems unassisted – that is
> the familiar protocol of standardized assessment, such as the
> Stanford–Binet. The child's *learning*, however, exceeds the reach
> of the developmental level and is to be found by assessing those
> additional problems that the child can solve with social assis-
> tance.

(p. 30)

In the first two statements, Tharp and Gallimore seem to be equating learning and development. For example, it is not clear what
distinguishes the 'developmental processes' from the 'discrete
skills' in which they can be observed. Nor do we learn anything

about how the Micronesian boys' navigation skills impact on their development. In the last statement, the authors state a position on learning and development strikingly reminiscent of Piaget: development is what can be measured by what a child can do unassisted; learning, they say, is what can be measured by the child's assisted performance. Never mind that Vygotsky made absolutely clear that, because of the ZPD, the child's developmental level could not be measured by what she/he could accomplish unassisted! Vygotsky's continuous search for method and his discovery of psychology's proper unit of study have, in our view, been pragmatized, calling into question both the scientific validity and the Vygotskianism of these studies.

Moving left on the continuum

Some researchers show far greater sensitivity to Vygotsky's insights into the relationship between learning and development – and the revolutionary nature of the ZPD. In reviewing how those involved in cooperative learning studies view the role of motivation, Forman and McPhail (1989) offer a Vygotskian critique of their dualism. Cooperative learning refers to a set of pedagogical practices in which students are grouped and urged to work together in order to facilitate active involvement in discussing, explaining, critiquing and defending different perspectives on a common theme. Findings consistently show greater learning than under conditions of less active or task-focused peer interaction (Slavin, 1983). According to Slavin, educational and developmental psychologists have different positions on the role of motivation; educational psychologists believe it is of critical importance in facilitating learning, while developmental psychologists downplay its significance. To the extent that they do recognize its value, they view 'extrinsic motivation' as potentially an inhibitor of development, and, instead, tend to advocate for learning that is 'intrinsically' motivating.

How does Vygotsky fit into this debate? Forman and McPhail's (1989) interpretation of some of Vygotsky's work in this area is useful in advancing our understanding of how some contemporary researchers, contrary to Vygotsky himself, maintain a dichotomy between cognition and affective factors, such as motivation, and have a dualistic understanding of 'social.' Forman and McPhail refer to Vygotsky's comments about teaching exceptional children (the mentally retarded and learning disabled) in which he addressed the issue of motivation. Little of his work in this area had been available until the recent translation of an extensive discussion (Vygotsky, in press), which Forman and McPhail use.

Vygotsky advocated a pedagogy that not only was radical for his time but, sadly, is still regarded as 'too radical' today in the United States, where special education increasingly employs reductionistic remediation of isolated cognitive skills practiced individually. Vygotsky's strategy was essentially a cooperative learning strategy. He created heterogeneous groups of retarded children (he called them a collective),[7] providing them not only with the opportunity but the need for cooperation and joint activity by giving them tasks that were beyond the developmental level of some, if not all, of them. Under these circumstances, children could create a ZPD for each other, something not possible if one takes developmental level as the basis for learning:

> It turned out that a teaching system based solely on concreteness [what retarded children are assumed to be capable of learning based on their developmental level] – one that eliminated from teaching everything associated with abstract thinking – not only failed to help retarded children overcome their innate handicaps but also reinforced their handicaps by accustoming children exclusively to concrete thinking and thus suppressing the rudiments of any abstract thought that such children still have. Precisely because retarded children, when left to themselves, will never achieve well-elaborated forms of abstract thought, the school should make every effort to push them in that direction and to develop in them what is intrinsically lacking in their own development.
>
> (Vygotsky, 1978, p. 89)

Forman and McPhail (1989) observe that, for Vygotsky, the advantages of cooperative learning go beyond what was just quoted, i.e. the enhancement of cognitive skills. He saw peer interaction as fostering self-regulation, self-direction and self-control and, in this way, it could counteract retarded children's problems of passivity, distractibility and perseveration. Furthermore, for Vygotsky, motivational factors – wants, needs, goals, interests – are not merely facilitators of cognitive development; rather, cognitive development is as much motivational (affective) as it is intellectual. It leads to a total reorganization of affect:

We often describe a child's development as the development of his intellectual functions... Without a consideration of the child's needs, inclinations, incentives, and motives to act . . . there will never be any advance from one stage to the next . . . It seems that every advance from one age period to another is connected with an abrupt change in motives and incentives to act.

(Vygotsky, in press; quoted in Forman and McPhail, 1989)

The importance of this cannot be overstated. Not only are educational theory and practice still marked by a cognitive–affective split – with learning understood as purely cognitive, emotions as states of mind that 'get in the way,' and motivation some vague semi-magical characteristic possessed only by certain children (with those who lack it often blamed for their poor performance and 'lack of motivation'). Vygotsky is frequently criticized for not paying attention to affective factors. Yet this passage makes clear that he did not view affect as separable from intellect. Furthermore, as we will discuss later, he provided a sophisticated critique of Piaget and Freud for making just this separation (see Chapter 6).

Forman and McPhail's recognition of the unity of intellect and affect is, we believe, a clue to the meaning Vygotsky gives to social. He stated more than once that all higher mental functions are internalized social relationships. Whether or not Vygotsky viewed emotions, affect, interests, volition and motivation as higher mental functions, he clearly saw them as social – socially produced, socially internalized, socially realized. For Vygotsky 'social' was not reducible to 'between people,' although much of his work explicitly dealt with interpsychological ('between people') processes and many researchers unfortunately take him at that level. In part because of this misunderstanding of social to mean interpsychological and/or interpersonal, the dominant form of observing the ZPD 'in action' has been with dyads, or pairs (e.g. mother–child, teacher–student or peers). The focus of investigation is often on dialogue and 'dialogic features' (similar to Wertsch's 'semiotic mechanisms') as one of the means by which the subjects' goals and understandings are established, negotiated and modified during the course of their joint activity, collaboration or cooperative learning.

With this (mis)understanding of social, the ZPD is used as a tool for understanding individual mental processes. Most often, what is of interest are the mental processes of one member of the dyad – the 'novice' – under conditions where the other member of the dyad – the 'expert' – has 'created the ZPD.' A tool for result methodology underlies the essentially interactionist (and, therefore, dualistic) perspective on learning, development and Vygotsky that is relied on and perpetuated in these studies of individuals in social, interpersonal settings. For the 'zone' is wrenched out of life, out of history, out of material reality, out of the social process that produces it: the individual (or 'mind') is ontologically and epistemologically separated from society and then the two are 'reunited' both in actual human development and in the scientific study of it. The ZPD is seen as a principle (a neo-Kantian category) for explaining the interaction between individual and society, as a means to answering the perplexing question of how an individual ever gets to learn anything given that she/he is fundamentally an individual. But the question itself and its perplexity have a history! It is only perplexing if one begins with the premise of a dualistically divided individual and society.

Wertsch, in much of his work, is sensitive to this issue. In a recent interview he observed how deeply rooted in our language is the primacy of the individual (quoted in Holzman, 1990). He pointed out that the very structure of linguistic construction conveys and perpetuates not only the dichotomy between individual and society but the deeply held bias in favor of the individual. In English, we must add a term to traditional psychological concepts if we want to convey that the study and/or the psychological process under study is social. For example, one has to say 'socially shared' cognition and 'collective' memory. The unmarked terms – cognition, memory – imply the individual; cognition and memory are seen and experienced as characteristics of individuals.

The significance of the ZPD, in our view, is that it is not premised on the individual–society separation; it is an historical unity. In fact, it methodologically destroys the need for interactionist solutions to the dualism of mind and society because it does not accept their ontic separation in the first place! The claim that learning takes place in the ZPD is neither a claim about learning nor about the ZPD. For the ZPD is not a place at all; it is an activity, an historical unity, the essential socialness of human beings expressed as revolutionary activity, as Marx put it. In Vygotsky's (1978) words: 'the method is simultaneously prerequisite and product, the tool and the result of the study' (p. 65).

ZPD research

There are a few research projects which are more closely allied to Vygotsky's position on the social nature of learning and development. Rather than taking the ZPD to be a factor in how individuals learn, these studies have investigated how collectives of people learn and develop through the self-conscious utilization of the ZPD, where the ZPD is understood to be the fundamental social-historical characteristic.

For example, Moll and Greenberg (1990) have been involved in a research project examining the social sharing of knowledge in households in a Mexican community in Arizona. The content and manner in which this knowledge is shared and transmitted – what Moll and Greenberg call 'the households' zone of proximal development' – is the main focus of the ethnographic component of the study. The two other components are an after-school 'lab' where researchers and teachers experiment with literacy instruction based on information from the community ethnography, and classroom observations examining existing methods of instruction and exploring changes in instruction based on what is learned in the after-school program.

According to Moll and Greenberg, the social sharing of knowledge (what they call the exchange of 'funds of knowledge') is an integral part of the households' functioning, and using it as a resource in classroom instruction is invaluable for advancing the skills and development of students, teachers and parents.

> Our analysis shows that families control their resources through social relations which connect households to each other and facilitate, among other functions, the transmission of knowledge among participants. We have termed these diverse, socially-mediated transactions the exchange of funds of knowledge. It is how these social systems of knowledge operate, these extended zones of proximal development, that has attracted our attention. These social relations of exchange are multi-stranded and flexible in that they involve many people and can be arranged or re-arranged depending on the specific needs of the participants.
> (1990, pp. 31–2)

Through the development of social networks for teaching [they continue] the teacher facilitated the intellectual contribution of parents and other adults in academic lessons. This parental participation, in turn, provided the teacher and students not only with an appreciation of the knowledge of the parents, but with an additional context for learning.

(p. 33)

The significance of their findings is that both the context for and content of learning were reorganized to be both more inclusive and beyond the developmental level of any individual student. This, in turn, reorganized the relationship between the students' learning and development, which is consistent with Vygotsky's critical claim that learning leads development – if it is properly, i.e. socially, organized.

Moll and Greenberg interpret their results as follows:

To be successful, the introduction of funds of knowledge into classrooms must facilitate the development of new, more advanced literacy activities for the students... We perceive the students' community, and its funds of knowledge, as the most important resource for re-organizing instruction in ways that 'far exceed' the limits of current schooling. An indispensable element of our approach is to create meaningful connections between academic and social life through the concrete learning activities of the students. We are convinced that teachers can establish, in systematic ways, the necessary social relations outside classrooms that will change and improve what occurs within the classroom walls. These social connections help teachers and students develop their awareness of how they can use the every-day to understand classroom content and use classroom activities to understand social reality.

(pp. 33–4)

An ongoing project by Hedegaard (1990) is another example of Vygotskian research that does not focus on the learning of individuals. She and her colleagues in Denmark are implementing a three-year curriculum for social science subjects (a combination of biology, history and geography) in a Danish elementary school classroom of third- to fifth-graders. The theoretical basis for this study draws upon Soviet educational psychologists as well as on Vygotsky's writings. For our purposes, what is of interest is that the conception of the ZPD underlying the research is close to Vygotsky's thinking in reference to the retarded presented earlier – the goal was to create a collective, classwide ZPD rather than to analyze the creation of 'an individual's' ZPD. The study is also concerned with the relationship of motivation to the ZPD:

> We attempted several times to produce a division of work in which the children would work on a number of different tasks in a group with a shared motive for the entire activity. This activity, in principle, is intended to develop a zone of proximal development for the class as a whole, where each child acquires personal knowledge through the activities shared between the teacher and the children and among the children themselves.
>
> (Hedegaard, 1990, p. 361)

Following Vygotsky's insistence that 'cognitive development is as much motivational as intellectual,' Hedegaard regarded the development of motivation and the transformation of interests and needs as essential and designed the curriculum with this in mind. Results of the first year of study (whose theme was 'the origin of species') indicate a developmental shift in the children's motivation in the hoped-for direction – from an interest in concrete material to an interest in developing principles which can then be applied to concrete material.

Hedegaard summarizes the results:

> In our teaching experiment, we saw that it is actually possible to make a class function actively as a whole through class dialogue, group work and task solutions. The teaching experiment differed from traditional instruction in that the children were constantly and deliberately forced to act. The research activity was central in these guided actions, which gradually led the children to critical evaluations of the concepts. We can conclude, therefore, that we have succeeded in building a common basis for the children in the class from which future teaching can be developed.
>
> (1990, pp. 369–70)

To Hedegaard, the ZPD is clearly more than a psychological construct; it is no abstraction. It itself is socially-culturally-politically determined. She has made the interesting claim that values are an integral component of the ZPD:

> The ZPD is a very valuable tool. It implies that we have to have some values and an idea of what a good life is if we are to educate children . . . if you read Vygotsky carefully, you see that the ZPD

is not just a general psychological law. The next 'zone' for the child is determined by the society in which we are living, the values and customs for the upbringing of youth, etc.

(Hedegaard, quoted in Holzman, 1990, p. 16)

Hedegaard and her colleagues offer an example of the dialectical relationship between values and the ZPD (Engestrom, Hakkarainen and Hedegaard, 1984). They challenge the prediction made by some researchers (for example, Papert, one of the leading experts in this area), that computers bode well for the future of education. The authors report that, according to Papert (1980), as computers increasingly become the private property of individuals, education will become increasingly privatized. He believes this will lead to greater opportunities for creativity as people will be able to place their ideas directly on the marketplace without the intermediary of bureaucracies. But Engestrom, Hakkarainen and Hedegaard point out that alienation from the school as an institution does not automatically lead to creativity! In fact, there is a contradiction between the fact that computers are potentially powerful intellectual tools and their commercial and consumer use – a contradiction between capacity and the reality that is characteristic of contemporary students' 'life-world.' It is not at all clear that this contradiction can be reorganized privately and individually, as Papert seems to think.

...to turn the tools of the life-world from consumptive to productive use . . . demands that the school *is turned into a collectively used instrument of grasping the life-world, the societal practice theoretically* . . . This cannot be accomplished by means of the forced individual togetherness of the traditional school, but only by *pooling the intellectual and practical activities and capacities of pupils and teachers* to form a *collective subject* of learning.

(Engestrom, Hakkarainen and Hedegaard, 1984, p. 144)

Both the Moll and Greenberg and the Hedegaard studies are excellent examples of research which attempts to heed Vygotsky's admonition that the search for method is both 'the tool and the result of the study.' Bakhurst put it nicely: 'Vygotsky believed that, since the psychologist must search for a method appropriate to the specific nature of his object, to address methodological issues is at the same time to enquire into the nature of the object itself' (1988, p. 82).

These two studies simultaneously addressed methodological issues and transformed the object they investigated – the ZPD. Moll and Greenberg explicitly tried to construct zones of proximal development by reorganizing the relationship between the existing social institutions and activities of home, community and school that are kept separate in traditional education. Similarly, Hedegaard intervened on existing classroom practices to reorganize the learning environment so that the children themselves could create a 'classwide' ZPD.

Vygotsky's left wing

We take it you will not be at all surprised to find out that we place ourselves at the 'practice, Vygotsky as methodologist' end, i.e. the revolutionary end, of the continuum. Thus far, we have presented portions of Vygotsky's own discussions of his discovery of the ZPD as well as summaries of contemporary Vygotskian researchers' use (and, on our view, misuse) of his work in their attempts to understand early childhood development and/or create educational environments and institutions which facilitate learning and (sometimes) foster development. Along the way we offered some Vygotsky-style critical analysis. It remains for us to expand on this critique as we present our view ('our Vygotsky') of the significance of the ZPD in developing a truly human science.

In Chapter 3 we proposed that revolutionary activity, far from being unusual or special, is 'the practical-critical activity of everyday life' (p. 41). Furthermore, this is the essential point of our new understanding of a psychology of human beings, produced from the synthesis of Marx's discovery of activity as practical-critical, revolutionary activity and Vygotsky's tool-and-result methodology: the object of study of a human science must be what is uniquely and specifically human, i.e. revolutionary activity. But we have not yet fully answered that most important question we raised in Chapter 3 – what do everyday, ordinary revolutionary activities look like? What method can we employ to find them, describe them, shape them, study them?

In our opinion, most of the neo-Vygotskians have more or less abandoned Vygotsky's insistence on discovering the proper unit of analysis. Some of his followers have replaced the ZPD as that unit with the environment, the scene or the individual (or two individuals, the interpersonal dyad) *as* the scene. As Vygotsky's social-historical unit(y) of study, the ZPD has a distinctly historical quality, being simultaneously that life space in which and how we all live, i.e. society-in-history. The key term here is 'in.' There is no society literally 'in' – included in or within the limits of – history just as there is no mind 'in' society, no noodles 'in' noodle soup and no colds 'in' one's head. The idea that there could be individuals separable from their societal environment and/or social history does not make sense to Vygotsky – or to us. Learning, by the same logic, does not take place 'in' the ZPD in an inclusionary or inter-actionist or mediated sense. Nor do reified ZPDs exist in anything or anyone. Phenomenological experience in contemporary, com-modified society notwithstanding, mind-in-society-in-history, or the ZPD, is the character of the monistic and activistic unity {individual-in-society-in-history}.

Thus (and in this sense) both development and learning must occur in the ZPD (the individual-in-society-in-history), and learn-ing worthy of the name must lead development. However, Vygotsky recognized that, just as many psychologists and educa-tors of his day did not understand the unity {learning-and-development}, so too the structure of schools and other critical societal institutions did not typically realize this unified organiza-tion of learning and development. Most instruction, Vygotsky saw, was not directed toward the child's development but toward the acquisition of a specialized skill in and of itself, a condition which limits rather than impels development. His empirical research with school-age children and the mentally retarded was, in part, focused on ways to reorganize instructional environments so that learning as a source of (in the service of) development could be more fully realized.

Despite his efforts, things the world over have gotten signifi-cantly worse in the last half century. How, then, is the societally biased misorganization of learning and development to be dealt with in practice? How is this profound misorganization of learning and development – where learning is institutionalized in such a way that the organization of its relationship to development is actually a fetter to development – to be transformed?

Vygotsky, for all his brilliance, did not, in our opinion, complete-ly delineate the dialectical unity {learning-and-development}. Had he lived longer (and had Stalin died sooner), perhaps he would have done so. As it turned out, however, Vygotsky left the door open to pragmatic objectification of the ZPD. It is our task to slam it closed!

REVOLUTIONARY UNITY

We understand human development to be the dialectical unity {meaning-making/learning-leading-development}. Meaning-making is the toolmakers' (our species') tool-and-result, a non-dualistic dialectic-in-practice of changing the many totalities which are determining the changer. For human beings are never fundamentally changed (i.e. never develop) except insofar as, by our revolutionary activity, we change the totality of our continued historical existence. This we accomplish not by the humanly impossible act of materially altering all the elements of history, but by the uniquely human activity of materially reorganizing what there is to create a new meaning for everything. It is the child's meaning-making by which 'instruction . . . impels . . . a whole series of functions . . . in the zone of proximal development' (Vygotsky, 1987, p. 212). Without this revolutionary activity of meaning-making, i.e. when the human capacity for changing totalities is not able to be expressed (due to various forms of societal coercion), when toolmakers become mere tool users, when we engage in behaviors (even of incredible complexity and sophistication) and no longer activity, then learning ceases to lead development; instead, it replaces development.

At first reading this may sound bizarre, both at the level of theory and in reality. However, we need only recollect traditional psychological theory to realize how pervasive is what we have called elsewhere the essentially religious belief that development ends (Holzman and Newman, 1985). Both Freud and Piaget (indeed, all stage theorists) take as *a priori* that development is not a life-long process. Freud was concerned to reinitiate what he took to be the developmental process of personality formation, blocked as it was by certain psychosexual mechanisms, so that the process of development could be completed (finished). Piaget's life work was that of a 'genetic epistemologist'; he traced what he took to be the normal and 'natural' course of intellectual development from its earliest stages to its end point, the scientific mind. With the ideal being the (unrealized) end of development, the reality has been the insane proliferation of learning as an end-in-itself, ironically producing, in contemporary society, an end to development.[8]

We can see in Vygotsky's work support for our contention that meaning-making is how learning does and can come to lead development. Recall, for example, his observations about children's imitations, i.e. that children do not imitate anything and everything, but only what is in the ZPD. In our view, what is significant about Vygotsky's claim and the contemporary empirical research which supports it is what it says about the process of language acquisition (potentially a life-long activity, we should note) as (revolutionary, practical-critical) activity. Imitation in the ZPD is the activity of making meaning, where the predetermining tools of the adult language and the resulting predetermined tools of mind are used by the child – the toolmaker – to create something that is not determined by them. The meaning in the emerging activity, not the linguistic or verbal behaviors, is what is essentially human. The parrot's imitations, even with their potentially unlimited complexity and length, are, at best, merely linguistic behaviors; they are determined by the predetermined and predetermining tools. The child's imitations, in contrast, are not determined by the predetermining tools; they are the use of such tools for results to create tools-and-results, to create meaning and, thereby, to reorganize thinking/speaking. While we do not know what the child means when she/he imitates what is proximal to her/his development, we do know that the child almost certainly cannot mean what the adult means – e.g. what it means to mean is not the same for a novice and an expert. It follows, then, that what we know – and this is most important – is *that* the child means, because for the child meaning is not yet separated from the total activity of meaning-making, as it becomes for the more fully alienated (societally adapted) adult.[9]

Thus the limitations on children's imitation, taken by the philosophical and psychological heirs of Plato and Kant as evidence of children's underlying knowledge of language (whether of a semantic, syntactic or pragmatic nature), is, to our understanding, evidence of their revolutionary practice, their manifest capacity to make meaning. And it is through this revolutionary activity that children acquire language. The contradictory nature of language development is that the process of becoming a language user – by and large, the process of participating in societally determined fixed verbal intercourse, i.e. of doing verbal behavior (the computer-like use of language as tool for result by tool for result-determined thinking) – occurs through the child's manifest ability to make meaning, to make tools-and-results (as opposed to using tools for results, i.e. making results). It is in early childhood that we can see most clearly the dialectical environment of human existence, where revolutionary activity/verbal behavior is the ongoing dialectical thinking/speaking environment of human learning and development. This is true not because of some special quality of childhood, but merely because the child is less societally determined than the adult. And it is precisely this revolutionary capacity which makes creativity possible for the adult of the species. Picasso's lament that it took half a lifetime to learn to draw as children do is not an idealization of childhood but a recognition of the revolutionariness of creativity.

Ironically, what Vygotsky left out of his discovery of the ZPD was Marx's understanding of revolutionary activity. We see this in his genetic approach, embraced (not surprisingly, without criticism) by the pragmatist neo-Vygotskians who equate it with Marx's historical approach. But in our reading of Marx ('our Marx') the two approaches are very different indeed. Marx's dialectical historical materialism is premised on the fundamentality of revolutionary activity or practice: 'The coincidence of the changing of circumstances and of human activity or self-changing can be conceived and rationally understood only as *revolutionary practice*' (Marx, 1973, p. 121). Vygotsky seems to substitute genetic explanation ('having a history') for historical explanation in the Marxian sense ('being in history'). His genetic approach was to study the history of things – the history of language, the history of thought, the history of the relationship between them, the history of the unity {learning-and-development}, etc. However, what this leaves out is these histories relative to the history of society; i.e. it leaves out the history of the history of things. For it turns out that the history of the history of things ('being in history') cannot be accounted for by a 'history of things' (genetic) approach; the genetic approach was not designed to give such an accounting. Only Marx's revolutionary method of simultaneously investigating and transforming social-historical totality – the fundamentality of human beings as historical producers of our world, i.e. as revolutionary activists – can do so. For psychologists, it is not enough to study the history of things; we must actively challenge in our new science turning history itself into a thing.

To begin with, the ZPD is not a 'zone' at all! As we have said, it is neither in anything nor is anything in it. Nor is it a model or a paradigm. It is, rather, an anti-paradigm – a unity, Vygotsky calls it. Specifically, it is an historical unity. Psychology's proper object of study is history. (Sadly, it usually has been quite the other way around – psychology all too often being history's object of study.) In our times, with society (institutionalized learning) overdetermining history (development), the 'social catalyst' necessary for the discovery of seemingly omnipresent history is revolutionary activity. But in fact there is no history independent of revolutionary activity; history (dare we risk mixing our metaphors and add 'at this point in time'?) *is* revolutionary activity. Revolutionary activity is, therefore, at once as abundant and as sparse as history. If psychologists (Vygotskians and otherwise) engage in (use) revolutionary activity (like a microscope), there is much to study. If they do not, there is nothing to study. Revolutionary activity is, as such, the psychologists' particular tool-and-result. Use it and there will be a result to study; fail to and there will be none.

Is this some profound idealistic deviation? Are we suggesting that microbiotic life did not exist until the microscope was invented? Surely not, although it is worth noting that microbiology did not exist until the microscope was available. Our characterization bears a closer resemblance to the discovery and study (not to mention utilization) of fossil fuels. Prior to the discovery of critical industrial tools, fossil fuels did not exist. The fossils did. But the fuels (like the products of the tool- and die-maker or toolmaker) did not come into existence until the tools of their discovery/development did. Psychology lingers in an extended state of pre-life precisely because the activity required of the psychologist in order to have a proper object of study is prohibited by the institutional organization of psychology – institutionalized learning dominates development in the field of psychology itself. No great surprise. Psychology, after all, exists within a particular set of societal arrangements. Yet psychology's proper object of study is history. If it is to exist at all (loudly declare both 'our Marx' and 'our Vygotsky'), then it must be revolutionary. Galileo, confronting a similar dilemma *vis à vis* physics, and an ultimatum from the church hierarchy, recanted. Only the emergence of a new and (at the time) progressive class, the bourgeoisie – which needed physics to advance technology further, as much as we now need psychology – permitted its development as a new science. Most modern psychologists, many unwittingly, have 'recanted'; the modern state is interested in neither revolution nor development.

What are revolutionary psychologists to do? Is revolutionary activity sufficiently commonplace to be a proper object of everyday psychology? What is the self-conscious, revolutionary activity that is the 'precondition' for creating the unity {meaning-making/learning-leading-development} – the ZPD?

It is helpful to think of the ZPD (and its production by revolutionary psychologists) as a language game, in the Wittgensteinian sense (1953; 1965). Just as we play a language game, though the game has no existence or significance independent of its playing – indeed, that is its very point! – so we (revolutionary psychologists) must create or organize a ZPD, though the 'zone' has no existence or significance independent of its creation or organization. The ZPD is the reorganizing ('simplifying,' in Wittgenstein's word and sense) of the socio-historical environment (a history game, perhaps) to make the 'mental mist which seems to enshroud' history (in contemporary society) disappear. Thus, a ZPD is created by 'putting together' (organizing) elements of the societal environment (scenes) in ways (often bizarre ways) which help us to 'see activities, reactions, which are clear-cut and transparent' (Wittgenstein, 1965, p. 17; see Chapter 3, p. 54). We are helped to see life (including language and other reified, fetishized elements of commodified society) as history, i.e. we are helped to see history because (and as) we make it, precisely as the toolmaker (as opposed to the tool user) does. In such newly developed 'liberated zones,' meaning is more plainly shown and seen as productive activity and meaning-making is more plainly shown and seen as a creative/productive activity.

This 'liberation' of meaning from 'the confusing background of highly complicated processes of thought' (Wittgenstein, 1965, p. 17; see Chapter 3, p. 53) sufficiently de-alienates the collective producers, making it possible to engage in the revolutionary activity of less than alienated working or less than alienated producing or less than alienated creating or less than alienated living in history. It is in history – and only in history – that learning leads development. For in an international environment as bloated with alienated knowledge as our own, development has been sacrificed on the Altar of Decreasing Profitability (financial and political). Once upon a time Big Business footed the bill for the creation of physics; now in its death throes it exploits psychology, as the medieval rulers in their own death throes did religion.

The creation of 'history zones' where history games (and, as an element thereof, language games) can be played (performed, we prefer to say) is somewhat analogous to the creation of the European-style university relative to the explosion of discoveries (mainly in the natural sciences) called modern science. That 'universal zone' served a particular class at a particular historical moment. The 'ZBD' ('Zone of Bourgeois Development') required an urban-based research-educational community directly connected to the most progressive forces in the social environment (the bourgeoisie) while simultaneously being protected from the most regressive (the church and the nobility). The European-style university ('ZBD') played such a bourgeois revolutionary role. But the 'ZPD' ('Zone of Proletarian Development') could not, ultimately, be the 'ZBD.' Thus, while the European-style university has been the home of many a proletarian revolution-in-name, it has also been the site of the most tragic sellouts of the working class. In this century traditional psychologists have often been in the forefront of both.

The complex evolution and dominance of science, technology and the 'ZBD,' i.e. capitalist ideology, are inseparable from the philosophical hegemony of believing and thinking (more generally, cognitive acts) and the closely related philosophical-psychological hegemony of perception (more specifically, seeing). As the formal solipsistic core of human identity ('I think therefore I am'), belief and sight are closely related in both metaphor and technological models within the empiricistic/observationalist paradigm of modern science and industry, 'I know' and 'I see' having become virtually synonomous. This is the case even as pragmatism overdefines human action. For while deeds are determining for pragmatists, what they determine is what one believes. Of course, this rationalistic and 'opticalistic' bias predates capitalism by centuries. It is, for example, plainly recognizable in Plato.[10] But the advent and extraordinary success of bourgeois science, economy and optics, or observation, elevated belief and sight to new levels of glory. Over the last several hundred years cognition and visual perception have become fundamental to secular human definition. No doubt great leaps forward from faith and the hearing of voices, they are no less (and in some ways even more) Eurocentric, racially biased and patriarchal than prior identity paradigms.

While Marx and Vygotsky share these nineteenth- and early twentieth-century capitalistic biases in many areas of their work, their methodology is a deliberate, thoroughgoing rejection of them. For the method of practice (Marx) and the practice of method (Vygotsky) 'tear asunder' the 'model of man' as judger/thinker/seer/asserter/observer in favor of social activity not as predicate (attributes of 'men') but as subject. It is as subject that MAN socially, politically and philosophically controls and coerces. Anglo-American philosophy and psychology (as well as the other 'departments' of the modern university) are still dominated by the biased cognitive/visual paradigm, though nowadays the university seems less a zone of bourgeois development and more a zone of bourgeois stagnation. But the ZPD itself (and Marx and Vygotsky, its forefathers) remains endangered by the Eurocentric, patriarchal cognitive-visual bias. Bulhan (1985) addresses this bias in traditional psychology clearly.

> In our view, the limited and uneven advances of this psychology derive from the essentially *solipsist* character of this basic assumption, methods of inquiry, and sources of experiential datum. *Solipsism* is the perspective that only the 'self' exists or can be proven to exist. The dominant psychology is founded and imbued with the outlook that (a) the Euro-American world view is the only or best world view; (b) positivism or neo-positivism is the only or best approach to the conduct of scientific inquiry; and (c) the experiences of white, middle-class males are the only or most valid experiences in the world. The first of these I call *assumptive solipsism*; the second, *methodological solipsism* and the third, *experiential solipsism*. These three types of solipsism interpenetrate and influence one another. Together they form the foundations of Eurocentric psychology.
>
> (pp. 64–5)

Revolutionary activity, not any form of solipsism, must be at once our practice and our object of study – a tool-and-result, a practice of method – if Marx and Vygotsky and, we would argue, our species, are to survive.[11]

Moll and Greenberg (1990) and Hedegaard and her colleagues (Hedegaard, 1990; Engestrom, Hakkarainen and Hedegaard, 1984) come much closer in their research than most Vygotskians to reorganizing environments via revolutionary activity which changes the meaning of key pedagogic language (and, thereby, of everything). Yet their independence remains limited. The state uses ideology (the non-developmental, learning-biased organization/institutionalization of the individual-in-society) to block the meaning-making revolutionary activity of our species by demanding that everything – every idea, every experience, every emotion, every event – be translated into its vernacular and comprehended in terms of its dictionary. The ZPD, like the language game, must not be transformed into a technique for individual or even group or community learning (a tool for result). The ZPD – a reorganizing of environmental scenes to create new meaning and a learning that leads development – is a tactic. It is not a tactic-in-itself (a tactic for achieving a particular end), but a tactic-for-itself. It is revolutionary activity creating the conditions for revolutionary activity; creating development; creating 'the working class' not as a socio-economic category of the bourgeoisie but as the class-for-itself activity of continued human development; creating psychology as the new kind of science, a 'harnessing' science, a revolutionary science. Learning that leads development implies development that is endless, for one and for all. The politics of endless learning and limited development is fundamentally conservative; it asserts that 'history is over' for us as individuals and as a species, that qualitative transformation is no longer possible. The politics of learning serving endless development is radical.

There are no hard and fast rules for creating a ZPD, precisely as there are none for creating a poem or a song. Yet there are things to be known about the creating-a-ZPD activity, just as there are studies relevant to the art of poetry-making or song-writing. Both Freud, with his idealization of the 'fully matured' and of 'analytical learning,' and Piaget, with his dedication to the 'pure' individual untainted by 'assistance,' treat the group and other social units as necessary evils which, when left to their own (de)vices, manifest the most bestial or least matured elements. The revolutionary psychologist, on the other hand, must organize ZPDs: environments which maximize both the presentation of the least mature and group or collective learning – and, therefore, learning leading development. We will say more of this in our concluding chapter.

Chapter 5

Playing in/with the ZPD

> . . . play is not the predominant feature of childhood but it is
> a leading factor in development.
>
> (Vygotsky, 1978, p. 101)

So begins the concluding section of Vygotsky's brief (twelve-page)
discussion of the role of play in development in *Mind in Society*.
Read it again, for its provocativeness might not be apparent from
a quick reading. No doubt readers are aware that many psychologists take play to be important for development (often, however,
because – in tautological fashion – they believe it to be the predominant feature of childhood). In common belief and common practice
in most industrial societies play is taken to be the main feature of
childhood, but little consideration is given to its relevance for
development or for learning. If this weren't so, there would surely
be much more play taking place in primary (not to mention secondary) schools.[1]

Vygotsky, as the above quote makes clear, accorded play a
critically important place in his overall theory of development. To
our Vygotsky, therefore, play is of concern as revolutionary activity. In this chapter we will investigate play in its specific
relationship to the dialectical unity {meaning-making/learning-
leading-development}, i.e. as an instantiation of learning leading
development in the ZPD. A critical question for revolutionary
scientists is how and under what conditions play is or can be
organized as product and process of producing activity settings
(creating ZPDs).

There has been very little Vygotskian-inspired research on play.
Several factors contribute to the paucity of work: Vygotsky himself
wrote so little on the topic; developmental psychologists (in our
opinion overly focused on cognitive development and pragmatic

methodology) have adopted an information processing definition of creativity (as generatively transformative); and Vygotskian developmental and educational psychologists and linguists, influenced by the issues which dominate their disciplines, have tended to focus on the discourse and semiotic aspects of Vygotsky's findings.

Those (non-Vygotskian) contemporary researchers on play and specialists in early childhood who believe that play is important for development typically identify the following characteristics as contributing to cognitive and social development in particular: (1) in play children suspend the constraints of reality; (2) through play children learn social norms; and (3) play is rule-governed.[2] As Vygotskians examining play, we wish to ask what is meant by reality and rules in particular. Further, we seek to examine the concept of play itself in order to understand Vygotsky's contribution and its various uses by contemporary Vygotskians and others.

Play is associated with a host of other concepts and activities: games, imagination, fantasy, symbolic representation, pretending, performing, pleasure and fun, to name but a few. There are also different conceptual frameworks in which the concept play 'lives.' At least three meanings of play are important for our discussion of play's role in development: play as 'free' play, the pretend and fantasy activities of early childhood; play as games, the more structured, explicitly rule-governed activities that become pervasive in the school years and which are the dominant form of how adults play; and play as theater acting or performance, also common in early childhood but becoming more exclusive and formalized in adulthood. Only the first two kinds of play – free play and game play – have been examined to any degree by psychologists, especially developmental psychologists and psychoanalysts; theatrical play (acting) or performance has rarely been researched by psychologists of any kind, although theatrical concepts have been employed in analyses of children's symbolic and dramatic play (Erikson, 1977; Sutton-Smith, 1976). In addition, some sociologists and anthropologists have studied theater and/or used theatrical concepts in the study of other institutions (e.g., Goffman, 1971; McDermott, 1976; Sacks, 1974).[3] For reasons we will elaborate on here and in Chapter 7, we believe all three types of play are of critical importance in development and, further, that Vygotsky's life-as-lived (the performance of his life) suggests that he recognized this.

VYGOTSKY AT PLAY

Vygotsky's analysis of play is most interesting. More evocative than definitive, this discussion is less unified than others, e.g. those on concepts or language and thinking. He makes note of how play both 'liberates' and constrains the child, yet he does not fully discuss the contradiction between these nor complete the dialectical unity.

In his discussion of play and its role in development, Vygotsky (1978) examines several relationships and characteristics which in his day had been assumed to be defining features of play – for example, that it is associated with pleasure, that it satisfies ungratified desires, that it is symbolic, that it is rule-governed – and finds them all lacking, except for the fact that play is rule-based. With respect to pleasure, for example, Vygotsky points out that activities other than play give pleasure (e.g. sucking on a pacifier) and that, conversely, play is not always pleasurable (e.g. playing a game or sport and losing). Ignoring needs, desires and subjectivity, however, and considering play only from the perspective of how it contributes to the development of intellectual functions can result in 'a pedantic intellectualization of play' (1978, p. 92). Again Vygotsky is emphasizing the social production of needs, motives, desires and wants; in the dualistic framework of traditional psychology, these are usually referred to as characteristics of emotional, as opposed to intellectual, development. Here he is also stressing the monistic character of human development. He goes on to specify the needs and desires that develop in relation to play, what he refers to as immmediately unrealizable desires, which, he argues, begin to develop only in the preschool years and thus are critical to but do not explain play from the perspective of its own developmental course or its role in development more generally. Finally, defining play as symbolic does not differentiate it from the many other sign- and symbol-using activities in which human beings engage.

Vygotsky also makes claims about play which, at first reading, are counter-intuitive – because, we would urge, our 'intuitions' are shaped by the dominant understanding of play. One is that, far from being 'free' in play, it is in play that the child exhibits the most self-control. Another is that in play what can be or stand for something else is not limitless, i.e. the child does not pretend or fantasize anything and everything. Vygotsky concludes that what is unique to play is the creation of an imaginary situation:

> Thus, in establishing criteria for distinguishing a child's play from other forms of activity, we conclude that in play a child creates an imaginary situation. This is not a new idea, in the sense that imaginary situations in play have always been recognized; but they were previously regarded as only one example of play activities. The imaginary situation was not considered the defining characteristic of play in general but was treated as an attribute of specific subcategories of play.
>
> (1978, pp. 93–4)

This defining characteristic of play – creating an imaginary situation – is linked theoretically with the presence of rules. Vygotsky claims that even the earliest forms of play contain rules and, further, that their importance grows with development. Any imaginary situation contains rules within its creation: 'Whenever there is an imaginary situation in play, there are rules – not rules that are formulated in advance and change during the course of the game but ones that stem from an imaginary situation' (p. 95). Thus even free play, where the creation of the imaginary situation dominates the child's activity, contains (hidden) rules. At the other end of the play continuum, every game with rules contains an imaginary situation.

> For example, playing chess creates an imaginary situation. Why? Because the knight, king, queen, and so forth can only move in specified ways; because covering and taking pieces are purely chess concepts. Although in the chess game there is no direct substitute for real-life relationships, it is a kind of imaginary situation nevertheless.
>
> (p. 95)

Vygotsky thus identifies the creation of the imaginary situation with the limitations placed on possible actions that occur in game play. It is in this way that rules and imagination are linked.

The developmental course of play is characterized by the changing positions of imaginary situations and rules in play activity: 'The development from games with an overt imaginary situation and covert rules to games with overt rules and a covert imaginary situation outlines the evolution of children's play' (p. 96). Play, then, begins with an emphasis on the imaginary situation and develops into the dominance of rules. What is the impact of this course of play development on development?

To answer, we must pursue the elements of this analysis further. Early play, according to Vygotsky, is very closely tied to reality; the imaginary situation is a reproduction or re-creation of a real situation. For example, when a child plays Mommy with another person or with a doll, she/he is re-creating what she/he has seen Mommy do. Similarly, when the child pretends that a stick is a horse and has it do 'horselike' actions, she/he is re-creating what she/he has seen horses do (or what people do with horses). Yet for the child to accomplish this re-creation entails operating with meanings separated from their usual, real life objects and actions (e.g. the meaning of stick and the object stick, the meaning of horse and the object horse, similarly of mother and child). The process of separating meanings from object and action in this way creates a contradictory situation which is of importance in understanding the role of play in development. On the one hand, the child detaches meanings from objects and, on the other hand, she/he fuses real actions and real objects. According to Vygotsky, the stick becomes a pivot for detaching the meaning of 'horse' from a real horse, which is then attached to the stick. This transfer of meaning, Vygotsky claims, is facilitated by the fact that for the young child the word is a property of the thing. At the same time, according to Vygotsky, it is through play activities like these that words become part of the thing.

> In play a child spontaneously makes use of his ability to separate meaning from an object without knowing he is doing it, just as he does not know he is speaking in prose but talks without paying attention to the words. Thus, through play the child achieves a functional definition of concepts or objects, and words become parts of a thing.
>
> (p. 99)

Paradoxes of play in reality/history

> In one sense a child at play is free to determine his own actions. But in another sense this is an illusory freedom, for his actions are in fact subordinated to the meanings of things, and he acts accordingly.
>
> (Vygotsky, 1978, p. 103)

In play – the creation of an imaginary situation – the child eman-
cipates her/himself from situational constraints, such as the
immediate perceptual field. Vygotsky describes this as the primary
paradox of play – 'the child operates with alienated meaning in a
real situation' (p. 99). But being freed from situational constraints,
the child, paradoxically, also faces constraints imposed by play: the
rules of imagination. One such constraint, as Vygotsky understands it, is to act against immediate impulse. 'At every step the
child is faced with a conflict between the rules of the game and
what he would do if he could suddenly act spontaneously' (p. 99).
The example he gives is refraining from eating a piece of candy in
a game where the candy represents something inedible. Subordination to rules and restraining spontaneous action – again,
paradoxically – is the means to pleasure. Here, Vygotsky seems to
be talking less about free or pretend play and more about game
play. It is when game play comes to dominate over performance
play, when, as Vygotsky says, rules become overt and the imaginary situation covert, that these paradoxes of play emerge. This
paradoxical 'moment' is highly significant for the child's development because

> play gives a child a new form of desires [rules]. It teaches her to
> desire by relating her desires to a fictitious 'I,' to her role in the
> game and its rules. In this way a child's greatest achievements
> are possible in play, achievements that tomorrow will become
> her basic level of real action and morality.
>
> (p. 100)

If this sounds strikingly similar to Vygotsky's description of the
relationship between instruction and development, it is not ac-
cidental. Does play create a ZPD? Yes, but not in the same way as
the ZPD is created in everyday nonplay situations. According to
Vygotsky, the critical difference is that in everyday situations of
real life, action dominates meaning, while in play, meaning dominates action. In play a child behaves differently from how she/he
behaves in nonplay. Action in the imaginative sphere, as we have
seen above, frees the child from situational constraints and, at the
same time, imposes constraints of its own. Strict subordination to
rules is not possible in real life, Vygotsky claims, but only in play.
In this way,

play creates a zone of proximal development of the child. In play a child always behaves beyond his average age, above his daily behavior; in play it is as though he were a head taller than himself.

(p. 102)

Vygotsky continues,

Though the play–development relationship can be compared to the instruction–development relationship, play provides a much wider background for changes in needs and consciousness. Action in the imaginative sphere, in an imaginary situation, the creation of voluntary intentions, and the formation of real-life plans and volitional motives – all appear in play and make it the highest level of preschool development. The child moves forward essentially through play activity. Only in this sense can play be considered a leading activity that determines the child's development.

(pp. 102–3)

Davydov and his followers (e.g. Davydov and Markova, 1983) in the Soviet Union and elsewhere have taken Vygotsky's claim that play is a leading activity and conducted investigations with children to show that learning activity is based on play activity (see also Engestrom, Hakkarainen and Hedegaard, 1984).

Lest we be tempted to see play as a 'social catalyst' or 'context,' or even as 'the basis' for learning-leading-development, that is, not a ZPD at all, recall that psychology's proper object of study is history and that its particular tool-and-result is revolutionary activity. Again, what we mean by history is human beings creating and producing activity/activity settings 'in' and 'out of' the materials present in the dialectical environment of human existence that is revolutionary activity/societal behavior. Play makes, and shows, history most clearly through the paradoxes of play Vygotsky describes. For both real life and play are at once societal and historical. When organized as a ZPD, play is thus simultaneously more real (coherent with the dialectical environment of history/society) and less like real life.

The centrality of rules in Vygotsky's analysis needs examination. The question is: what kind of rules? We cannot accept the concept unexamined. For just as there are different kinds of tools – tool for result and tool-and-result – so too there are different kinds of rules. This 'for'–'and' distinction, critical to our understanding of the entire Vygotskian enterprise and to his specific discoveries regarding learning and development and thinking and speech, is useful, by analogy, in understanding play. We propose that rules are to the imagination what tools are to reality; there are *rules for results* and there are *rules-and-results*.

To our understanding, early play is characterized by rules-and-results – the imaginary result informs the mode of performance (playing) as much as the performance informs the imaginary result. It is only later (when, as Vygotsky says, rules dominate) that the transformation from rules-and-result to rules for result occurs – in game play where rules are the how-tos, the instrumentation to an end result separate from, yet determined by, the mode of performance of the game. In this way, game play, like language-making, is a means of adaptation to reality, for it is nothing less than the repression of revolutionary activity – meaning-making, creating rules-and-results (imagination) – even as its development is made possible by revolutionary activity.

Armed with our new conceptual tool (-and-result) of the distinction rule for result and rule-and-result, we can view Vygotsky's analysis of the developmental course of play – from the primacy of creating an imaginary situation to the primacy of subordinating oneself to rules – and its significance for human development as an instantiation of the unity {meaning-making/learning-leading-development}. Imagining, playing, performing, playing games – these are some of the uniquely human tool-and-result activities made possible by meaning-making and the unity {meaning-making/learning-leading-development}. Creating an imaginary situation, regardless of its content, is revolutionary activity – although not all revolutionary activity is imaginary. Unlike beavers, who don't pretend (although they might play), our toolmaking, rule-making species creates in imagination rule-and-result; we use the predetermining elements of the life space in other than a predetermined way to create something other than what is predetermined. Recall Vygotsky's description of the rules of early, free play: 'Not rules that are formulated in advance and change during the course of the game but ones that stem from an imaginary situation' (1978, p. 95). The rules (-and-results) of play create the imaginary situation even as they stem from the creation of the imaginary situation. These rules (-and-results) are incomprehensible apart from the process of their development. The child playing at being Mommy is a rule(-and-result)-maker – the rules of playing at being Mommy are inseparable from playing at being Mommy. We propose that what Vygotsky identifies as action dominating meaning in real life is the revolutionary activity of creating tools-and-results; what he identifies as meaning dominating action in the imaginative sphere, we propose, is the revolutionary activity of creating rules-and-results. Free play (rule-and-result play, revolutionary activity, meaning-making) is necessary for the further development of play, i.e. game play (rule for result play, subordination to rules, societal behavior), because, and as, learning leads development in the ZPD.

Playing at Mommy and Daddy, even if following rules and imitating social roles, disrupts the organization of the life space. After all, the child is not Mommy. And Mommy doesn't play Mommy, she is Mommy. The strict subordination to rules (-and-results) of early play is the means by which the child is able to be more actively a producer of her/his own activity than in nonplay situations where action dominates. Vygotsky describes the situation where the child plays at what she/he is doing and gives the example of pretending 'it's night-time and we have to go to bed' to 'facilitate the execution of an unpleasant action' (1978, p. 102). He says that in play the child liberates her/himself from reality. Such liberation could mean an escape from reality or a means of getting closer to reality. We believe that in play the child gets closer to reality, because it is an attempt to make things more historical and less societal. By this we mean that it is more coherent with the dialectical environment history/society and less overdetermined by societal arrangements.

Play is at once an adaptation and an opposition to the adaptation. It is thus a conflicted response to alienation, for adapting to society is adapting to alienation – the separation of the process of production from the product. In everyday life one is guided – indeed, overdetermined – by perceptual, cognitive and emotional behaviors and is therefore less directly the producer of one's own activity. In play, as the producer, one has more control in organizing the perceptual, cognitive and emotional elements. In this sense, play is much more a performance than an acting. When children, for example, play Mommy and Daddy they are least like Mommy and Daddy because Mommy and Daddy are not playing or performing; they are acting out their societally predetermined roles. We are all cast by society into very sharply determined roles; what one does in a role is act it. Performance differs from acting in that it is the socialized activity of people self-consciously creating new roles out of what exists for a social performance. Children playing Mommy and Daddy are not acting but performing – creating new roles for themselves, reorganizing environmental scenes. In this sense, 'ZPD play' is a history game – the putting together of elements of the social environment in ways which help to see and show meaning-making as creative, productive activity – which produces learning-leading-development. In Chapter 7, we discuss further the history game and the significance of performance.

In an essay on the development of imagination written in 1932, based on a lecture delivered in that year, Vygotsky exposes the flaws both of the 'old' psychology and what he saw as the idealistic psychology of his contemporaries, including Freud and Piaget. Here he links imagination and thinking to the development of consciousness. In a concluding section, he describes the increasing complexity of forms of imagination in a way that is suggestive of our discussion:

> Alongside the images that are constructed in the immediate cognition of reality, man constructs images that he recognizes as part of the domain of imagination. At advanced levels in the development of thinking, we find the construction of images that are not found in completed form in reality. By recognizing this, we can begin to understand the complex relationship between the activity of realistic thinking and the activity of advanced forms of imagination. Each step in the child's achievement of a more profound penetration of reality is linked with his continued liberation from earlier, more primitive forms of cognition. A more profound penetration of reality demands that consciousness attain a freer relationship to the elements of that reality, that consciousness depart from the external and apparent aspect of reality that is given directly in perception. The result is that the processes through which the cognition of reality is achieved become more complex and richer.
>
> (1987, p. 349)

THE WRITING GAME

> ...drawing and play should be preparatory stages in the development of children's written language.
>
> (Vygotsky, 1978, p. 118)

We have departed somewhat from Vygotsky's own analysis of play and imagination. Recall that he claimed only that instruction (learning) leads development and that play leads development. Our discovery of the unity {meaning-making/learning-leading-development} 'leads' us (in Vygotskian fashion) to posit a more specific relation between the two developmental processes – that play is an instantiation of learning-leading-development. Our argument is strengthened, we believe, by Vygotsky's (again brief) discussion of 'pre-written language' (1978). It not only is fascinating in its own right, but it provides further insight into his understanding of play and its role in development.

Vygotsky claims that becoming proficient in written language, however complex, disjointed or confusing it may appear on the surface, is not discontinuous but a unified process of development: 'In the same way as children learn to speak, they should be able to learn to read and write' (1978, p. 118). He presents experimental evidence of his own and others for the continuity from gestures to drawing to writing and for the preschoolers' capacity for 'primitive' written language (they can 'write' before they know how to write 'properly'), and urges that 'children be taught written language, not just the writing of letters' (1978, p. 119).

Central to Vygotsky's understanding is the difference between first- and second-order symbolism. He explains this distinction simply. First-order symbols directly denote actions or objects: a stick for a horse, pencil dots on a paper for running; second-order symbols denote symbols: written signs representing spoken words, a scribbled spiral for smoke. Both drawing and writing in the earliest stages are first-order symbolism. They are not representational, but indicatory; arising out of gestures, they are 'graphic speech.' Vygotsky describes the process of learning written language as one where first-order symbols become second-order symbols (the child comes to discover that one can represent spoken language by written abstract symbolic signs), only later to become first-order symbols again at a higher level of psychological process:

> [The] higher form ... involves the reversion of written language from second-order symbolism to first-order symbolism. As second-order symbolism, written symbols function as designations for verbal ones. Understanding of written language is first

effected through spoken language, but gradually this path is curtailed and spoken language disappears as the intermediate link. To judge from all available evidence, written language becomes direct symbolism that is perceived in the same way as spoken language. We need only try to imagine the enormous changes in the cultural development of children that occur as a result of mastery of written language and the ability to read – and of thus becoming aware of everything that human genius has created in the realm of the written word.

(1978, p. 116)

He cites experimental findings as well as anecdotal evidence from studies in which very young children were challenged to use written symbols to remember and/or represent objects. For example, Vygotsky's colleague Luria conducted experiments which created the moment of discovery that 'one can draw not only things but words' (p. 115). Children not yet able to write were given tasks in which they had to remember a certain number of phrases that exceeded their memory capacity. When the point was reached where the child was convinced she/he could not remember them all, she/he was given a piece of paper and told to record the words in some way. Although many of them were bewildered by the request, when aided by concrete suggestions from the experimenter, they complied. For the most part, the youngest children (3- to 4-year-olds) did not utilize the marks they made; they didn't even look at them when trying to remember. Nevertheless, as Vygotsky notes in summarizing Luria's results, there were occasionally 'some astonishing cases' where the child makes meaningless (to adults) lines and squiggles 'but when he reproduces phrases it seems as though he is reading them; he refers to certain specific marks and can repeatedly indicate, without error, which marks denote which phrase' (p. 114). To Vygotsky, this memory technique is the first precursor of written language. Children gradually replace these kinds of marks with pictures and figures, and then signs (letters and numbers).

Vygotsky also believed that play – specifically the pretend games children play – was another link between gesture and written language. He viewed children's play as a complex system of 'speech' through gestures that indicate the meaning of things – as, for example, when a pile of clothes becomes a baby through the child's own motions and gestures, e.g. of holding or feeding a baby.

'It is only on the basis of these indicatory gestures that playthings themselves gradually acquire their meaning – just as drawing, while initially supported by gesture, becomes an independent sign' (p. 108).

In another section of his discussion, Vygotsky offers more support for his view that make-believe, gestures, drawing and written language comprise a continuum of development. He describes the oft-observed developmental sequence of children's drawing aligned with speech – from initially communicating the basics in both marks on the paper and speech (Vygotsky likens the earliest children's drawing to telling a story), to drawing or scribbling something and suddenly discovering its meaning, to announcing beforehand what one is about to draw. Vygotsky also notes that children sometimes write separate phrases or words on separate sheets of paper, paralleling speech patterns, as further evidence that speech provides the model for writing.

Two observations concerning the relationship between speech, written language and play led Vygotsky to make strong recommendations as to how written language should be taught. First, speech initially dominates writing in children's earliest drawing and 'writing'; second, children are able to learn to write through discovering that they can draw speech. In that case, writing dominates speech. This is, we think, an interesting dialectical relationship. Vygotsky does not highlight it yet we believe it informs his contention that written language should be taught by 'exploiting' the continuity of the unity (pretend play, drawing and writing) through creating environments in which reading and writing are necessary for play.

Vygotsky makes one other point about the importance of play in the development of written language. He cautions that without an 'inner understanding' of written language, it will be mere learning: 'Of course, it is necessary to bring the child to an inner understanding of writing and to arrange that writing will be organized development rather than learning' (p. 118). To do so, he argues, requires that drawing and play be organized so as to be preparatory stages in the development of written language. The concept of 'writing as organized development' is, to us, profound (and profoundly Vygotskian). To explain why, we summarize a contemporary Vygotskian study of written language and present our analysis of its use and misuse of Vygotsky.

McLane (1990) describes one of several recent research projects that explore writing as a social process.[4] Working with sixteen children (most aged 6 to 8) and two group workers in an after-school program in a poor, inner-city community of Chicago, McLane observed and intervened in supportive and creative ways in the organization of the after-school program so as to enhance the children's writing experiences. The study is rich in useful ideas for teachers and child-care workers. We will concentrate on how McLane understands/uses Vygotsky's discovery regarding play and how it creates a ZPD.

According to McLane, the various writing activities in which the children and adults were involved suggest that 'adults in non-school settings can support children's writing by helping them discover connections between more familiar symbol-using activities such as drawing, play and talking, and the less familiar one of writing' (p. 317). Moreover, McLane found it was necessary to support the adults to develop new ways of seeing the writing process, including their own relationship to it. She makes the important point that one must consider 'how to negotiate zones of proximal development with the children *and* the adults who work with them' (p. 317).

In discussing the significance of 'playful uses of writing,' McLane makes the following observation:

> Finally, play encourages the player to act as if he or she were already competent in the activity under consideration, to act, in Vygotsky's words, 'as though he were a head taller than himself' (1978, p. 102). Playing with the processes and forms of writing seems likely to give children a sense of 'ownership' of – or 'entitlement' to – this complex cultural activity. Through playful uses and approaches to writing, children may come to feel that they are writers long before they have the necessary skills and knowledge to produce mature, fully conventional writing. Such positive and proprietary feelings are likely to nourish assumptions and expectations about learning to write, as well as the motivation to work at developing increasing competence in writing.
>
> (p. 312)

Here we have a description of play that comes very close to identifying its meaning-making character, yet it misses the mark. The difference between McLane's extension of Vygotsky and ours turns on the seemingly slight distinction between 'as' and 'as if.' What McLane considers important in playful uses of writing is that children act *as if* they were writers. 'As if' establishes a separation between what is – they are not writers – and what might be – they could be writers; it accepts the duality of reality and fantasy; it locates the developmental aspect of play in the child's mind. We, on the other hand, take the significance of playful uses of language to be that children perform *as* writers, not 'as if' they were writers. Unlike 'as if,' 'as' embodies the dialectical relationship between being and becoming, between what is and what can be, between reality and pretense; it locates the developmental aspect of play in the child's activity. Following Vygotsky, we view play as an environment in which children perform beyond themselves. In play children learn/play that they are learners/players; they are performing as writers. Play is a ZPD for the unity {meaning-making/language-making}.

But McLane persists in identifying play with changes in mental states, not in activity. For example, she emphasizes the 'sense of "ownership" of the cultural activity' that can come from acting *as if*; we emphasize the expression of revolutionary activity that comes from performing *as*. Ownership of an activity is effectively an expression of alienation. In order to own an activity which one produces, the activity must be reified and made into a product (commodified), separated from the process of its production (and thereby its producer). Furthermore, ownership of an activity implies a separation of oneself from the historical process of human productive/creative activities; it separates the one who owns from others. The situation is even more complex than this, because under capitalism one of the things human beings do is own; things, ideas, feelings and people have become commodities – why not activity? This means that the very process of production (including the process of the production of understanding production) which distances one from the human species – ownership of an activity – also brings one close to it, because human beings are, societally speaking, owners as much as we are writers.

McLane's assertion that 'children may come to feel that they are writers' in such play situations as she is describing (as when children play with language and writing) is not attentive to the meaning(-making)fulness of play that Vygotsky identified. Children may come to feel that they are writers 'through playful uses and approaches to writing,' but why is how children feel what is of critical importance? The word 'feel' in this context implies that there is a mismatch between feelings and the actual state of affairs. It does not merely emphasize feelings; it implies that the children, in fact, are not writers – they only feel that they are. But this denies the critical factor that makes learning lead development in the ZPD.

Children's writing activities of the sort McLane describes are evidence of children performing as historical writers (meaning makers). Not to see them as such is to take 'mature, fully conventional writing' (societal writing) as what writing is. It is to deny the unity {meaning-making/learning-leading-development} as the critical force behind language-making/thinking (which includes but is not reducible to 'mature, fully conventional writing'). It is children's play with written language that makes it possible for them to learn, eventually, the 'workings' of written language.

Another study employing Vygotsky's discovery that play creates a ZPD was conducted over a five-year period by McNamee (1990). Working with staff, parents and children at Chicago community centers that had Head Start and day care programs, McNamee set out to discover 'how story dictation and dramatization activities carried out in a literacy-rich preschool classroom environment that emphasized play as the main context and approach to learning might help children considered at risk for school failure and illiteracy' (p. 292). The report is replete with examples of classroom activities, teachers' stories and reports, and McNamee's own observations. It is valuable in its emphasis on the collaboration that developed among the teachers and researcher in the creation of ZPDs: 'ZPDs took shape between us as we acted together, spoke together, and wrote with and for each other' (p. 293).

However, when McNamee attempts to explicate Vygotsky's discovery, like McLane (1990) she 'elevates' activity to the realm of thought and thereby obscures the very point Vygotsky was making. Here is McNamee's interpretation of Vygotsky on play and the ZPD: 'Vygotsky says that play creates a ZPD; he meant that in order to grow and develop people need to be able to think of themselves in a way that is different from the way they are now' (1990, p. 288). To corroborate her faulty thesis – there is no evidence Vygotsky meant this – she draws on the work of Paley, who explained why she told a child to '"pretend" you are a boy who knows how to share' in the following way: '"Pretend" disarms and enchants; it suggests heroic possibilities for making change, just as in the fairy tales' (Paley, 1984, p. 87). McNamee comments, 'Like Mrs Paley, Ms Stevens had discovered a way of speaking that helped her and the children establish a footing from which to change and grow in their classroom ZPD' (1990, p. 301).

In ascribing primary significance to what goes on in the child's mind, and attributing the power of pretending to the story the child acts out, McNamee misses what is in fact the extraordinary developmental occurrence that takes place 'in' play (and every other ZPD): meaning-making activity.[5]

Reform and revolution in the study of thinking and speech

Between 1962, when Vygotsky's *Thought and Language* first appeared in English, and 1987, when the complete version was published as *Thinking and Speech*, Western scholars (following Wertsch, who was familiar with the original Russian manuscript) have taken pains to note the error in the original translation of the title.

Vygotsky used the active terms 'thinking' (*myschlenie*) and 'speech' (*rech'*), not the conceptual nouns 'thought' (*mysl*) and 'language' (*iazyk*). As should be clear by now, Vygotsky understood these complex psychological processes as activities. But what are activities? What is activity? Have we finally answered these questions? We think not. For the task of answering them is ongoing. It is easy enough to compare and contrast 'activity' with, say, 'passivity,' or 'process' with 'things.' It is much more difficult to articulate in a positive fashion what activity is. And what is history – the totality or, more precisely, totalities of activities?

For 'our Vygotsky' history is psychology's object of study, and activity – history's radically monistic unity – is revolutionary activity. But the historical Vygotsky, perhaps because he was so much in the midst of the Russian Revolution, and, therefore, subjectively very much in history and in activity, failed to let the revolution in fully.

Wertsch (1991), in his important recent work *Voices of the Mind*, makes the point this way:

> Because Vygotsky and his colleagues were influenced by Marxist theory, one would expect their account to extend to broader historical and economic forces; this seems to be precisely what motivated Luria's concern with the social and historical forms

of human existence. But Vygotsky and his colleagues did relatively little to elaborate this claim in concrete ways.

(p. 34)

Yet Vygotsky's failure to include substantive economic and historical elements is less troublesome to us than his occasional inconsistency in employing the revolutionary method(s) of Marxism, including his own anti-instrumentalist tool-and-result method. For the Vygotskian unity (brilliantly used in his polemic with Piaget and others and in his own experiments) must itself be continuously united with revolutionary activity.

We do not think that history is a force to be included or extended to. It is not an environment 'in' which everything happens. It is, rather, the broad revolutionary activity of reorganizing environments that determine us. As such it is far closer to the truth to say that history is in everything than that everything is in history.

Speaking (verbalizing, using a language) is, perhaps, the single human performance that best exemplifies the dialectical dynamic that is history and society, the form and substance of the life space of everyday human performance, the ZPD. Therefore, the study of this kind of performance in all its complex detail demands, on our account, the most consistent and rigorous use of the revolutionary tool-and-result method.

A tool-and-result analysis of tools (e.g. language) must not be replaced by or conflated with (consciously or not so consciously) a tool for result (instrumentalist) analysis of tool-and-result. Indeed it is the claim and conclusion of 'our Vygotsky' (even if he rarely mentioned and inconsistently used tool-and-result methodology and revolutionary activity theory) that speech and language must both evolve and be studied as tool-and-result if the learning and use of language and speech is to have happened (and be understood as having happened) at all.

Vygotsky's approach, then, contrasts sharply with the dominant philosophical and psycholinguistic views of language and language learning, for they take language and linguistic elements to be the tools out of which meaning is derived, produced, created and constructed. Vygotskians, too, are prone to see meaning as evolving from language, interpreting the significance Vygotsky accords signs, symbols and other semiotic elements as due to their use as instrumentalist tools for the creation of meaning. However, Vygotsky's investigations into thinking, speaking and consciousness reveal that meaning is not a (tool for) result of language, but rather that *the revolutionary activity of meaning-making is the precondition for language-making*. The purpose of his investigations was to answer not questions about meaning, e.g. 'What does this language mean?,' but questions about activity, e.g. 'What language completes this meaning?' He says, for example, 'we must now analyze not the development of meanings and their structure, but the process through which *meanings function in the living process of verbal thinking*' (1987, p. 249). His complex and detailed discussions of egocentric and social speech and thought and of word meaning, to be presented shortly, stress the tool-and-resultishness of meaning, thinking and speaking.

Vygotsky identifies the earliest pre-speaking, pre-thinking activities of the human infant (e.g. babbling, pointing) as pre-intellectual and pre-speech. For Vygotsky and for us a study of meaning is historical; it is a study of meaning-making, of activity, not a study solely of societally appropriate word–object relations. Long before children do what is recognized as speaking, they are making meaning; they are reorganizing the determining environment, which includes linguistic elements. It is by virtue of children reorganizing these elements that they learn the societal use of them (language-making/thinking). While sounds and words may be necessary tools for language-making, meaning-making is its historical precondition.

In the language of 'our Vygotsky,' then, the specific though highly complex revolutionary activity of meaning-making is the historical learning that leads the societal development of language-making and without which there would be no language-making and, therefore, no language worthy of the name at all. The unity {meaning-making – leading-language-making} is one critically important instantiation of Vygotsky's discovery that learning leads development.

Our distinctly unstylish recommendation for the title of Vygotsky's extraordinary work published in English in 1962 is, therefore, neither *Thought and Language* nor *Thinking and Speech* (whatever happened to 'speaking'?) but the less elegant though more accurate *Meaning-Making/Language-Making*. The historical production of meaning-making is dialectically related to the societal production of language-making. As Vygotsky says, meaning-making 'leads' – in a categorically anti-causal sense – language-making as 'learning leads development.'

EGOCENTRIC THOUGHT AND EGOCENTRIC SPEECH

The task of psychology, however, is not the discovery of the eternal child. The task of psychology is the discovery of the historical child.

(Vygotsky, 1987, p. 91)

But what is meant by 'the historical child'? Does 'historical' here mean simply 'real' or 'actual' as opposed to 'eternal' or 'abstract'? Vygotsky's focus on individuals and dyads of children and his genetic accountings (explaining by giving the linear history of the particular child or social phenomenon) suggests this limited understanding of 'the historical child.' Yet the substance and style of Vygotsky's experimental conclusions and writings, taken as a whole, impel us to understand 'the discovery of the historical child' to mean that the child and her/his development *is* history. Learning to speak *is* history. Vygotsky's critical (though incomplete and inconsistent) discovery that the child's acquisition of speech not only occurs in a social context, but is itself history – a social-historical human activity – is exemplified well in his analysis of egocentric speech and thought.

The orthodox perspective on these matters presents Vygotsky's position as directly opposed, once again, to Piaget's. (Indeed, there is some basis for seeing it this way; at times, Vygotsky himself was prone to expressing the argument in a framework of opposites.) In point of dialectical fact, however, Vygotsky stood Piaget on his head (precisely as Marx overturned Hegel). And being turned upside down is not the same as being negated (being an opposite). Yet before we get caught up in the precise nature of Vygotsky's rejection, let us ask more simply (and once again): what is Vygotsky's problem with Piaget?

Piaget – particularly in his early works (the only ones with which Vygotsky was familiar) – begins with the premise and argues for the empirical validity of the essential egocentricity of the child's thinking and thought-governed activity. According to Piaget, developmental characteristics of the child's thought follow from its egocentric nature. Piaget defined egocentric thought as intermediate between autistic and rational thought. He regarded egocentric speech – speech 'for oneself' with no communicative function, which is said to characterize the child's speaking behavior until the age of 7 or 8 (when social speech supposedly emerges) – as evidence for egocentric thought:

This characteristic of a large portion of childish talk points to a certain egocentrism of thought itself... And these thoughts are inexpressible precisely because they lack the means which are fostered only by the desire to communicate with others, and to enter into their point of view.

(Piaget, 1955, p. 206)

Further, Piaget's observations that egocentric speech declines with the emergence and increase of social speech led him to conclude that egocentric speech disappears but that egocentrism as such does not; rather it is displaced to another level, that of abstract thinking.

Noting that 'This issue of the function and fate of egocentric speech constitutes the vital nerve of Piaget's entire perspective on this phenomenon [egocentrism],' Vygotsky attacked Piaget's thesis from 'above' and 'below' (1987, p. 69). That is, ever mindful of the task he set himself – the search for method and, thereby, a new science – Vygotsky considered the particulars of Piaget's analysis from the vantage point of the totality of the Swiss psychologist's methodology:

...we must attempt a critique of the theory and the methodological systems that provide the foundation for Piaget's studies. Within this framework, the empirical data will concern us only to the extent that they are basic to theory or concretize methodology.

(1987, pp. 55–6)

Vygotsky conducted his own studies of children's speech, and came up with very different findings from those of Piaget. His experiments were similar to Piaget's, with one critical difference. Interested in how egocentric speech is produced, Vygotsky introduced into the experimental task factors that increased the difficulty of the task for the child. For example, if the task involved drawing, paper or pencil might be absent. Vygotsky found that egocentric speech occurred nearly twice as often when there was such an impediment. The child would talk to her/himself – 'Where's the pencil? I need a blue pencil...' Why should egocentric speech increase in these circumstances? Vygotsky concluded that, far from being functionless, purely expressive, or merely a form of 'discharge' or accompaniment to the child's activity, egocentric speech becomes fused with thinking and activity. It can serve as a guide to or plan of action.

He gave the following example to illustrate how the data he gathered informed his analysis.

> In one of our experiments, a child of five-and-a-half was draw-ing a picture of a tram. While drawing a line that would represent a wheel, the child put too much pressure on the pencil and the lead broke. The child attempted, nonetheless, to com-plete the circle by pressing the pencil to the paper. But nothing appeared on the paper other than the imprint of the broken pencil. As if to himself, the child quietly said, 'Broken.' Laying the pencil aside, he took a paint brush and began to draw a broken tram car that was in the process of being repaired after an accident, continuing to talk to himself from time to time about the new subject of his drawing. This egocentric utterance is clearly linked to the whole course of the child's activity. It constitutes a turning point in his drawing and clearly indicates his conscious reflection on the situation and his attendant diffi-culties. It is so clearly fused with the normal process of thinking that it is impossible to view it as a simple accompaniment of that thinking.
>
> (1987, p. 70)

Thus for Vygotsky, egocentric speech is not a primitive, asocial form of speech which gradually disappears as the child becomes social. Unlike Piaget, who made the extraordinary statement that there is 'no real social life between children of less than 7 or 8 years' (1955, p. 40), Vygotsky thought very young children were intensely social. To him, egocentric speech is critical in the historical transi-tion from purely social speech (in which the child, no Robinson Crusoe, begins to participate at birth) to inner speech and thought. When the child's activity *is* history rather than merely the function-ing of an essentially 'egocentric' unit *in* history, the psychologist 'discovers the historical child.'

The orthodoxy says the child lacks the ability to plan, to stay on course, to not be distracted by the immediate situation. Underlying this metaphysical analysis is the 'eternal child,' the 'idealized child,' the 'naturally egocentric child.' For the historical child, following Vygotsky, thought and action are fused. The historical child, unencumbered by any egocentric oak in her or his Kantian-Piagetian acorn, is busy making meaning, changing the determining totality, letting her/his revolutionary activity create more revolutionary activity. Figuratively speaking, when the pencil breaks Piaget stops the experiment; Vygotsky begins it at that moment. For the capacity to reorganize what we have, not the ability merely to use what is given, is the essential situation for the historical child and the historical adult.

The reformers' Vygotsky

In expanding on his earlier work that explores the semiotic mechanisms through which joint activity is created, Wertsch (1991) offers a particularly sophisticated analysis of the Vygotskian enterprise. It is nevertheless a dualistic reformulation of what we take to be Vygotsky's methodological practice.

As many other Vygotskians do, Wertsch regards mediated action as Vygotsky's main building block; it is central to his own sociocultural approach to mind. Such an approach, Wertsch writes, 'begins with the assumption that action is mediated and that it cannot be separated from the milieu in which it is carried out' (1991, p. 19). From a societal point of view, the assumption that action is mediated makes perfect sense. But from the vantage point of history it does not. For the historical unit of analysis is revolutionary activity, not mediated action. The tools, such as language, used to carry out everyday revolutionary activity could not possibly be instrumentalist mediators – although that is certainly what they are 'within' alienated society. But to see them only, or fundamentally, as such is to bias the very practice and form of psychological analysis in favor of society and thereby to deny *a priori* the fundamentality of history and the dialectical dynamic that is history/society, the form and substance of the life space of everyday human performance (ZPD).

Here we need to analyze further the history/society dialectic in order to understand precisely what is so problematic about mediated action. To Marx, *socialization* is the process of the human species becoming more social, that is, producing more varied and complex relations of cooperation in the remaking of its life (Marx and Engels, 1973, see especially pp. 48–68). The need to adapt to an existing society, what we call *societization*, is both a product of and produces socialization. The two processes, socialization and societization, are in constant interplay in the development of human beings as individuals and as a species.

Societization (the child's adaptation to and assimilation by society) is the dialectical opposite of socialization. In contemporary society, where societization dominates socialization and the adaptation to capitalism intensifies the socialization/societization opposition, socialization tends to move 'inward' – producing (at best) creativity and abstract thinking, and (at worst) various forms of psychopathology. Meanwhile, societization moves 'outward' in the form of alienation (of process from product), of behavior (as opposed to activity), and of an increasingly coerced conformity.

On Vygotsky's account, thought and meaning,[1] as manifest in the word and its semantic analysis, is the unity of 'inner' and 'outer.' But this unity has been misconstrued to rationalize the dualism of inner thought and outer meaning when in point of dialectical fact the unity thought-and-meaning is the ultimate disproof of dualism. Marxian-Vygotskian method forces the Cartesian 'I think, therefore, I am' dualism underlying much of Western thought and thought about thought (since Kant, through Piaget and beyond) to give way to a radical historical monism that eliminates both the 'I' and the 'therefore' of the Cogito and leaves us with dialectical historical meaning-making/language-making/thinking human beings 'not in any fantastic isolation and rigidity, but in their actual, empirically perceptible process of development under definite conditions' (Marx and Engels, 1973, pp. 47–8).

In his discussion of mediation by tools Wertsch (1991) leaves out Vygotsky's critical concept of tool-and-result. That omission overdetermines Wertsch's comprehension and use of mediation. Perhaps, as Wertsch says, 'human action . . . is mediated by tools' (p. 19). But human activity is not, because human activity is not mediated at all.[2] Human activity – tool-and-result activity, practical-critical, revolutionary activity – is history. Wertsch may be correct in his explication of Vygotsky's analysis of mediated action, and Vygotsky's claims about mediated action may also be valid. However, Wertsch does not follow Vygotsky's tool-and-result methodology all the way, just as Vygotsky himself did not go all the way with Marx's concept of practical-critical, revolutionary activity. It is precisely this dialectical interplay between mediated societal action and practical-critical, historical activity that informs revolutionary Vygotskians' thinking about a new science. For Vygotsky the analysis of human life activity and the creation of a new science are inseparable; they are yet another unity.

Marx, Vygotsky and Wittgenstein lead us to believe that what is actually required for a new human science is:

- a unit (actually, a unity) of study which is inseparable (revolutionary activity, history);
- a method of study which demands inseparability (tool-and-result);
- a mode of understanding and an organization of understanding which are themselves seamless (a unity {learning-leading-development} and, more generally, the ZPD); and
- an experimental activity the performance of which makes history more than it does alienation (the language game and/or the history game – self-consciously created life environments, not experimental situations).

What is needed, as well, is a new science – perhaps several, perhaps a whole new understanding of what the science activity is – which is as rigorous in its approach to the child's (and adult's) historical-ness as Galileo's approach was to nature's motion-ness.

Rosa and Montero (1990) speak of a *new alliance* in science:

Even distinguished scholars of the natural sciences advocate change in the orientation of the conception and practice of the sciences. Ilya Prigogine, 1977 Nobel Prize winner in physics, in his most interesting book *La nouvelle alliance* (see Prigogine, 1984) points out the historical preeminence of mechanistic thinking in physics and the current incoherence of this explanatory mode both within the discipline and in relation to others. As he indicates, thermodynamics has demonstrated, with the concept of entropy, that time is not reversible and that chemistry reveals the undeniable existence of objects with negative entropy. This leads to the impossibility of applying an automatic and deterministic causality to all physical phenomena and reveals the existence of random behaviors in matter and points of bifurcation in the history of matter. This amounts to nothing other than the emergence of new behavioral modes of matter that contradict existing knowledge in various disciplines of the physical sciences, in short, the appearance of a historical dimension in matter and in the very laws that govern the way it functions. As Prigogine states, this puts physics in a position similar to that of the human sciences. It is essential to look for a new alliance among the diverse branches of knowledge once we see that they are all faced with the same challenge: the existence of an irreversible time that changes the behavioral modes of matter and a world open to random behavior with points of bifurcation in which human activity can play a central role.

It is somewhat surprising that, when psychology has spent a good part of its history as a science trying to imitate explanatory models derived from physics, one of the most distinguished physicists of our day indicates the necessity of incorporating explanatory models from social sciences into physics and calls for an integration of sciences and humanities. It appears that the gap between natural sciences and social sciences created in the last century is ready to be bridged.

(p. 83)

Revolutionary Vygotskians are speaking here of a new concept and practice of science, not a return to eighteenth- and nineteenth-century idealism – neither the Berkeleyan nor the Hegelian version – nor a rerun of twentieth-century positivism or empiricism, but a Marxian recognition of 'the this-sidedness of . . . thinking in practice,' as Marx put it in his second thesis on Feuerbach:

The question whether objective truth can be attributed to human thinking is not a question of theory but is a *practical question*. Man must prove the truth, i.e., the reality and power, the this-sidedness of his thinking in practice. The dispute over the reality or non-reality of thinking that is isolated from practice is a purely *scholastic* question.

(1973, p. 121)

The new revolutionary science activity must be practical, not pragmatic. Practicality (of the critical variety) is to be found neither in society nor in history but in their contradictory interplay – an interplay (a ZPD) in which, to paraphrase Vygotsky, history *leads* society. Piaget's societal child, full of eternal, egocentric, teleological predispositions, is well treated by Wertsch. But Vygotsky's historical child is abandoned. For it is not enough to knock down walls. Only when the humanistic bridge of a new science (activity) is built will the historical child be able to walk across. A principal architect of that yet to be built bridge is, of course, Lev Vygotsky, the revolutionary scientist.

The philosophy of the fact

Vygotsky further investigated the origins and development of egocentric speech in another series of experiments. In them he looked at the relationship between egocentric speech and what Piaget called the 'collective monologue,' referring to the phenomenon of egocentric speech occurring in the presence of peers, as when children playing or working next to each other are talking 'to themselves' and not attending to one another. One interpretation of this phenomenon is that the collective monologue represents an intentional isolation from the collective, that the child's egocentric speech stems from the egocentrism and inadequate socialization of his thinking. If so, then one would expect egocentric speech to increase when the collective was less present, i.e. under conditions more suitable to the expression of the child's essential egocentrism.

However, Vygotsky found the opposite was the case. For example, egocentric speech dramatically decreased when children were placed with other children who were deaf or spoke a different language, when they were placed either far from other children or in isolation, and when they were told to whisper. He understood these conditions as ways in which vocalization and the illusion of understanding (said to be characteristics of egocentric speech) were eliminated from the situation. Far from being pre-social, Vygotsky concluded, egocentric speech 'cannot live and function in isolation from social speech' (1987, p. 264). When the possibility for or illusion of understanding – a critical feature of social speech – is eliminated, egocentric speech 'atrophies.' Vygotsky hypothesized that the source of egocentric speech is the inadequate individualization of speech for oneself. He took this as the basis for his claim that egocentric speech is transitional between social speech and inner speech. Here again, we see the impact of his insistence that speech is socially organized and produced, that the child is historical, that learning to speak is history, that thinking/speaking is a sociohistorical activity which produces the 'inner' acts of mind, not an 'outer' expression of a species fundamentally egocentric-in-nature.

The significance of Vygotsky's findings goes well beyond identifying the character of children's early language: they challenge the very foundation of Piaget's work. For Piaget's claim that the child's thinking is essentially egocentric is largely based on his assumption of the link between egocentric speech (which he took to be functionless) and egocentric thought. According to Piaget, the extent to which the child's speech is egocentric is the extent to which the child's thinking is egocentric. Vygotsky refuted this faulty logic empirically:

> The phenomenon of egocentric speech, as we conceptualize it, cannot provide support for an argument concerning levels of egocentric thought. The intellectual function of egocentric speech, which appears to be directly linked with the development of inner speech and its functional characteristics, is not a direct reflection of egocentrism in the child's thought. On the contrary, it demonstrates that under appropriate conditions egocentric speech can be utilized as a means of realistic thinking at a very early age.
>
> (1987, pp. 72–3)

He is clear about the implications: 'with the severing of this link between egocentric speech and egocentric thinking, the empirical foundation for the conception of childhood egocentrism is lost' (pp. 72–3).

Vygotsky makes clear that the goal of his own empirical studies was not mere critique, but the development of a more fruitful approach to (a new science for) the study of children's thinking. He readily acknowledged that he presented little empirical data with which to refute Piaget, but believed that what was known about development supported his conclusion quite forcefully. This is an important methodological as well as psychological point. Vygotsky is not objectifying method, not separating method (tool) from result. He is saying that one cannot conduct investigations or experiments, gather data, look at those data as things-in-themselves and draw conclusions about whether the data support or refute a particular hypothesis. That is the traditional tool for result scientific method, the arbitrary separation of fact from theory. It is not Vygotsky's methodology. His method of verification for any particular inquiry is to stay grounded in the overall perspective on development, based on the totality of what is known and how it is known.

> Fact and philosophy are directly interrelated. This is particularly true of facts such as those that Piaget has discovered, reported and analyzed because they concern the development of the

child's thinking. If we want to find the key to this rich collection of new facts, we must first clarify the philosophy of the fact, the philosophy of its acquisition and interpretation. Otherwise the facts will remain silent and dead.

(1987, p. 55)

Look at Vygotsky's philosophy of the fact of development:

> The initial function of speech is social, that of social interaction or social linkage. Speech affects those in the immediate environment and may be initiated by either the adult or the child. The first form of speech in the child, then, is purely social. The notion that speech is socialized is incorrect in that this implies that speech was originally non-social, that it becomes social only through development and change... It is only after an initial stage where the child's speech is a purely social phenomenon, only in subsequent growth and development, that we begin to see a sharp differentiation of social speech into egocentric and communicative speech . . . egocentric and communicative speech are equally social; they simply have different functions. In accordance with this hypothesis, egocentric speech develops in a social process that involves the transmission of social forms of behavior to the child. Egocentric speech develops through a movement of social forms of collaboration into the sphere of individual mental functions.

(1987, p. 74)

Vygotsky summarizes Piaget's view succinctly and shows its close connection to psychoanalytic theory. For Piaget, the child's initial thinking is private, personal and autistic; only gradually does it become socialized. The egocentric stage of speech and thinking is transitional in the development from autistic to logical forms of thinking; from the intimately individual to the social. What is reflected here, Vygotsky points out, is a psychoanalytic manifestation of the fundamental dualism between the individual (the private) and the social – the bifurcation of the child's world(s) into inner needs and objective reality. For Piaget and the psychoanalysts, the child first is motivated to satisfy inner needs and only later is forced to adapt to objective reality. But, says Vygotsky, needs and their satisfaction do not exist separate from objective reality; the very notion that they do is pure metaphysics:

When Piaget borrows Freud's concept that the pleasure principle precedes the reality principle, he adopts the whole metaphysic associated with the concept of the pleasure principle. Here the principle is transformed from an auxiliary or biologically subordinate characteristic into a kind of independent vital force, into the prime mover of the whole process of mental development.

(1987, p. 77)

Piaget is then forced by logical necessity into yet another abstraction – pure thought. Having divorced needs and satisfaction from the process of adaptation to reality, he is left with realistic thinking dangling in air, completely cut off from the needs and desires of the child. But Vygotsky holds fast to Marx's historical monism and to the historical child. Need and adaptation must be considered in their unity. 'In the child, there exists no form of thinking that operates for the sake of pure truth, no form of thinking divorced from the earth, from needs, wishes, and interests' (1987, p. 77).

Further, if one carefully traces the development of thinking, as Vygotsky does, one can see the traditional dualisms breaking down. For example, Vygotsky notes that far from autistic thinking being separate from and prior to realistic thinking, the development of autistic thinking requires the development of realistic thinking. Here he is referring to the observation that trying to satisfy in imagination needs that have not been satisfied in life is a relatively late development. He also challenges the bifurcation of emotions and intellect, whereby emotions are traditionally associated with autistic thinking (because they are understood as essentially private) and rationality with realistic thinking. Note how Vygotsky holds to the unity of needs and reality in an earlier (1932) work:

When associated with a task that is important to the individual, when associated with a task that somehow has its roots in the center of the individual's personality, realistic thinking calls to life much more significant emotional experience than imagination or daydreaming. Consider, for example, the realistic thinking of the revolutionary contemplating or studying a complex political situation. When we consider an act of thinking concerned with the resolution of a task of vital significance to the personality, it becomes clear that the connections between realistic thinking and the emotions are often infinitely deeper, stronger, more impelling and more significant than the connections between the emotions and the daydream.

(1987, pp. 347–8)[3]

To summarize, in his complex investigation of egocentric thinking and speech (only sketches of which we have presented here), Vygotsky at his best examines the philosophy of the fact. He self-consciously employs new tools (method, concepts and analysis):

Activity and practice – these are the new [distinctly Marxian] concepts that have allowed us to consider the function of egocentric speech from a new perspective, to consider it in its completeness. They have enabled us to identify new factors in the development of the child's thinking, factors which – like the other side of the moon – have generally remained outside the observer's field of vision.

(1987, p. 78)

Vygotsky's radical rejection of the bifurcation between inner and outer (mind and society) can be seen in his understanding of reality and how the child comes to know it:

Piaget has argued that things do not influence the mind of the child. But we have seen that where the child's egocentric speech is linked to his practical activity, where it is linked to his thinking, things really do operate on his mind and influence it. By the word 'things' we mean reality. However, what we have in mind is not reality as it is passively reflected in perception or abstractly cognized. We mean reality as it is encountered in practice.

(1987, p. 79)

The philosophy of the fact! Still another extraordinary formulation of 'our Vygotsky.' As Aristotle liberated Plato's essences from a Greek heaven and located them in earthly objects, as Galileo and others freed motion from its subsidiary and chimerical role of 'serving' objects, as Wittgenstein saved language from the slavery of 'being about' something, so Vygotsky, following Marx, embraces the historical child and rescues both the fact and philosophy from abstract reality and brings them home to history. For the philosophy of the fact is the recognition that fact and reorganization of the philosophical framework – which is at once the tool for discovering the fact *and* the result of the fact being discovered – are continuous in the activity of a truly human science. Kuhn's paradigmism, and Quine's sophisticated pragmatism, which dualistically and temporally distinguish the revolutionary or philosophical period of scientific discovery from the fact-gathering phase, may have some vague, perhaps heuristic, relationship to the origins of modern physics and chemistry. But it is the philosophy of the fact which best exposes the continuous humanistic process of discovering/reorganizing totality that is the revolutionary, practical-critical essence of human activity and, therefore, of a new human science.

Vygotsky's critique of Piaget's analysis of egocentric thought and speech is not the only place where we can see Vygotsky's practical-critical method-in-use and Piaget's dualism. The entirety of Vygotsky's exploration of the relationship between thinking and speech is, in point of (philosophical) fact, a revolutionary critique of the position that speech is a reflection of thought, which was Piaget's view.[4]

THINKING AND SPEAKING

Why has there been so much interest in the relationship between thinking and speaking? No small part of the concern among psychologists, linguists and philosophers stems from what we referred to earlier as the seemingly perplexing question – how does anyone ever develop at all? How does the 'inner' get expressed outwardly? How does the 'outer' (culture, norms, values) become 'inner'? As we have said before, these questions are meaningful (and thereby perplexing) only societally, i.e. only to the extent that one assumes a separation between the individual and society. One must figure out how the inner and outer are mediated only if one accepts the metaphysical reality of inner and outer! The dominant ways of positing the relationship between language and thought, between thinking and speaking – Does language mirror thought? Or does language shape thought? Or, for that matter, are both true? – are philosophically dualistic in their assumptions.

Vygotsky's interest in the relationship between thinking and speech stemmed from no such *a priori* assumptions. His embrace of Marx's non-propositional premises ('men . . . in their actual empirically perceptible process of development under definite conditions'), his own version of Marx's methodological critique in the 'Theses on Feuerbach' (perhaps we should collect them as Vygotsky's 'Theses on Piaget'), and his break with dualism – his discovery and practice of tool-and-result methodology – enabled Vygotsky to recognize that the revolutionary activity of meaning-making and the unity {meaning-making/language-making/ thinking} held the key to development. He was not seeking a resolution of the dualists' dilemma – the illusory interactionist linkage of inner and outer; rather, Vygotsky saw that the activities of speech, word meaning, signs and language are the exquisitely and infinitely practical (in Marx's practical-critical sense) psychological tools-and-results created by our species, individuals-in-society-in-history, that make human learning and development (both toolmaking and tool-using) possible.

We look next at Vygotsky's understanding of word meaning and its role in the development of thinking and speaking. To begin with, he is very clear that the relationships between thinking and speaking are not a precondition for either phylogenetic or onto-genetic development; there is nothing primal or innate about the connections between thought and word:

> They are not something given from the outset as a precondition for further development. On the contrary, these relationships emerge and are formed only with the historical development of human consciousness. They are not the precondition of man's formation but its product... This connection [between word and thought] emerges, changes, and grows with the development of thought and word.

> (1987, p. 243)

These products (the relationships between thought and word) are, in the language of meaning-making, the toolmaker's tool-and-result. It is defined not by or in its use but in the productive activity of its development. Blurring the distinction between use and activity misidentifies the relationship between thought and word Vygotsky posits, for example, by using instrumentalist conceptions (e.g. of tool, mediation and use).

Wertsch's (1991) introduction of Wittgenstein's tool imagery is an example of this blurring. He quotes one of Wittgenstein's well known statements about words:

> Think of the tools in a tool-box: there is a hammer, pliers, a saw, a screw-driver, a rule, a glue-pot, nails and screws. – The

functions of words are as diverse as the functions of these objects. (And in both cases there are similarities.)

Of course, what confuses us is the uniform appearance of words when we hear them spoken or meet them in script and print. For their *application* is not presented to us so clearly.

(Wittgenstein, 1953, p. 6; quoted in Wertsch, 1991, p. 105)

Notice, however, that these tools are all store bought, and the application (the use) is what 'is not presented to us so clearly.' For Wittgenstein (and, as well, for 'our Vygotsky'), the problem is not that the use of the tool is obscure, nor even that the production of the tool is hidden, but that the self-reflexive practical activity – the tool-and-resultishness, the sensuousness, the subjectivity, the practical-criticalness of the tool – is transformed into an instrumentalist 'glue-pot.' For Wittgenstein, 'meaning' is not 'use'; meaning is more closely identified with activity.

Activity without use is, to be sure, ultimately existential, Sisyphean motion. Yet use without activity is the conservative pragmatic valorization of the societal status quo. Language as 'tools in a tool-box' is not identical to language as a played game – Wittgenstein was clear about the distinction. To conflate them is to distort Wittgenstein, Vygotsky, Marx and, most importantly, the historical child. For example, Wertsch prefaced the above quote from Wittgenstein in the following manner: 'In *Philosophical Investigations*, Wittgenstein addressed the difficulty of distinguishing one language game from another and the issue of how language games could be conceptualized as being organized in a tool kit' (1991, p. 105).

What does Wertsch mean by saying that Wittgenstein 'addressed . . . the issue of how language games could be conceptualized as being organized in a tool kit'? Plainly it is words, and not language games, that are organized (as Wittgenstein says, can be thought of as being organized) in a tool-box. Tools in a tool-box (thinking of them) helps us to understand the use of language (e.g. words) in society. Language games help us to see the activity, not the societal use, of language. Wittgenstein, Vygotsky and Marx understand, in varying ways and to varying degrees, the activity/use dialectic of activity leading use (although Wittgenstein would be most unhappy, we suspect, with the word 'dialectic').

Only a few pages after the passage quoted by Wertsch from *Philosophical Investigations*, Wittgenstein goes on to say:

But how many kinds of sentences are there? Say assertion, question, and command? – There are *countless* kinds: countless different kinds of use of what we call 'symbols,' 'words,' 'sentences.' And this multiplicity is not something fixed, given once and for all; but new types of language, new language games, as we may say, come into existence, and others become obsolete and get forgotten. (We can get a *rough picture* of this from the changes in mathematics.) Here the term 'language-*game*' is meant to bring into prominence the fact that the *speaking* of language is part of an activity, or of a form of life.

(p. 11)

A language game is not to be found in a tool-box (analogically or any other way) any more than an activity in alienated society can be found in its product. It is in the contradictory unity of history/society (not in the tool-box) that the language activity and other forms of life are to be found. Meaning derives from the social activity of language-making (language games), even as it is expressed or used (taken from the tool-box) in society in ways that are meaningful. Conflating use and activity leads to strange formulations like 'language games . . . organized in a tool kit.' And much worse. It is toolmaking – the activity – not tool-using – the behavior – which is fundamental for the anti-instrumentalist Marx, Vygotsky and Wittgenstein. Tool-and-result tools are not to be found in the tool-box; language games (and history games) are not to be found in verbal behavior; revolutionary activity is not to be found in societally overdetermined institutions. The historical child uses what she or he can obtain from society. But her or his activity is not determined by what there is to use.

The unity of thought and word

What is the connection between thought and word? For Vygotsky, thinking and speech are not separate processes that at some point in development come together; rather they are, once again, a unity. And this unity {thinking/speech} is reflected in word meaning, the unity {thought/word}. The importance of identifying word meaning in this way, according to Vygotsky, is that it enables us to discover that word meaning itself develops:

The discovery that word meaning changes and develops is our new and fundamental contribution to the theory of thinking and speech. It is our major discovery, a discovery that has allowed us to overcome the postulate of constancy and unchangeableness of word meaning which has provided the foundation for previous theories of thinking and speech.

(1987, p. 245)

Vygotsky, of course, could not have foreseen the advances that would be made decades later in studies of language acquisition in general and semantic development in particular. Nowadays, only the most extreme behaviorists still believe that word meaning does not take a developmental course. Yet Vygotsky's discovery is no less a significant and up to date contribution to the theory of thinking and speech because of this. Indeed, he discovered nothing less than the tool-and-result that produces what is uniquely human: meaning-making/language-making/thinking. This is what makes possible both revolutionary activity in general (adaptation to history) and behavior (adaptation to society) – the ongoing dialectical thinking/speaking environment of human learning and development.

We organize our discussion of Vygotsky's lengthy, rambling analysis of word meaning (the topic appears in almost every chapter of *Thinking and Speech*) around three of his observations/ conceptions concerning thinking and speech: the differentiation of two planes of speech; word and object; and generalization and social interaction.

It was an unexplored axiom among Vygotsky's contemporaries that speech combines the functions of social interaction and of thinking. Using tool-and-result methodology, he asked: How? Why? What is their developmental course? While agreeing with his colleagues that speech is a means of social interaction, Vygotsky insisted that social interaction proper (communication) requires understanding and intention. He thus distinguished between the social interaction of humans, which does have these properties, and so-called social interaction among non-humans, which, he argued, does not, and is more correctly called 'contamination.' For the cry of the frightened animal, while it rouses its mate to flee, is not the communication of a thought or experience, but contamination with its fear.[5]

According to Vygotsky (following Marx), human speech emerged historically with the need to interact socially in the labor process and has evolved into the prototypical systematic means of social interaction. But, paraphrasing Kant, while the labor process may well be the 'occasion' for the emergence of human speech, it does not follow that the labor process is the 'cause' of human speech.[6] Indeed, human speech is a triadic relationship of human to human to nature – a mode of human to human activity that is itself an historically dialectical unity with the human interaction with nature that is labor (Chapter 3, note 12). Meaning-making, in unity with language-making/thinking on the one hand and with generalizing, referring and communicating on the other, is historically unified with the labor process as human activity, unlike the beaver building a dam or the bee making a hive. All of these complex and complexly unified activities spring into being at once, so to speak. Thus while labor is basic for Marx, there is no human labor without revolutionary activity (meaning-making, thinking, speaking, generalizing, denoting, communicating).

Vygotsky's historical tool-and-result analysis of word meaning led him to disagree with those psychologists who assumed that sign, word and sound are the means of social interaction. To be sure, social interaction is impossible without signs, Vygotsky saw, yet it is equally impossible without meaning. The flip side of the dialectical coin of word meaning is generalization.

> To communicate an experience or some other content of consciousness to another person, it must be related to a class or group of phenomena... Social interaction presupposes generalization and the development of verbal meaning; generalization becomes possible only with the development of social interaction.
>
> (Vygotsky, 1987, p. 48)

In the case of young children just learning language, then, it is the lack of a particular generalization or concept, not the lack of words or sounds, which sometimes makes it difficult for them to express themselves.

Word meaning, therefore, takes on added developmental significance. For not only is word meaning the unity of thinking and speech, as Vygotsky previously argued, it is also *a unity of generalization and social interaction, a unity of thinking and communication* (1987, p. 49). This unity of generalization and social interaction –

word meaning – is a tool (-and-result) in understanding the actual connection between cognitive and social development.

> The relationship of thought to word is not a thing but a process, a movement from thought to word and from word to thought... Thought is not expressed but completed in the word. We can, therefore, speak of the establishment (i.e., the unity of being and nonbeing) of thought in the word. Any thought strives to unify, to establish a relationship between one thing and another. Any thought has movement. It unfolds.
>
> (1987, p. 250)

Vygotsky believed that in order to understand the movement of thought to word in early development, one must distinguish between the external or auditory plane of speech and the inner or semantic plane of speech. Development of speech consists of movement along these planes in opposite directions. In the auditory plane, the movement is from the part to the whole, from word to sentence – the child utters first single words, then two or three words, then phrases. In the semantic plane, the movement is from sentence to word; the child begins with the whole – a whole phrase, semantically, even if a single 'word' auditorally – and moves to mastery of particular units of meaning, separate words. In their complex relationship to each other, these two planes form the unity of speech. And this unity both reflects and restructures the relationship of speech to thought:

> The structure of speech is not simply the mirror image of the structure of thought. It cannot, therefore, be placed on thought like clothes off a rack. Speech does not merely serve as the expression of developed thought. Thought is restructured as it is transformed into speech. It is not expressed but completed in the word. Therefore, precisely because of the contrasting directions of movement, the development of the internal and external aspects of speech form a true unity.
>
> (1987, p. 251)

This notion of completing (thought completed in the word) is both an extraordinary discovery in itself and a magnificent example of what Vygotsky means by unity; it is a concept of unity that is distinctly anti-metaphysical and dialectically, historically materialistic.

Of course, the two planes of speech which we are distinguishing are not distinguished for or by the child. In fact, the child must learn to separate the unity of speech into these two aspects – learning this is what becoming socialized/societized as a language user involves. Children's meaning-making is what makes their language-making possible. Vygotsky put it clearly:

> The partitioning of speech into semantics and phonology is not given at the outset. It arises in the course of development. The child must differentiate these two aspects of speech. He must become consciously aware of the different nature of each to permit the gradual descension that is presupposed in the living process of meaningful speech. In the child, we initially find a lack of conscious awareness of verbal forms and verbal meanings. The two are not differentiated.
>
> (1987, p. 253)

Vygotsky goes on to discuss a well known phenomenon of child language – that young children take the name of a thing to be one of its characteristics. Asked if you could call a cow a dog, the preschooler responds no, because cows give milk and dogs don't. Here, again, we find Vygotsky oriented toward his overall task, i.e. understanding the critical role that the relationship between thinking and speech plays in development. His analysis is deeply humanistic; it is an analysis of an active self-reflexive and dialectical process of development, not of a linear or teleological process. Rather than focusing on what the child cannot do relative to the adult, he focuses on the sensuous process of self-reflexive production of the word–object relationship. Many psychologists see only what is 'missing' in the child. Piaget based his entire enterprise on children's inability to decenter. His 1929 compilation of children's answers to questions about words and objects (material things such as the sun, moon and wind, and subjective things, such as dreams and thoughts) is highly influential in contemporary research into semantic and comparative development (Piaget, 1929).

For Vygotsky, the fusion of word and object is evidence that *'the auditory aspect of the word is an immediate unity for the child*, that it is undifferentiated and lacking in conscious awareness' (1987, p. 254). Recall that, initially, the auditory (which moves from the part to the whole) and the semantic (which moves from the whole to the part) planes of speech are unconnected and far apart. Relatively early in speech (language) development, however, they begin to move towards one another, coming closer and closer together until they merge. This is the moment we are discussing here – when word and object are fused. An important characteristic of continued speech development (and, therefore, of thinking as well) is the gradual differentiation of this unity and conscious awareness of the two planes of speech.

The culmination of Vygotsky's complex analysis of word meaning in early development is to link the child's developing differentiation and conscious awareness of the two planes of speech with the social interaction that occurs through speech. He notes that the fusion of word and object, as when the child calls a dog with horns a cow – 'With the kind of dog that is called a cow there must be little horns' (1987, p. 254) – is also the fusion of meaning and object relatedness. At this point, words function only in an indicative or nominative manner. Later in development word and word meaning become separable and separated from the object, i.e. meaning becomes independent of reference and words have many more functions than merely denoting. Vygotsky makes note of the seemingly opposing implications of the child's fusing of word and object. The child's word is more closely connected to the object than the adult's – it is, indeed, part of the object. Yet precisely for this reason, it is, while part of the object, more easily isolated from the object than the adult's word; 'it can more easily take an independent place in thought, more easily live an independent life' (1987, p. 255). In other words, the child can more easily make meaning with words than can the adult because the child, being not yet overdetermined by the societal norms, rules and uses of language, is therefore closer to the essential characteristic of language as activity – meaning-making, playing language and/or history games.

The extraordinary paradox of human development is that it is the revolutionary activity of children – their meaning-making, their 'disruption' of the societal organization of signs and symbols and sounds – that makes their adaptation to societal organization, including language-making/thinking, possible. This is precisely what we mean by the fundamentality – or leadership, in Vygotsky's sense – of revolutionary activity. Revolutionary activity is necessary for (leads) adaptation to society (non-revolutionary activity) – including the labor process. One cannot participate in the patterns of socialization/societization which are the adaptation to society, whatever shape it may take, without traveling the

'revolutionary road.' Vygotsky was describing the dialectical relationship between revolutionary activity and societal behavior as it
is organized in early childhood. He did not foresee a world – late
twentieth-century international society – in which that dialectical
relationship has been transformed so that adaptation to society
dominates adaptation to history. In such a world there are few
environments that support revolutionary activity; when it occurs
it is regarded as bizarre, problematic, anomalous. The irony is that
when society completely eliminates revolutionary activity through
deprivation or coercion, ultimately no societal adaptation is
possible.

Initially, the child does not differentiate either between word
meaning and object or between the meaning and the sound of the
word. The differentiation occurs, Vygotsky says, in accordance
with the development of generalization. When the child develops
true concepts, the complex and varied relationships between the
separate planes of speech arise. He concludes:

> This ontogenetic differentiation of the two speech planes is
> accompanied by the development of the path that thought
> follows in the transformation of the syntax of meanings into a
> syntax of words. Thought imprints a logical emphasis on one
> word in a phrase, isolating the psychological predicate. Without
> this, no phrase would be internal to the external plane. Under-
> standing presupposes movement in the reverse direction, from
> the external plane of speech to the internal.

> (1987, p. 255)

At the end of *Thinking and Speech* Vygotsky summarizes the long
and circuitous route he has taken in this investigation. As is typical,
his summary reorganizes the totality of what preceded it. Reitera-
ting the central discovery or claim that thought is not expressed
but completed in the word, Vygotsky introduces the concept of
mediation, but in a distinctly non-instrumentalist fashion. He won-
ders whether, in those instances when thought remains
uncompleted, thinking occurs. Does the person know what he
wanted to think? Yes, but only in the way someone who wants to
remember something – but fails to do so – knows. Has he begun to
think? Yes, but only as someone begins to remember. He says,

> Thought is not only mediated externally by signs. It is mediated
> internally by meanings. The crux of the matter is that the

immediate communication of consciousness is impossible not only physically but psychologically. The communication of consciousness can be accomplished only indirectly, through a mediated path. This path consists in the internal mediation of thought first by meanings and then by words. Therefore, thought is never the direct equivalent of word meanings. Meaning mediates thought in its path to verbal expression. The path from thought to word is indirect and internally mediated.

(1987, p. 282)

The developmental path that Vygotsky has analyzed above is, of course, recognizable as the developmental process of socialization/societization which we have identified as meaning-making/language-making/thinking. The difference, to the extent that there is any, lies in our insistence that the revolution, activity, be let in. Vygotsky is describing what happens in the course of the child's everyday life, where she/he experiences language (speaking, verbal behavior) in its most essential way, as activity, and is able to make use of it, to make meaning, in order to learn to use it eventually in its less essential, more alienated, more societally adapted ways – the infinite number of linguistic behaviors and uses which then become dominant. By this we, and Vygotsky, mean that children (and most adults, we might add) obviously do not experience the structure of language. Thus, children do not initially make the separation between the auditory and semantic planes of speech, nor the separation between word and object, because they do not yet know that this is something language, as a societal institution, does. What they do is grasp language activity, take the elements in their life space, including language, and reorganize them to create something other than what previously existed. This is the revolutionary activity of making meaning via revolutionary language activity.

We agree with Vygotsky that thought and object come into existence together. The internalization of the process just described is what thinking is and what makes thinking possible. The unity {meaning-making/language-making/thinking} is what makes adaptation to society (language-using) possible. Societal adaptation accelerates once children (through their revolutionary activity, language and history games) become able to think. Each instance of learning a new concept teaches far more than the particular concept. It is a means of socialization/societization to the cultural norms (including the complex set of meaning and conceptual categories that become, societally, what it means to think); it teaches that there are concepts, and it teaches that one of the things it means to be a human being is to think via concepts. As the twentieth century nears its end, adaptation to post-modern society has become so coercively encompassing and overdetermining that the everyday life experience of most human beings after the first two or three years offers precious little opportunity for the ongoing adaptation to history, meaning-making/language-making/thinking. Linguistic behavior has come to dominate meaning-making/language-making/thinking, just as adaptation to society (behavior and societization) has come to dominate adaptation to history (activity and socialization). Total domination may well be 'the end of history' and therefore, ironically, of an international society (a new world order) that advocates the termination of history.[7]

It should come as no surprise that, on our view, meaning-making and language-making in early language development differ in a critically important, qualitative way. Meaning-making, language-playing, the revolutionary activity of using the predetermining tools of language to create something other than what is predetermined, of disrupting the current organization of sound, syntax and meaning, is a critical component of the adaptation to history (socialization). Language-making, occurring as it does through meaning-making, is a critical component of the process of adaptation to society (societization). It is coming to use the predetermining tools in their less essential though more societal, more descriptive, more communicative, more generalized, predetermined ways – learning to separate word from object, learning the rules, structure and function of various linguistic forms. To repeat, it is only through making meaning (revolutionary activity) that children become able to make language and become mature language users and, thereby, to engage fully in societal behavior. Meaning-making leads language-making. It is the specific human activity that makes language-making completing thinking possible. One must participate in revolutionary activity (play language games, adapt to history) in order to be adapted to society. In the increasingly meaningless life of monadic individuals in our alienated culture, language (the societal institution) has come more and more to dominate (lead) monistic and collective meaning-making (the historical, playful, revolutionary activity of our species).

How does all of this take place? The way we have been talking (following Vygotsky, to some extent) has focused on 'the child' to the point of seeming to ignore the continuous reorganization of the environment that is the tool-and-result of the unity {meaning-making/language-making/thinking}. Yet recall that 'our' child is the individual-in-society-in-history, the historical child sometimes forgotten by Vygotsky. Joint activity, the creating of new ZPDs (language and history games), the ongoing reorganizing of the social environment in ways which make it possible to see life as history because (and as) we make it is the critical revolutionary activity of the child-in-society-in-history.

It remains for us to say more about what this ordinary, everyday, revolutionary activity – creating new ZPDs (the unity {meaning-making/language-making/thinking}) – looks like. To do so, we turn first to traditional views of language and language acquisition and their impact on how human beings speak and think, because we believe that the pervasive pragmatic perspective, including the pragmatic misuse of Vygotsky's insights concerning the development of speech and thinking (and their role in overall human development and learning), is to a large extent perpetuated by a tool for result, instrumentalist conception of language and thought. We will then contrast such 'pragmatized,' neo-Vygotskian work with the revolutionary Vygotskian approach we have been urging.

UNEQUAL PARTNERS IN DIALOGUE: ANOTHER LIBERAL REFORMIST INTERPRETATION OF VYGOTSKY

Once the 'discovery' that language is social transformed the study of language and cognitive development in the 1960s, a great deal of attention went into studying the nature of conversational and communicative exchanges children typically engage in and what kinds of things they are learning through such exchanges. What occurs through the joint activity of adults and children that makes it possible for young children to become language users?

Bateson's concept of 'deuterolearning' is extremely useful (1942). Deuterolearning refers to the fact that in learning a particular thing (how to wave bye bye, how to pilot a plane) people are also learning how to learn. Each particular act of problem-solving is a piece of simple learning, but in the activity of solving such problems people also learn how to solve problems. The conventional wisdom has it that adults create an environment which facilitates the acquisition of language by children, and that children are able to learn language remarkably easily because each instance of conversational exchange teaches them not only something particular (about sound, sense, syntax, discourse) but something more general, such as doing what an adult asks, taking turns and interpreting the intentions of others. Bruner (1985) reviews some of the research and findings in this area, including his own, and, adding a neo-Vygotskian touch, asserts that 'When the child masters a new task, he masters its means–end structure; he too now knows the goal, although at any moment he may be unclear about how to get there' (p. 31). Bruner's significant contribution to contemporary developmental psychology is the creation of a construct that is taken to have explanatory value for how the child comes to learn and learn how to learn language – how to use language. We wish, for a moment, to consider his work, for to us it is a clear and quite sophisticated instrumentalist revision of Vygotsky's non-instrumentalist conceptions, particularly the ZPD, the unity {thinking/speech}, and the activity/use distinction.

Bruner believes that Vygotsky's self-conscious goal (which he did not live long enough to achieve) was to 'delineate the transactional nature of learning, particularly since learning for him involved entry into a culture via induction by more skilled members,' and that, unlike other psychologists, Vygotsky was struck 'with how much learning is quintessentially assisted and vicarious and about social conventions and intellectual prostheses in the manner of Popper's World Three' (1985, p. 25).[8]

We are reminded here of Wertsch's insight concerning psychologists' allegiance to the primacy of the individual. For if much learning is 'assisted,' 'vicarious' and 'about . . . intellectual prostheses,' then some learning, presumably 'real' learning, must be individual and unassisted. Furthermore, Bruner views the revolutionary activity, the unity {learning-leading-development} that occurs in the ZPD, as rule-governed behavior, namely, the induction of a child into the culture by the adult. Joint activity which occurs therein he describes as a 'transaction.'

Bruner took the social-constructionist, functional view of language acquisition farther than most. To aid Chomsky's LAD (Language Acquisition Device, the mental apparatus that supposedly innately programs human beings to a universal grammar, thus making it possible for us to speak and comprehend language),

Bruner created a sister (!) he called LASS (Language Acquisition Support System):

> The development of language, then, involves two people negotiating. Language is not encountered willy-nilly by the child; it is shaped to make communicative interaction effective – fine tuned. If there is a Language Acquisition Device, the input to it is not a shower of spoken language but a highly interactive affair shaped . . . by some sort of an adult Language Acquisition Support System.
>
> (1983, p. 39)

And,

> LAD is what makes it possible for the child to master the constitutive rules of his native language without a sufficient sample of instances to support his inductive leaps. Without it we would be sunk, for there is no unique grammar that can be logically induced from any finite sample of utterances in any language. The function of LASS is to assure that the input will be a form acceptable to the recognition routines of LAD, however those recognition routines may eventually be described.
>
> (1985, p. 28)[9]

LASS is not exclusively linguistic, but is part of an overall system 'by which adults pass on the culture of which language is both instrument and creator' (1983, p. 120). According to Bruner, the culture, including language, is 'passed on' to children through a complex set (system) of rules.

This characterization of culture, and language as part of culture, as being rule-governed, is, in our opinion, an idealistic and pragmatic methodological error which explains how it is that Bruner and others can so widely (and instrumentally) miss Vygotsky's dialectical mark. For it does not follow (either logically or historically) from the fact that language can be described as governed by rules that (1) it is, in fact, governed by rules; (2) children learn it because it is (or can be described as) rule-governed; or (3) children are learning the rules (or the description of language as governed by rules) – any more than it follows from the fact that young children act as if the name of a thing is a characteristic of the thing that the name really is a characteristic! This commitment to rule-governedness as *a priori* and necessary to understanding is pervasive, even among those like Bruner who see the language acquisition process as active, as a social construction. Bruner's actors are not human beings (i.e. revolutionary activists) but two computer-modeled logical systems. And what they produce is not meaning, but matches between 'input' and 'recognition routines.'

Vygotsky's tool-and-result and Wittgenstein's language game allow us to break thoroughly with the conception of rule-governedness, not to reform or socialize it, i.e. not to come up with a better set of rules or a more active conception of rule-governedness itself. It is important, therefore, to ask: Where does this commitment come from? What are the alternatives? What does Vygotsky say about rule-governedness? In Holzman and Newman (1987) we provided some direction for answering these questions. There we argued that prevalent views of language have been overdetermined by a commitment to rule-governedness. In some instances, language is explicitly modeled after formal logical systems (e.g. Bloom, 1970; Bruner, 1975; Chomsky, 1957; 1965; Labov, 1972; Lyons, 1981; Wittgenstein, 1961 – the earlier Wittgenstein of the *Tractatus*). The idealized language, the model from which the actual language is viewed and to which it supposedly (and vitalistically) strives to conform, is consistent, coherent, rational, formal and logical. This epistemological commitment to rule-governedness, we wrote, is

> inseparable from the fact that the overdetermining variable in the relationship between language, thought and history has been language in both social history and the history of the individual. For the most part, thought has become increasingly divorced from its origins, i.e. history, and more and more modeled after language.
>
> (Holzman and Newman, 1987, p. 106)

We need think for only a moment to recall how quickly and 'naturally' research whose goal was to see if computers could 'think' like people transformed into its opposite: computer capacities have become the model for many human mental capacities. This generalization, while extreme, highlights the way the view of language as systematic has overdetermined how we think and speak (about language, thought, their relationship, and most other things). It is now commonplace to assume that there is a rule-governed relationship between how one speaks and how one thinks. Even Labov's (1972) impressive refutation of the racist claim that black children cannot think because they speak an 'illogical' language did not challenge this language-overdetermination; he merely showed one of the premises of the argument to be false by providing a wealth of evidence that black English is, indeed, as logical (i.e. rule-governed) as any language. He did not challenge the invalidity of the general position that rule-governedness is the essence of language and thinking.

In addition to rejecting rule-governedness as being conceptually necessary for understanding language, thought and their relationship constructively,[10] following Marx we argued that what actually characterizes the life space in which human beings live, speak, think and understand (the dialectical speaking/thinking environment) is *organized contradictoriness*. The overriding contradiction is that of history and society, the human life space (Holzman and Newman, 1987) – Vygotsky's ZPD. This is what has been increasingly denied in contemporary society – language is less and less capable of expressing the contradictoriness of historical/social reality; thought has become increasingly overdetermined by rational computer-modeled views of language (and, therefore, it too is less and less capable of expressing contradictoriness); and history, according to Fukuyama (1989) and others, is a thing of the past. Understanding language and thought in a way which divorces them from their social origins constrains and distorts how we think and how we speak. Rule-governedness has become how we learn, understand, think and speak; it is a means – an instrument, a tool for result – to resolve contradiction; it is, like all societally overdetermined products, alienated. In Chapter 8 we discuss further the pseudo-resolution of contradiction as a means of coercive clinical adaptation to society via the sophisticated linguistic-logical tool for result called meta-analysis.

Bruner's understanding of the self-reflexivity of the learning process – that in learning a particular thing, one is learning how to learn (being culturally inducted) – is, on our view, exceedingly conservative; it takes human beings to be instrumentally active and social, i.e. to be nothing more than exceptionally good tool (and/or rule) users. It is a misuse and/or misunderstanding of Vygotsky's tool-and-result methodology.

In discussing the significance of the ZPD, Bruner considers what he sees as the contradiction embodied in Vygotsky's claim that the only 'good' learning is in advance of development:

On the one hand the zone of proximal development has to do with achieving 'consciousness and control.' But consciousness and control come only after one has already got a function well and spontaneously mastered. So how could 'good learning' be that which is in advance of development and, as it were, bound initially to be unconscious since unmastered?

(1985, p. 24)

Bruner goes on to resolve this contradiction. He claims that what happens in the ZPD is that the adult or more competent peer serves as

a vicarious form of consciousness until such time as the learner is able to master his own action through his own consciousness and control. When the child achieves that conscious control over a new function or conceptual system, it is then that he is able to use it as a tool. Up to that point, the tutor in effect performs the critical function of 'scaffolding' the learning task to make it possible for the child, in Vygotsky's word, to internalize external knowledge and convert it into a tool for conscious control.

(pp. 24–5)

It seems to us that Bruner is talking here about tool for result-type tools and tool for result-type learning when he asserts that 'consciousness and control come only after one has already got a function well and spontaneously mastered.' In so doing, we think Bruner mistakenly attributes to Vygotsky a tool for result methodology – internalized knowledge is converted into a tool for conscious control. But Vygotsky emphasized the human capacity for toolmaking in producing consciousness and control. In fact, he speaks frequently of the production of consciousness or conscious awareness through/by/in activity, as we have tried to make clear in the discussion of spontaneous and scientific concepts in Chapter 4, as well as in this chapter's discussion of egocentric and social speech and thought (e.g. the development of autistic thinking requires the development of realistic thinking) and of word and object. Recall that 'thought is not expressed but completed in the word.' Vygotsky's 'world view' is a dialectical one. As we have said, his instrumentalism is practical-critical, not pragmatic. Through joint activity where learning leads development, the child is able to 'do things' beyond her/his development level. The seeming contradiction Bruner points to is not in need of resolution; it is in need, conceptually, of completion. Marxian practical-critical activity is what completes it: not only do human beings and the products we produce have a history, but – as Marx points out – we are in history. Indeed, we *are* history. Learning, for Vygotsky, does not causally lead or produce development. Rather it is a premiseless historical precondition for development. Thus, 'in learning something, for example, how to talk about the world, children are not just learning two things – how to talk about the world and how to learn – but they are also learning that there is such a thing that human beings do called learning how to talk about the world' (Holzman and Newman, 1987, p. 116). They are learning the essence of human activity in general and in particular. Three things, therefore, not just two, are learned when one learns something. Thus, 'good learning' is and must be learning in advance of development precisely because and as one learns that one is a learner (inseparable from being related to as a learner) through revolutionary activity – making meaning – in the ZPD.

The orthodox ways of viewing language activities and learning activities deny the revolutionary characteristics (the historicalness, the activity) of human beings – our meaning-making; what is viewed and described is not activity at all but societally overdetermined behavior. But regardless of description (scientific, pseudo-scientific or otherwise), it is by virtue of the language activities and learning activities we engage in that we are human beings. It is this feature of our species' life space that is contradictory. This 'organized contradictoriness,' as we have said, needs no resolution; it needs merely to be reorganized so as to allow for the completed expression of the self-reflexivity of human learning. In infancy and early childhood, one learns that one is a learner and the activity of learning simultaneously with learning to wave bye bye and say 'Mama,' and with learning how to learn. However, school learning, for all too many of our children, resolves the contradictoriness by eliminating learning that one is a learner and the activity of learning. Learning that you are a learner and the activity of learning – essential for learning leading development, and, therefore, for development and therefore for learning – are thus lost or not developed sufficiently to continue to learn new development.

Vygotsky's description of the process of development of the unity {thinking/speech}, coupled with his detailed analysis of the development of concepts, is a picture of what everyday revolution-

ary activities look like in early development. Human social interaction is joint activity (say, between adult and child); it is the
tool-and-result of human development. Like the researchers we
discussed in Chapter 4 who misuse Vygotsky by turning joint
activity into activity settings, Bruner also misuses Vygotsky. He
jettisons the ongoing dialectic and self-reflexive speaking/think-
ing environment; the reorganizing-transforming-disrupting of the
organization of environmental elements; the meaning-making
(created as much by the child's revolutionary activity as by the
adult's societally determined behavior, as much by the adult relating to the child as being capable of doing more than she/he can do
as by the adult doing more of the task than the child). In place of
that richness Bruner gives us a vastly impoverished – albeit systematic and orderly – 'transaction' of rule-governed behaviors
concerned with combining elements between the culturally produced mental apparatuses (the LAD and the LASS) of two unequal
partners: 'it is precisely the combining of all elements in constrained situations (speech and non-speech alike) that provides the
road to communicative effectiveness' (1983, p. 29).

As we have said, revolutionary activity is both as abundant and
as sparse as history. The difference between conceptualizing language – the social institution – as systematic, rule-governed and
rational and conceptualizing meaning-making/language-making
– the activity – as systematic, rule-governed and rational is the
difference between having much to study and few good tools-and-
results to do so and having little to study and infinite tools for
results (glue-pots) to do it. But what we must do is study – as
historical adults – the historical child. Then we will have both much
to study and much to study with. Then we will be making history
even as we study it. Says Marx: 'The philosophers [we must add,
'and the psychologists'] have only *interpreted* the world, in various
ways; the point is to *change* it' (1973, p. 123). We would argue that
the point is to *make* it. Such is the essence, as we see it, of revolutionary science in general and of revolutionary psychology in
particular.

Chapter 7

Completing the historical Vygotsky

We have been working to answer the central question: what does everyday, ordinary revolutionary activity look like? Vygotsky's investigations into the daily thinking, speaking, drawing, writing, playing and imagining activities and behaviors of early childhood – the ZPD (where and how the unity of learning- and- development takes place) – have helped us come closer to an answer. They have also helped us see and show the historical necessity of history leading society (the unity {meaning-making/learning-leading-development}) even as we recognize the contemporary societal deconstruction by which this unity (necessary for progress) is rapidly being destroyed. And in this way we have further come to know 'our' Lev Vygotsky.

In Chapter 4 we asked a closely related question: what are revolutionary psychologists to do? We argued there that the task of revolutionary psychologists was to make history – to create ZPDs (self-conscious, revolutionary activity as the 'precondition' for reinitiating the unity {meaning-making/learning-leading-development}). It remains for us to delineate further the unity of everyday revolutionary activity and the work of the psychologists, to say more sensuously what the 'search for method' by revolutionary psychologists can and should and does look like, to distinguish the historical method from the experimental method. For without this, the unity which is the analysis of human activity and the creation of a new human science remains not unfinished, for unless civilization ends it will always be so, but incomplete (in Vygotsky's radically anti-teleological sense).

IMITATION

How can we complete Vygotsky? We know that we must 'reorganize what we have, not use what is given' (we must be historical, not experimental) – but how do we do it? How do we move beyond connection to completion? How do we make revolution?

To answer these questions we return to an exploration of Vygotsky's great psychological discovery – that learning leads development in the ZPD. In Chapter 4 we cautioned against turning the ZPD into a technique for learning (even if it be group or collective learning). We stated there that the ZPD is not a technique or an experiment, but a reorganizing of environmental scenes to create new meaning and a learning that leads development; the ZPD is the seemingly contradictory process of revolutionary activity creating the conditions for revolutionary activity.

But the pull to turn the ZPD into an experimental technique is very strong, and closely tied to how one understands learning-leads-development, since the learning-leading-development activity *is* the ZPD. But what does 'lead' mean? What meaning is Vygotsky making?

In ordinary language, 'leads' (or 'leads to') most often connotes chronology, linearity, hierarchy or cause (e.g. 'One thing leads to another'; 'She led me to the house I was looking for'; 'The United States leads the world in...'). Not surprisingly, as we have seen, many Vygotskians and neo-Vygotskians understand learning-leads-development ultimately to mean that learning precedes and/or causes development. When Vygotsky says, for example, that learning is 'ahead of' or 'in advance of' development, it is easy to understand him to mean temporally or linearly ahead of or in advance of. In the totality of his work, however, in which dialectical unity (not metaphysical duality) is the central paradigm, or anti-paradigm, it is highly unlikely that 'leads' in 'learning-leads-development' is meant to express a temporal 'in advance of' or a linear 'ahead of.' No, 'leads' for Vygotsky (and for us) expresses the dialectical unity of learning-and-development, where one is not the cause but the historical 'bicondition' for the other; learning cannot exist without development and development cannot exist without learning (just as in tool-and-result methodology, the tool and the result are historical 'preconditions' for each other). Recall Vygotsky's eloquent conception of the relationship between thought and word: 'Thought is not expressed but completed in the word' (see Chapter 6). The unity relationship of learning and development is also one of completion – learning 'completes' development, while development 'completes' learning – though they do not complete each other in the same way. They could not – since learning leads development. This Vygotskian conception of completion helps us to understand better what 'leads' means. But even so, we must ask, can Vygotsky be completed – can development be reinitiated given the state of the world? Our social–psychological–political analysis of contemporary society as essentially underdevelopmental raises again and again this most critical question: given the world conditions, which do not promote the creation of ZPDs and, therefore, learning-leading (completing and being completed by)-development, is it possible to reorganize these conditions so that human beings can reinitiate the meaning-making activity necessary for (and produced by) the continuous creation of ZPDs and thereby learning-leading-development?

With the help of our more completed understanding of 'leads' and, therefore, of the ZPD and, therefore, of Vygotsky – and many years of practice – our answer is 'yes.' But how do we create ZPDs in such a deadly environment? ZPDs – Vygotsky's psychological discovery about the nature of human activity – and the environment(s) for creating ZPDs – the ZPD 'factory' – must be created simultaneously. But what could this possibly mean? Isn't the environment for creating the ZPD simply another (perhaps a meta-) ZPD? The traditional logic of linearity suggests that what we have here is a hopeless contradiction. Vygotsky's (psycho-)logic of completion tells us otherwise. For in real, historical human development (as opposed to metaphysical, representational interpretations of development) we must be and can be 'ahead of ourselves.'[1] We must do 'more than we are capable of.' We must and can do A and A's preconditions, presumably Ã, simultaneously.

The discovery that learning leads development is not a simple negation of the Piagetian causal theory that development leads learning. Rather it is a full-blown rejection of the causal-linear model of human development which systematically confuses representation with history. Learning is not 'ahead of' development.[2] Learning is not temporally related to development at all. Rather the 'two' form a unity – an active historical completeness.

ZPDs and the environment necessary for their development can be, and indeed must be, built together (as tools-and-results) because the activity of being ahead of ourselves is the very 'essence' of revolutionary, practical-critical, human practice. What is extraordinary and profoundly revolutionary in Vygotsky's work is that he begins to uncover the actual, historical dynamic of the being ahead of ourselves activity as a bicondition for human development. In Vygotsky we have no neo-Hegelian philosophical analysis of history as abstraction. Rather we have a consistent, though less than fully developed, historical analysis of human development. As we noted earlier, Vygotsky sometimes overlooked Marx's idea of revolutionary activity but he exemplified revolutionary activity in practice (his life-as-lived) and, furthermore, provided us with a practical-critical analysis of revolutionary activity by completing Marx's socio-economic account with a psychological one. The unity which is the environment-for-building-ZPDs/ZPDs, therefore, is not a 'logical impossibility' but is the continuous performance of tool-and-result toolmaking. It is the self-conscious performance of making history by whatever means possible and/or necessary.

Let us then carefully re-examine Vygotsky's analysis of the being ahead of ourselves activity as we complete 'our Vygotsky,' the historical Vygotsky. In Vygotsky's time and place, history moved 'way ahead' and a desperately backward society (Russia in transition) could not and did not keep up. Vygotskian psychology did not prevail in Stalin's USSR (by and large conservative psychologies did) and a more and more conservative society held history back. In our historical moment we must be ahead of ourselves as history comes to a virtual standstill. Vygotsky's psychology is more desperately needed than ever. Which is where imitation and performance come in.

We learned from Vygotsky's analyses of the development of thinking, speaking and playing in early childhood that these psychological processes (indeed, all of learning and development) are ontologically social. It is helpful to repeat two important formulations by Vygotsky, the first a question, the second a statement. 'What new forms of activity were responsible for establishing labor as the fundamental means of relating humans to nature and what are the psychological consequences of these forms of activity?' (1978, p. 19); and 'Every function in the child's cultural development appears twice: first on the social level and later, on the individual level; first *between* people (*interpsychological*), and then *inside* the child (*intrapsychological*)' (1978, p. 57).

In Chapter 3, we noted that Vygotsky's experiments, observations and analyses shed light on the development (if not the history) of the ongoing production of the fundamental means of relating humans to humans to nature. Vygotsky identifies instruction as, if not the most important, then one of the most important means of relating humans to humans to nature. Instruction is the means by which the child is organized to act (perform, we would say) 'ahead' of her/himself – the historical child leads the eternal child.

> When we observe the child's development and instruction in school, it becomes apparent that each subject demands more than the child is capable of, leading the child to carry out activities that force him to rise above himself. This is always the case with healthy school instruction. The child begins to learn to write when he does not yet have the mental functions that are required for written speech. It is for precisely this reason that instruction in written speech calls these functions to life and leads their development.
>
> (1987, p. 213)

Vygotsky does little by way of describing what instructional or collaborative interactions look like; he pays little attention to what the adult is doing that contributes to the child engaging in activities that are developmental (ahead of her/himself). Indeed, in this passage as well as others, Vygotsky sometimes appears to be attributing the 'leading' characteristic to the subject matter. Nevertheless, his understanding of imitation as an active and interactive process that has such a significant impact on development is suggestive, to us, of his sensitivity to the joint activity that occurs in/creates the ZPD. Recall that Vygotsky distinguished between the imitations of the parrot and the child; children do not imitate anything and everything but only what is in the ZPD. He put great stock in the power of imitation for learning-leading-development, arguing that imitation is 'the source of instruction's influence on development' and 'instruction is possible only where there is a potential for imitation' (1987, pp. 211–12).

Why is this so? Why is imitation so important? What happens when the child (or the adult, for that matter) imitates in the ZPD what someone else does or says immediately, or hours or days later? We gave a partial answer earlier, when we argued that imitation in the ZPD, far from being rote behavior, is the revolutionary activity of making meaning (Chapter 4). To Vygotsky imitation is what makes it possible for the child's capacities to develop by virtue of doing what she/he cannot yet do. In early childhood, then, the predominant joint revolutionary activity that occurs in the ZPD is imitation. It is fundamental to the unity {meaning-making/learning-leading-development} because and as the child does what she/he is not yet capable of doing. Yet as we stated earlier, learning leads development because and as one learns that one is a learner; learning that you are a learner is inseparable from being related to as (performing as) a learner (Chapter 6). In the imitative activity/interaction itself (language games), the child learns that she/he is a learner and speaker – inseparable from being related to as a learner and speaker. Imitation is an extremely complex activity, in spite of the ways it has traditionally been viewed as non-transformational behavior of the behaviorist or cognitive variety.[3] In imitating (in the ZPD) – saying what someone else says or picking up a pencil and 'writing' the way a skilled writer does – the child is performing as/being related to as/relating to herself as/learning that she is a learner and a speaker of words and phrases or a writer. The child (or adult) is learning that she/he is a revolutionary.

Imitation, then, is a critically important developmental activity because it is the chief means by which in early childhood human beings are related to as other than and in advance of who they are.[4] Mothers, fathers and other adults relate to infants and babies as capable of far more than they could possibly do – they relate to them as speakers, feelers and thinkers. In the case of language that is imitated, for example, adults relate to young children not as parrots, but as speakers, as the following interaction between a 21-month-old boy and an adult illustrates:

Child: (opening cover of tape recorder) open/open/open
Adult: Did you open it?
Child: (watching tape recorder) open it
Adult: Did you open the tape recorder?
Child: (watching tape recorder) tape recorder
                    (Bloom, Hood and Lightbown, 1974, p. 380)

Relating to infants as communicative human beings is how they get to be so. We suggest, then, that a critical feature of the fundamental means of relating humans to humans to nature (revolutionary activity) is that one is related to as other than and in advance of one's development – as a revolutionary activist, i.e. someone capable of revolutionary activity. This is the chief sociological characteristic of Vygotsky's psychological discovery that learning leads development in the ZPD.

Imitation is developmental because and if it is organized in such a way that something new is created out of saying or doing 'the same thing.' Imitation in the ZPD is revolutionary activity because it is organized such that the 'product' is not a product of imitation at all – which would be, after all, nothing qualitatively new, being merely 'an imitation' – but something which is other than (beyond) imitation, not unlike the labor activity under capitalism which produces more than the inputs. (As such, the organized exploitation of labor is capitalism's most creative discovery.) If this were not the case – if imitation were not, under the specific circumstances of infancy and early childhood, revolutionary activity – then there would be no answer to how it is that we ever stop imitating and/or start developing. The 'something new' that is created is the process and product (tool-and-result) of (a) meaning-making, (b) learning that leads development, and (c) revolutionary activity.

Yet imitation is not always revolutionary activity. In the absence of ZPDs, i.e. within traditional institutions, imitation is mere societal behavior – mimicking or repeating that does not create something other than what is determined by the predetermining tools (the sounds, words or actions being imitated). Until a certain age or perceived developmental stage, exchanges like the one above seem perfectly acceptable to most adults; they are not related to as mere mimicking or as meaningless, but as communicative exchanges not only in a dialogue but in the building of an actual social relationship with a child. In modern post-industrial society, however, there comes a point when children's imitations cease to be understood and related to as creative and communicative; it is no longer acceptable to repeat what someone else says or does. Once children begin school, and for many long before then, they are taught or behavior modified to 'do it yourself,' 'make your own' and 'stop copying.' Imitation no longer is, nor is it understood as, creative or a way to 'express oneself.' Ironically, the majority of traditional school tasks are in fact imitative (copying from the board, repetition). Yet imitation is more and more pejoratively identified as cheating. This is but one expression of the destructively contradictory nature of the contemporary organization of schooling, a place (most frequently a self-perpetuating institution, surely not a ZPD) where the activity/use dialectic of human development is instrumentally and pragmatically misorganised.

Imitation in the ZPD – mimicking or repeating that does create something new and that is ahead of oneself (or oneselves) – both demands and makes possible the building of the environment (precondition) for creating ZPDs and of the ZPDs simultaneously; it is this activity of creating A and A's preconditions ($\bar{A}$) that makes the reigniting of development in a reactionary historical moment possible. At such a moment *we must imitate revolutionary activity itself*. Scientifically speaking, imitated revolutionary activity (it is hard to imagine that any other kind is possible at this time, at least in capitalism's core) is the historically precise tool-and-result which builds the ZPD 'factory' and the ZPDs simultaneously.

It is this activity – imitating revolutionary activity, in all its complex variations – which we identify as performing. We take great pains in our own psychological, cultural and political work, which we will discuss shortly, to distinguish performing from its dialectical opposite, acting. Acting, dramaturgically speaking as well as within the roles of traditional society, is fundamentally representational – it is copying, mimicking, repeating without being ahead of oneself. It is not revolutionary activity; it is a conservatizing activity. Performing (in 'our' school, theater, therapy sessions, production factories, electoral campaigns) is the varied and creative imitation of revolutionary activity, i.e. making history, making meaning, to reinitiate a learning (cognitive, emotional, cultural) that leads development. To speak, to write, to create, to work, to play, the historical child and adult must, through imitation in a socially collectivized environment (a ZPD), do something that goes beyond herself, himself, themselves, ourselves. We can do so because our species alone can both imitate and engage in revolutionary activity. At a time when speaking, writing, creating, working, playing – human activity itself – are being systematically negated, it is revolutionary activity which must be imitated – performed – if psychology and human life, which it must properly account for, are to continue developmentally. How children and adults actually learn and develop is, of course, inseparable from how psychologists (both revolutionary and non-revolutionary) explain/understand/change how children and adults learn and develop.

One such historical child and adult was Lev Vygotsky himself. How did Vygotsky, the revolutionary psychologist, learn and develop? How does our deepened analytical understanding of Vygotsky's work help us to grasp more clearly this man's life-as-lived? Conversely, can our picture of Vygotsky teach us about the relationship between revolutionary psychology and the human life process? What of the women and men living in post-modern international society who read this book – what of your lives-as-lived? What of our – Holzman's and Newman's – lives-as-lived? What are our radically varied practices? Is it impossible or improper or indiscreet to engage such questions? Are they too personal? Are they too political? Can we take seriously what we have said so far if we do not try?

VYGOTSKY'S PRACTICE: HIS LIFE-AS-LIVED

Practice belongs to the deepest roots of scientific operation and restructures it from beginning to end. It is practice that poses the tasks and is the supreme judge of theory; practice is the criterion of truth; it is practice which dictates how to build concepts and how to formulate laws.

(Vygotsky, 1982, pp. 388–9)

Vygotsky's scientific, psychological, methodological practice was of enormous depth, as we have tried to show in Chapters 3 to 6. Yet his life-as-lived (briefly considered at the beginning of this book) is even more remarkable when we realize the tremendous breadth of interest and work which accompanied his analytical depth. We have focused on learning and development and thinking and speech, areas of scientific investigation in which Vygotsky's influence has been most strongly felt and on which his life's work of building a truly human psychology was centered. It remains for us, however, to deepen our portrait of Vygotsky-in-use (as-lived) by considering the breadth of his interests and influence.

Lev Vygotsky had a social vision; certainly, the revolutionary epoch in which he lived both clarified and at times clouded it, but this vision – of a new human being – was integral to his entire life. From all reports, he lived as a revolutionary. For us, as for Vygotsky, to be a revolutionary is to be a Marxist scientist/organizer, not an idealist romantic. Clearly, we want to avoid the trap some Vygotskians have been accused of falling into, that of creating and/or contributing to a cult of personality around Vygotsky.[5] For, in our opinion, Vygotsky's self-conscious life practice was revolutionary activity (not cult-making), the dialectical unity {meaning-making/learning-leading-development}. We choose not to 'locate' Vygotsky in his social context (in Cole and his colleagues' phrase, his ecological niche), for he is inseparable from his historical notch, his practical-critical activity. 'Our Vygotsky' is neither a cult figure nor an alienated product of his times; ultimately, he was not a reformer. Rather, he was a self-conscious organizer of socio-historical conditions (a revolutionary scientist): Lev Vygotsky made history.

While Vygotsky wrote volumes, as Blanck (1990) notes, an autobiography was not, as far as anybody knows, among them. Unfortunately, none of his contemporaries wrote about his life either and 'a war that destroyed half a continent buried many of his life's documents. He seemed condemned to have no biography; his history, therefore, must be reconstructed from fragments that form pieces of a puzzle' (Blanck, 1990, p. 31). The biographies of Vygotsky that we have are based on facts and anecdotes gathered from people who knew him personally, e.g. his sisters; his daughter; his childhood friend, Semyon Dobkin; his student and colleague, Alexander Luria; and many of his followers in the fields of psychology and pedagogy, and those who knew his work or that of his collaborators. In the last decade, several biographies and biographical sketches (e.g. Blanck, 1990; Kozulin, 1986b; 1990; Levitan, l982; Luria, 1979; Rosa and Montero, 1990; Van der Veer and Valsiner, 1991; Yaroshevsky, 1989) have been published using these sources as a foundation; with each new sketch more information is added. What is emerging is indeed a fascinating life. Perhaps because Vygotsky's life and writings capture so vividly the social motion of such a tumultuous historical period, in recent years – which have seen the endless reappraisal of those earlier times – this new information has raised questions and speculation. Hypotheses and explanations are put forth concerning his genius, charisma, magnetism, commitment to human progress and socialism, his consistency (or inconsistency), his Marxism (or abandonment of Marxism), his kowtowing to Stalin (or firm stand against Stalinist dogma), his universal relevance (or Eurocentrism), his Jewishness, his Russian-ness.

Vygotsky's parents are reported to have created not only a close-knit family with/for their eight children, but to have made their home a center of culture in Gomel, the small town in Byelorussia where the Vygodsky family[6] settled one year after Lev's birth. Gomel was within the Pale – the territory in which Jews were restricted to live under the czar. The repression and anti-Semitism of pre-revolutionary Russia were vulgarly manifest, as were the growing civil unrest and agitation for revolution. Biographical information suggests that 'Vygotsky's ZPD' during his childhood and youth included people, relationships and activities centered on Jewish culture, human rights and opposition to the czar. For example, Kozulin reports that in 1903, after a full-scale pogrom, the Jewish residents of Gomel fought back and eventually defeated their attackers. At the trials that followed, Vygotsky's father is reported to have said in his testimony: 'As long as Jews did not talk about this, all was good, but when they started to consider themselves as people like others and talk about their human dignity, the attitude toward them has changed' (Kozulin, 1990, p. 14). The persecution of Jews in pre-revolutionary Russia nearly kept Vygotsky from entering Moscow University, in spite of his excellent grades, and from pursuing studies in areas he loved, such as history and philology, that would have led to a teaching career (Jews were barred from government positions). Vygotsky's primary education was conducted in his home by Solomon Ashpiz, a private tutor who had been exiled to Siberia for his revolutionary activism, and the last two years of his secondary education were in a Jewish private school (Blanck, 1990, p. 32).

In 1914, when he went to Moscow to study medicine (at his parents' urging, because it was a profession which held some promise of security), Vygotsky quickly changed to law and simultaneously studied at Moscow University and Shaniavsky People's University. The latter was an unofficial, 'alternative' institution created in 1906 after students who had participated in an anti-czarist revolt were expelled from Moscow University. In protest, nearly a hundred leading scholars left and established a 'People's university' (Blanck, 1990). In 1917, the year of the October Revolution, Vygotsky graduated from both universities and returned to Gomel. There he was now able to teach, anti-Semitic legislation having been abolished by the Revolution. For the next seven years he remained in his home town, teaching those subjects in which he had become expert – literature, Russian, logic, psychology, aesthetics, art history and theater – at adult schools, technical schools and institutes specializing in the education of teachers and workers. He was the key organizer of the intellectual-cultural life of the new society in this small town, one of thousands where – if only for an all too brief period of time – a radically humanistic reorganization of every aspect of life was taking place.

Vygotsky's intelligence was noticed early in his life and no doubt was nurtured by his family (Blanck, 1990). From his mother he learned to speak German and to love poetry; each of his professors at school tried to steer him in the direction of their own discipline because he showed such a gift for it; his friends related to him as their intellectual leader and teacher, calling him, at age 15, 'little professor' because he organized stimulating intellectual discussions. What seems to us significant about Vygotsky, however, is not his intellect (although we do not dispute those who say he was a genius), but his intense socialness as expressed in his work as an organizer.

What comes across from anecdotes and facts about his accomplishments and personality is the consistency with which, throughout his short life, he organized the elements of his environment – what existed: the people; social institutions; cultural, political, intellectual traditions; his own development and capacities – in creative and not obvious ways so as always to be advancing learning and development. Here is a man who, while an adolescent, staged Gogol's *The Marriage*, published literary critiques, wrote an essay on *Hamlet* which became the basis for his dissertation, led a Jewish study circle (where it is said he first became interested in Hegel and then Marx); who could read and speak eight languages, including Esperanto; who during his twenties founded several literary magazines, authored a theater column, lectured on history, literature, theater and science, read widely in philosophy, linguistics, history and psychology, and corresponded with some of the leading European thinkers while teaching in Gomel; who, after becoming a renowned psychologist in Moscow, returned to medical school as a first-year student, co-directed an art seminar, consulted frequently with film director Eisenstein, held numerous political and scientific posts, and conducted practical educational intervention with handicapped and retarded children. But Vygotsky was no dilettante. Far from flitting from one subject or discipline to another, he added, advanced and built on everything at his disposal. The intensity and excitement of the revolutionary socialist task – building a new society – for those, like Vygotsky, who were willing to go all the way with it, meant building a new culture, new ways of relating, of learning and working and playing, of thinking and feeling, by reorganizing the totality of material conditions.

This revolutionary activity was carried out under tremendously difficult conditions. First, there was the extreme hardship of the post-revolutionary period – famine, the lack of other essentials, such as water and heat, and, of course, invasions by foreign armies and the Civil War. Vygotsky's family, like almost everyone, suffered the effects. In 1918 his brother contracted tuberculosis, and in 1920, when he was 24, Vygotsky himself had the first of several serious attacks of the disease, which periodically confined him to a hospital for up to a year at a time and ultimately killed him. In addition to this kind of hardship, the calcification and distortion of Marxian practice and the abandonment of real (revolutionary) socialism (which began almost immediately with the birth of the first socialist state, if not sooner) was another hardship with which Vygotsky and other revolutionary practitioners had to contend.

As one pieces together the different periods of Vygotsky's short life, what emerges is a continuous deepening and widening of experiences, people, traditions and ideas stemming from this struggle and from his understanding of and commitment to Marx's methodology – radical monism and historical dialectical materialism – and creating a psychology in the service of a new society. His inclusion of Western (bourgeois) thinkers, such as Freud, Piaget, James, Durkheim, Stern, and others whose names have been forgotten, has been seen by some as suggesting that Vygotsky wavered from Marxism and the reason that his work was suppressed under Stalin (Joravsky, 1989, pp. 263–4). We view it differently: as his 'search for method,' as his practice of Marxism – the reorganization of totalities (what there is). Inevitably influenced by the centuries-old dualistic tradition he inherited, Vygotsky nevertheless kept his self-conscious goal of a unified, general psychology at the forefront (Levitan, 1982; Rosa and Montero, 1990).

Vygotsky clearly was the leader/organizer of the many collectives of committed, creative people with whom he worked in Gomel, Moscow, Karkhov and other cities. He created new zones of proximal development; he organized environments where individuals with different levels of development and expertise in a wide variety of subjects were able to work together to take what existed and create something new. Blanck suggests that the root of

Vygotsky's discovery of the zone of proximal development was his tutor Solomon Ashpiz's unique teaching technique, which was based on the Socratic dialogues (1990, p. 32). It is more likely that the root of the ZPD (which we do not take to be a dyadic teacher–student relationship) was Vygotsky's life-long practice of creating and organizing ZPDs. The conceptualization of the ZPD as how/where real learning (learning that leads development) takes place was perhaps a tool-and-result of Vygotsky's revolutionary activity. His capacity to inspire others seems to have stemmed from his activity of organizing environments in which they could participate in the collective learning and development necessary to create a psychology for and of the new human being. Vygotsky provided the leadership to what has been described as very exciting research and educational environments, such as the initial 'troika' of Vygotsky, Luria and Leont'ev, later joined by the 'pyatorka' (group of five), students who carried out experiments based on the ideas the troika came up with in their discussions (Luria, 1979). These students later became prominent in Soviet psychology (Cole, 1979, p. 206).

Vygotsky's enduring significance is often attributed in part to his having been an innovator in so many fields of inquiry and practice, someone with many diverse interests. But it is the fields that are diverse; human existence is seamless. The compartmentalization of human existence creates the illusion that someone who lives and investigates its totality has a diversity of interests. Vygotsky's revolt against dualism is apparent not only in specific analyses of particular psychological phenomena (such as those we have so far discussed), but also in what others identify as the breadth of his interests and influence. He did not abandon any of his interests when he entered a 'new' field, but rather allowed the new to reorganize the totality of his existing knowledge and activity. Thus, his interest in and pursuit of ways that retarded and otherwise handicapped people could be helped to develop, how dialectical historical materialism could be portrayed visually in film, why certain theatrical works move people emotionally across cultures and social organization, the roots of artistic creativity and abstract thinking in children's scribbles, the methodology of psychoanalysis, and the nature of psychopathology, including schizophrenia, were not diversions from his main revolutionary task of creating a Marxist psychology, but tools in his search for method.

Vygotsky's famous speech of 1924,[7] when he burst onto the psychological scene with a provocative analysis of the crisis in psychology, is significant for its compelling argument on behalf of a unified psychology and its insistence that issues of methodology are not peripheral to psychology, but an integral part of developing a general, unified psychology (Blanck, 1990; Kozulin, 1986b; 1990; Levitan, 1982). To Vygotsky, psychology was not limited to what comprises it as a discipline; the totality of how people live their lives – and this includes their creative, emotional and artistic development (and underdevelopment) – needed to be reorganized and investigated if there was to be a new human being and a new human science.

COMPLETING VYGOTSKY

How do we use (not instrumentally, of course, but as tool-and-result), how do we historically connect with or complete, Vygotsky – his life-as-lived, his writings, methodological discoveries and psychological insights, his revolutionary activity? What method do we as revolutionary psychologists practice to produce the unity {meaning-making/learning-leading-development} in the ZPD? How can we – as students, educators, researchers and clinicians – lead others in the continuous creation of ZPDs?

These questions, if they are taken seriously, cannot be separated from questions about our own environment – the general historical moment in which we all live and the particular environment in which the authors live. 'What is your environment – your ZPD?' readers will no doubt ask. 'It's clear that the historical moment in which Vygotsky was practicing and writing was "officially" revolutionary. But the time and place in which you are working and your book is being written are, I suspect, very far indeed from revolutionary. Where did these ideas come from? What is your ZPD?' We would be less than radically self-reflexive if we did not try to answer these important methodological questions in general and in particular.

Despite the social-political-economic-cultural differences in historical periods, there are parallels and connections between Vygotsky's life-as-lived and ours. Just as Vygotsky created the environment in which he made his discoveries – inseparable from making the discoveries – so too our analysis and discoveries could not have been made without creating the particular environment which made their discovery possible. We could not be writing this book without having built, with many others, the specific environment which makes it possible to write it. Our book is a work-in-progress report from a functioning ZPD.

Like Vygotsky, we too have a social vision of a new society and a new human being, and the distinctly non-revolutionary epoch in which we all currently live at times clarifies it, at times clouds it, as his epoch did for him. Unlike his challenge – staying grounded in the history/society dialectic (the human life space, the historical notch) while revolutionary history dominated moribund and dysfunctional European society (revolutionary activity whirled at such speed and with such intensity in the first thirty years of the twentieth century in Russia that the critical dialectic history/society could be, and frequently was, forgotten, with tragic results) – our challenge has been to stay grounded in that dialectic while society thoroughly dominates history (as we have noted, history has been declared over and done with) and represses revolutionary activity. The challenge has been to reshape the history/society dialectic so as to see and show and make history at a time when history does not seem makeable, to organize the social-historical conditions – increasingly (quantitatively and qualitatively) destructive of humanity (existentially and essentially) – into something usable for continued human growth, learning and development.

There are serious impediments and obstacles. The near century since Vygotsky was born has seen the production of the most sophisticated and powerful tools (for result) of ideological coercion and control the world has ever known – pop psychology, pop culture and mass media.[8] Psychology and psychologized culture – the form currently taken by the secular world view that emerged long before Vygotsky's time – have come virtually to replace religion (even religion has been psychologized these days) as the dominant guide to everyday subjective or 'moral' life. During capitalism's heyday (a prolonged period of extraordinary economic expansion) psychology was to some extent able to function as the servant of political-social liberalism. Now, in a time of profound and, in our opinion, irreversible capitalist crisis and decay, psychology is more and more a tool for an international ruling class rapidly moving towards (neo-)reaction.[9] The privilege of economic wealth enjoyed by the United States and other core capitalist societies in the earlier years of this century (generally, a time of capitalist growth) created the environment not only for the development of so-called traditional psychology but also for liberal challenges to it in the form of movements for social reforms and cultural and social experimentation, including, for example, 'the psychological and cultural revolution' of the 1960s. But in the last quarter of a century, as wealth turned to debt, liberalism waned and psychology – ever the instrumentalist tool – exposed more and more its essentially pragmatic character. A psychology that valorizes the individual (as an egocentric tool user par excellence, a commodity, a societal behavior but not an historical activity) and that contains within it the means for rationalizing the destruction of human progress (obliterating the unity {meaning-making/learning-leading-development}) is the historically lawful accompaniment to a 'free market' economy. Bulhan (1985) addresses the issue well in his important book *Frantz Fanon and the Psychology of Oppression*:

> From the fourteenth century to the present, Europe and its descendants have been embarked on an unprecedented mission of violence and self-aggrandizement throughout the world. Meanwhile, an intellectual debate on the human condition had been raging in academic circles. A discipline called 'psychology' emerged by the sixteenth century, when Philipp Melanchthon, a friend of Luther, coined the term, even though the roots of this new discipline reach back to ancient civilizations. In time, the new discipline flourished and proliferated in various aspects of society. It developed its own concepts, won numerous adherents, evolved its own tradition, won a measure of respectability, and defined a jealously guarded turf. As Europe conquered much of the world, the European imposing as the only honorable model of humanity, the discipline of psychology too emerged as a powerful specialty and a scientific arbiter of human experience.
>
> The discipline of psychology did not of course emerge in a social vacuum unrelated to Europe's history of conquest and violence. From its beginning to the present, the discipline has been enmeshed in that history of conquest and violence. This fact is all too often unappreciated and conveniently avoided. Yet for a discipline known for its commitment to unmask the repressed and for its profusion of studies, such neglect and

avoidance of human history and the role of psychologists in that history are curious indeed.

(p. 37)

Euro-American psychology molds (by a sickening mixture of coercion and rationalization) the subjectivity necessary for adaptation to alienation and commodification. It also functions in its liberal guise as the pseudo-scientific underpinning for the 'granting' of bourgeois individual rights.[10] It fosters a societal myth of democracy, which effectively covers over the deepest contradictions of capitalism – the historical process – by portraying the fundamental contradictions of life in history/life in capitalist society as mere societal dilemmas or problems. For in late capitalist society lingering liberal values may still allow individuals the 'freedom' to choose, but never the freedom to determine what the choices are, how they are determined, and by whom. We (or an elected representative, so-called) can choose to take drugs or not, to buy a cassette player or a CD player, to run or vote Democratic, Republican, Labour, Conservative or Liberal-Democrat, but we are by and large prohibited from exercising the freedom to determine (produce) whether these are the choices we want to make or the things about which we want to have the freedom to choose. We cannot choose (within the deadly constraints of the psychological-/ideological paradigm of late capitalism) to alter the totality of a socio-historical system. Thomas Jefferson's disingenuous eighteenth-century polemic in support of periodic revolution has transformed into grade B Reagan–Bush (Thatcher–Major) moralisms here at the end of the twentieth century.

In a period of economic development and growth, capitalism sustained itself and withstood challenges such as dissatisfaction among its more privileged middle-class white members, who wanted to see a better, more equitable world (it allowed them to speak out for an end to war, for civil rights, for sexual liberation), and frustration among its least privileged and most oppressed members, who demanded justice and equality. But as Rosa Luxemburg made clear in her brilliant analysis of the dynamics of the accumulation of capital,[11] when the limits of capitalism's progress are reached, as they have been during the past twenty-five years or so, the living contradictions become more difficult to cover over. The economic crisis of contemporary capital has placed severe limits even on societal development, to the point of limiting not only activity but also behavior (e.g. individual choice in such things as employment, education and life style). However, the limited 'freedom' people experienced as individuals during the recently ended period of capitalist development makes it possible in this period of zero growth destabilization and reactionary political transformation to experience sensuously (if not yet to 'see' or understand cognitively) the utter hypocrisy and contradiction of our historical life space.

At such a moment as this, individual rights and privileges themselves become a threat to the status quo. In their total unrealizability they no longer serve to adapt people to alienation, much as alienation no longer serves so well to adapt people to exploitation. Valorization of the individual, still traditional psychology's primary and arguably most pragmatic adaptational task and tool, must then transform into a justification for curtailing even bourgeois individual rights, if it is to continue to serve its masters. Late twentieth-century pragmatism – a synthesis of bastardized existentialism, 'what is, is' (popularized into a billion dollar profit-making rationalization for oppression, injustice and deprivation by the likes of EST impressario Werner Erhard, Jimmy Swaggart and other pop psychology spinoffs and religio-psychological TV 'ministers'), and the most vulgar pragmatism, 'what works,' dominates – the banal dictum of post-modern human understanding has become 'what works is what is and what is is what works.' George Bush's New World Order is the CIA's choice of Voltaire's and Leibniz's best of all possible (post-modern) worlds. Liberal psychology's façade of humanity crumbles as human beings are forced to adapt to conditions which increasingly and more and more obviously are against not only their own interests but those of the human species as a whole. Violence, homelessness, unemployment, drugs, starvation, destruction of the environment and racial injustice are clearly non-developmental and anti-progress. Yet without new tools for changing/understanding the growing unviability of adaptation to society while ignoring adaptation to history, people become 'sicker' – the effect of living solely in a sick society.[12]

Still another characteristic of the unique environment that is late twentieth-century US society and the New World Order of which it is the heartless heart is the lack of a working class, and thereby class-consciousness – yet another manifestation of how society totally dominates history in these times. The popular front social reforms of the 1930s in the United States produced, ultimately, the destruction of working-class institutions: unions, newspapers, schools, cultural groupings (such as theater) and political parties. With the destruction of its organized activities, the working class was destroyed. For, following Marxian and Vygotskian methodology, we take the working class itself to be an activity, not a socio-economic category. Marx and Engels make the point this way:

> As individuals express their life, so they are. What they are, therefore, coincides with their production, both with what they produce and with how they produce. The nature of individuals thus depends on the material conditions determining their production.
>
> (Marx and Engels, 1973, p. 42)

And:

> The ideas of the ruling class are in every epoch the ruling ideas, i.e., the class which is the ruling material force of society, is at the same time its ruling intellectual [and emotional] force. The class which has the means of material production at its disposal, has control at the same time over the means of mental production, so that thereby, generally speaking, the ideas of those who lack the means of mental production are subject to it.
>
> (p. 64)

If people's production (the what and the how) is determined more and more by the ruling-class, then what is produced will be an expression of ruling class interests and beliefs. As those beliefs become more and more neo-fascistic, what, if anything, can be done? Revolution is the answer. But the question remains – how can that be done?

In a word, we share (it should be clear by now) a politic with Vygotsky. We share a class analytic, dialectical historical materialist political-methodological analysis. In a name, we share Marx and Marxism with Vygotsky. Yet so do many others. What makes it possible for us to complete (obviously not to finish) Vygotsky's work in reactionary times such as these is a shared understanding of what politics in general and Marxism in particular are. For Vygotsky and for us, Marxism worthy of the name is a theory and practice of revolution. It is neither an abstract analysis of capital ('a stringing together of quotations') nor a programmatic politic of a dogmatic sectarian party and/or state bureaucracy. It is an everyday practical guide (for ordinary people) to transforming the world progressively, to making history. It is about building alternatives, not only *in* the society but *to* the society. It is not primarily about society; it is about our relationship to history. It is not reducible to a centralized planned economy. Indeed, it is not reducible to anything, economic or otherwise. It is practical, i.e. practical-critical, i.e. revolutionary.

We need not in any way deny Marxist materialism to affirm Marxist dialecticalism. The relationship between superstructure and base (endlessly discussed directly and indirectly in orthodox Marxist literature) is not reductionistic but one of dialectical unity. As the composition of post-industrial capital and capitalist labor transforms, 'popular' psychology and culture (the contemporary form of ideology) become more and more the method of capitalist control and, thereby, the point of revolutionary production. To create a new historical-human psychology is not an interesting application of Marxism; it is a completion, a continuation, of revolutionary Marxism. And to create a new psychology and/or a new culture one must continuously build the ever changing environments – the ZPDs – within the societal mainstream so that history and revolution can be made.

The environments that produced the conditions (the what and the how of the production of our practice) include the traditional and orthodox progressive 'community.' For the most part, progressive activists and academics – lacking the Marxian-Vygotskian practical-critical revolutionary tool-and-result methodology – have been, like their revisionist Stalinist (and anti-Stalinist) counterparts in the former Soviet Union and elsewhere, overdetermined by the determining totality rather than leaders in the fight for freedom (i.e. revolutionary activists changing social totalities). For example, no small part of the failure of the US left to sustain a movement and an organization that can impact on the body politic, that can change the lives of oppressed and working people, is that its own understanding of psychology is as Freudian as the psychology of any Park Avenue psychoanalyst, as instrumentalist as the psychology of Henry Ford, and as anti-Marxian as the psychology of the FBI's notorious J. Edgar Hoover. It has focused largely on tactics for mentalistic change – consciousness raising and educational campaigns – rather than on organizing environments and/or institutions for the creation of a progressive, working-class politic (psychology and culture).[13]

That focus is, as we see it, a manifestation of the left's bourgeois psychology, one in which learning no longer leads development; instead, abstract programmatic learning (what happens in society, including opposition to society – the class-against-capital) *replaces* development (history). Progressives in the United States, and to a lesser extent worldwide, have historically left issues such as sexuality, the family, depression, violence and abuse alone, substituting vulgar economic analysis and/or explanation (deadly language) for life itself. But as Reich (1970) made plain, the failure to engage directly fundamental issues of everyday life leaves people (of all classes) open in moments of socio-economic crisis to being organized by fascism.[14] In the absence of the revolutionary activity of building the tools (of the tool- and die- maker variety) to create a new psychology that leads a revolutionary politic, the pseudo-progressive politics of the revisionist US and international left have been transformed by pragmaticized psychology into a sometimes left-slanted, not-so-radical bourgeois psychology (F. Newman, 1991a). Such a liberal radical tool for result is no match for pragmatism-turned-Terminator.

Yet even as 'the Movement' failed to bring about socialist revolution, liberation or racial justice, the 1960s had a tremendous impact on US culture. For the first time since the 1930s, people began to 'talk radical politics' and reclaim their social histories. Many ideas were thrown up, some by way of resurrecting Marx, Lenin and Mao; others were newly created by the Black Panthers, Malcolm X and other African-American revolutionaries, and by feminists and gay activists, European and American Marxist intellectuals, and African, Asian and Latin American revolutionaries. Equally important, there were new opportunities for people who ordinarily would not come in contact with or be touched by such ideas to be influenced by them.

We, in fact, are two such people. One of us (Newman), having grown up in a poor, inner-city working-class Jewish family and gone to work as a machinist, was among the millions to whom higher education was opened up after the Korean War through the GI Bill, which allowed veterans access to free schooling. Winding up in the mid-1960s a young philosophy professor, Newman was radicalized, as were so many others – outraged by racial injustice and the Vietnam War, he anarchistically gave all As to students to keep them from being drafted and was fired from one university after another. The other of us (Holzman) benefited both from the improved standard of living and suburbanization of America following World War II, as her working-class Jewish family entered the middle class (and became assimilated), and from the impact on American society of the feminist, civil rights and anti-war movements in the '60s. She had the opportunity to obtain a PhD and to hold professional positions at prestigious institutions, and, like some women of the day, to break out of the traditional roles marriage socializes women to (which typically are intellectually, as well as socially/psychologically, constraining) and thus be open to the radical ideas produced by and productive of the environment.

This is, very broadly, the transitional moment in history which was/is the environment out of which the conditions for creating 'our Vygotsky' (and, dear readers, perhaps, by this point, 'your Vygotsky') were organized. 'Our Vygotsky,' inseparable from our practice as the completion of our learning-and-development, is very much a product of the 1960s, not merely societally but historically.

Like Cole (see Chapter 2), Newman realized that one could not create a new psychology (a revolutionary psychology) without simultaneously creating the environment which makes the building of that new psychology possible. Unlike Cole, however, Newman recognized that a critical characteristic of this environment was that it be as free as possible from the ties and constraints of traditional, legitimate institutions which, he believed, were becoming more and more reactionary; he set about building a new kind of *anti-institution*. Like Vygotsky, Newman had participated in alternative 'people's universities' and political actions, and had made a thorough study of Marx as well as of bourgeois philosophers, experiences which (along with having been an apprentice toolmaker) contributed to his learning from each in the learning-leading-development sense, i.e. not abandoning one for another, but allowing each 'new' experience, activity, person and idea to reorganize the totality. This Marxian principle, as expressed in Vygotsky's life-as-lived, is the guiding radically democratic principle of this new kind of institution – an anti-institution, a ZPD.

The anti-institution is at once mainstream and radically independent. It is community-supported and -funded (the collective appeals, for example, directly to the public for dollars) rather than receiving its funds from – and thus owing its very existence to – institutions whose function is to maintain the status quo, such as the government, universities, corporations and foundations. The Institute for Social Therapy and Research, founded in 1978 (by the two of us and others), was the first center where social therapy, a psychology based in Marxist methodology, was practiced. It engendered the development of many other independent anti-institutions of education, culture and law, and itself eventually transformed into the East Side Center for Social Therapy and the East Side Institute for Short Term Psychotherapy (the international training center in the social therapeutic approach).[15] Independent but not 'alternative' (not havens attempting to be separate from the dominant culture), these ZPDs overlap with, intersect and informally include traditional institutions such as mental health facilities, hospitals, schools and universities and traditional political parties, heightening the contradiction between people's deep-rooted desire to be helpers/curers/creators/educators/changers (our 'inherent' revolutionary activism) and the growing impossibility of doing so at these deadly total institutions which exist merely or primarily to perpetuate themselves[16] and/or to control people's lives. The anti-institutions offer the dually located community/ZPD members the opportunity to participate in the construction of the new environments necessary for building a new science activity – in Rosa and Montero's words, 'forging new alliances' (1990).

Vygotsky's study circles, his Gomel 'community' theater and 'troika' of revolutionary scientists – these were the shapes his ZPDs took, as he used what was available in pre-and post-revolutionary Russia to organize environments where individuals with different levels of development and expertise in a variety of subjects were able to work together to take what existed and begin to create a socialist psychology for the new human being, for what they felt certain was to be a new kind of society. Independent anti-institutions in the mainstream – whose self-conscious task is to build an environment, a tactic, a ZPD for the continuous inclusion of a diversity of people participating in the collective meaning-making/learning-leading-development necessary to create a constructive (a practical-critical) activist critique of bourgeois society and a revolutionary practice in a deadly reactionary international society – is the shape of *our* ZPD.[17] As we see it, our extensive work in theater, the visual arts, education, politics and health is (like Vygotsky's) not a diversion from our main task – creating a Marxist psychology – but a practical-critical recognition of the seamlessness of human development and the tools in our search for method.

The diversity of people is one of the more striking features of our ZPDs. For the ZPDs – which intersect with traditional institutions and overlap, themselves forming a ZPD (we call *it* Community and *them* communities, and will discuss this later) – not only bring together subjects that are societally and dogmatically separated (such as politics, psychology and culture), but groups of people whom society and societization tend to keep apart, such as working and poor people and middle-class intellectuals, straight and gay people, people of color and white people, academics and activists, people with widely varying political perspectives (nationalist, bourgeois liberal, socialist, conservative). Our radically monistic understanding of revolutionary activity as necessary for revolutionary activity, of human beings as builders, toolmakers, meaning-makers and revolutionaries, has been continuously confirmed, deepened and 'completed' by creating environments where all kinds of people use who they are/whatever they have to create something new. Thus, women and men of color, particularly the poor, who have been brutalized and abused by the sexism and racism of this society yet remain caring and risk-taking, are able to contribute all of that to the building of the ZPD (Fulani, 1988); middle-class women who have had to deform themselves to approximate the ideal woman are able to use their skills and savvy and their repressed humanity to build the ZPD; men, gay and straight, those who successfully learned how to be 'men' and those who failed to learn how to be 'men', can contribute their learning-and-(mis)development, their privilege and their underdevelopment; racism, sexism, homophobia, anti-Semitism and classism, structural components of the organization of learning-and-development in the United States which are both product and productive of real differences among people, can themselves be used to build ZPDs (Holzman and Newman, 1985). As people of color throughout the underdeveloped world use US waste products to construct their homes (flattened Coke and Pepsi cans are a primary building material on the periphery), so too contemporary capitalist core society produces so much that is painful, destructive and violent that if it were all eliminated as potential material for the masses to reorganize into something new (development), there would be precious little to build with. Recall that for Vygotsky the totality of people's lives had to be reorganized if there was to be a new human being. At the historical juncture and in the culture in which he lived – a moment of hope, optimism, creativity, human potential and social progress – the dominant 'mentalistic' materials included their creative, emotional, intellectual and artistic development. At the current historical juncture – an epoch of decline, cynicism, panic, technological control – the totality of people's lives includes not only their modest development but huge doses of creative, emotional, intellectual and artistic undevelopment and underdevelopment as well.[18] These must be our building materials.

The concrete method we, as revolutionary Vygotskians, have developed to reinitiate the meaning-making activity (imitation that is meaning-making and imitating revolutionary activity) necessary for the continuous creation of ZPDs and environments for making ZPDs, and thereby learning-leading-development, is a synthesis of: (1) the basic Vygotskian model (especially learning leading development in the ZPD); (2) Wittgenstein's language game (which clears away the 'mental mist' so as to make it possible to see and show language as activity); and (3) our 'history game.' The history game is a method (a tool-and-result) that engages and changes how the self-reflexivity of human learning is repressed. While it is by virtue of the learning activities we engage in that we are human beings, this revolutionariness and historicalness of our species – the continuous reorganization of the 'organized contradictoriness' of the human life space – is more and more denied and eliminated in favor of societally determined behaviors, as we are increasingly maladapted to history by virtue of being superadapted to society.

The history game (making history) allows for the creation and completion of this self-reflexivity of human learning. It is the performance of meaning-making and/or revolutionary activity. If the material conditions rarely allow for meaning-making beyond the first few years of life, i.e. if what is 'natural' (societal) is revolutionary activity (adaptation to history) making possible non-revolutionary behavior (adaptation to society) which then overpowers/overdetermines/represses further revolutionary activity, then it is necessary to create environments where and how revolutionary activity can generate more revolutionary activity, i.e. to support people being 'unnatural' (performing meaning-making).

The history game grows out of the psychological, educational and cultural work of the Castillo Cultural Center, the East Side Center for Social Therapy and the East Side Institute for Short Term Psychotherapy, under the direction of Newman, and the Barbara Taylor School, under the direction of Holzman (all of them anti-institutions located in New York City). Newman and Castillo believe that psychology and culture are practical-critical tool(s)-and-result(s) for bringing revolutionary activity into being. Newman's (1989a; 1992) recent work as a playwright and producer-director of what he calls 'the theater of the unorganized' is the activity of challenging the institution of culture – its mode of production and practice – through organizing the predetermining conditions and tools of theater (e.g. actors, audience, props, stage) into something not predetermined by them – into 'culture ZPDs,' 'comedy ZPDs,' 'drama ZPDs.' Such ZPDs, collectively created, are simultaneously the creation of the 'results' – culture, comedy, drama. It is the collective which is creative, funny, dramatic. The organizing/directing of this environment/activity organizes the participants as producers/actors in the play, where the shared sense of creating an environment which, they did, in fact, create, produces the 'moral authority' to 'act' (perform) in this environment.

Newman's work, fundamentally a performatory mode of theater as opposed to an acting mode of theater, has been much informed by his social therapeutic work; in turn, it has important implications for psychology. What we have developed overall is a Vygotskian performatory method of learning-leading-development, an educational, clinical and cultural psychology-in-practice.

Performance

> To be natural in bourgeois society is to be dead-in-life. Unnaturalness is required if we are to live at all. But if such is the case – if life is performance – then what is performance?
>
> (F. Newman, 1989a, p. 6)

The profound and ever more totalistic repression of our humanity – revolutionary activity, the unity {meaning-making/ learning-leading-development} – produced by and productive of extreme levels of alienation and dehumanization of our species requires that we *perform everyday life*. The pragmatic world view has so successfully become woven into the fabric of America's institutions that its instantiations in everyday life seem 'perfectly natural.' For example, the Piagetian paradigm of development – development is both untouched by and thoroughly determining of learning – has become equated with what development is. Indeed, it seems and is unnatural to challenge it. As we hope our ongoing discussion has shown, Vygotsky's challenge to Piaget was brilliant, practical-critical and unnatural: Marxian-Vygotskian methodology – an historico-experimental activity the performance of which makes history more than it makes alienation – is nothing if not unnatural in a world so dominated by pragmatism.[19] Our challenge to the Kantian-Piagetian-Chomskian paradigm is in this tradition. Performance is the historically specific antidote to super-alienation; with revolutionary activity repressed in everyday life after earliest childhood, we must perform it. We must self-consciously produce a performance (a revolutionary imitation) of speaking, reading, playing, loving, writing, working, creating. We must use what is 'natural' and alive in childhood to combat what has become 'natural' and dead-in-life thereafter.

The experimental scenes set up at the Rockefeller University laboratory and the numerous other university-affiliated 'ecological niches' around the world attempt to create situations that are as similar to 'real life' as possible. By contrast, our history games – creating historical (not experimental) environments – attempt to produce scenes as unlike 'real life' as possible.

The theirness of building community

Consciousness is considered solely as their consciousness.
(Marx and Engels, 1973, p. 47)

Of course, Vygotsky's tool-and-result is not all process. (We disagree with those who find Vygotsky easily compatible with Dewey, e.g. Goodman and Goodman, 1990. There is, we must remember, a product, albeit a dialectical one. Thus, in order to make possible the performance of scenes (the experience and activity of life as seamless performance, the imitation of revolutionary activity {meaning-making/learning-leading-development} in the ZPD), it is necessary to create environments that foster and nurture such revolutionary activity. The unity of

ZPD 'factory' and ZPDs, the revolutionary activity of continuously creating and shaping ZPDs reinitiated by imitating revolutionary activity, we call building community. To us (following 'our Vygotsky'), community is a ZPD. More important (following 'our Marx' and 'our Wittgenstein'), it is an environment where creating ZPDs – playing language games/history games, performing life – is supported in ways typically not supported in alienated society. If we take Vygotsky's ZPD seriously, then it – and human development – is a social process, development is the activity of creating the conditions for development, and the unit that engages in this activity is the collective.

Most groupings of people – institutions such as the family, the school and the workplace, and what are called communities in ordinary language – are not environments conducive to creating ZPDs. They are typically predefined; they impose themselves, through their definitions and rules and roles for result, on themselves and the members who comprise them. For example, the women's community, the black community, the middle-class community, the academic community, are all defined by certain characteristics of the members who are in the community because they conform to these rules and roles. Often people voluntarily create new communities or join existing ones because they seek 'a haven in a heartless world,' to use the expression originally applied to the twentieth-century family by Lasch (1976). Yet if there is no haven (we are among those who do not believe there is), no escape from the cruelty and pain of contemporary life, then to seek one is to allow revolutionary activity (meaning-making, changing the determining totality, including the cruelty and pain) to turn into societal behavior.

The kind of community we have been building is self-defining, self-generating and radically self-reflexive. It constantly changes its shape, its definition, its activity. In Vygotskian fashion, we understand/practice community not as a location, but as an activity. It is the specific activity of supporting people who, far from seeking a haven in a heartless world, want to engage its cruelty, to do something to change it, to create a world in which havens are not necessary. In this sense, community is 'a heart in a havenless world' (F. Newman, 1991b). It is the activity of human beings taking what exists and creating new things out of it; not any new things but new things which – in their being created – help to change our relationship to the cruelty and pain and injustice and underdevelopment of the world in which we live and thereby create the possibility for doing something about those conditions. The human activity of community is changing that which is changing, which is changing that which is changing.

Such community – activity – is not without structure, although its structure is not of the tool for result, rule-governed kind. Rather, its structure is, like the human life space, like the ZPD, dialectical and radically self-reflexive; it is the structure of a tool-and-result. For when people collectively build community they build not just community but community that builds – Community.

Chapter 8

Logic and psychotherapy

If we are to complete Vygotsky, we must take care not to limit his discoveries to what he wrote most 'about' (what the discipline of psychology has isolated as cognitive or intellectual processes). The unity {meaning-making/learning-leading-development} is not an analytic tool to be applied to some aspects of human development but not others. Indeed, it is not a tool to be applied to anything but is rather the tool-and-result of human development. Furthermore, it must itself be continuously united with revolutionary activity, i.e. history. This uniting takes place in the self-defining communities (self-consciously created life environments where language games/history games can be played) to which we referred earlier. They do not deny but rather 'celebrate' the fundamentality of history and the dialectic that is history/society. The rules-and-results for playing such games (the tools-and-results of building community/creating ZPDs) are:

- the unit is not the individual but the social collective;
- the activity is the tool-and-result of playing the game (building the environment for playing the game is inseparable from playing the game); and
- in order to play, one must perform an historical role-and-result, rather than more or less naturally act out a societal role – really a role for result.

All kinds of ZPDs/communities can be and are created. As revolutionary psychologists concerned to create the 'new human being' and to nurture 'the historical child' – and adult – we have concentrated in our practice on aspects of the human life space which are especially vulnerable to the repression of revolutionary activity – subjectivity, education (learning) and culture – to create 'emotional ZPDs,' 'educational ZPDs' and 'cultural ZPDs.' Such ZPDs are necessary to eliminate interpretation – what Wittgenstein called 'the mental mist' – so that emotional, educational and cultural activity can be the tool-and-result of development.

THE LOGIC OF SYSTEMS AND THE LOGIC OF COMPLETION

Social therapy – our emotional ZPDs/ZPD factory – bears a striking similarity to its dialectical opposite, meta-analytic systems therapy, particularly as developed by Watzlawick and his colleagues (Watzlawick, Beavin and Jackson, 1967; Watzlawick, Weakland and Fisch, 1974). We complete our completion of the historical Vygotsky with an examination of both. To do so requires a brief discussion of logic, which plays a central role in essentially pragmatic systems psychotherapy.

Logic in crisis

From Aristotle to Boole logic has traditionally been understood as a description of the laws of thought with hardly a concern (ironically) for the historical process of thinking and thinking about thinking – how ways of understanding the relationship between how the world is and our accountings of how the world is were/are produced. Logic and psychology, then, have long been at odds with each other, with logic smugly establishing *a priori* what much of traditional psychology believed could only be determined by observation. Some logicians and methodologists were forever trying to put psychologists out of business by denying the existence (or at least the verifiability) of the very things (mental acts) which some psychologists studied. Psychology has, for this and other reasons, almost always been in crisis. But logic found itself in crisis in the early years of this century. In their intense efforts to provide precise and formal (and ultimate) logical characterizations of mathematics (to give mathematics even greater *a priori* certification), a handful of nineteenth- and early twentieth-century logicians and mathematicians discovered deep-rooted contradictions in logic and mathematics themselves. Some pragmatic psychologists, such as Watzlawick, saw in these logico-meta-mathematical contradictions nothing less than 'the ultimate paradox of man's existence' (Watzlawick, Beavin and Jackson, 1967, p. 270).

What was the paradox? Whitehead and Russell (1962) in their monumental work *Principia Mathematica* attempted to show that mathematics could be reduced to logical constructs and operations, that mathematics was a purely formal (rule-governed) system, i.e. that it had no substantive content based on features of the empirically observable real world. For example, the truths of addition $(2 + 2 = 4, 9 + 11 = 20)$ were not based on how the world is but on purely formal definitions (of 2, +, 4, 9, 11, =, 20).

One of the logical constructs (axioms, presuppositions) used by Whitehead and Russell (and by others doing similar meta-mathematical work) was the concept of a 'set.' A set is a highly abstract conception best analogized to an aggregate, collection or grouping of things (members of the set). We can imagine a set of all the people in the world with red hair which would have many members, a set of all the people named George Washington who crossed the Delaware in the late eighteenth century which has (as far as we know) at least one member, a set of the numbers 7, 42 and 19 which has exactly three members, or a set of all even numbers, 2, 4, 6, 8, 10..., which we presume has an infinite number of members. We can also imagine a set of the above sets since there is no reason, given the abstract definition of set, to exclude sets as members of sets. Indeed, in order to reduce mathematics to logic (in Whitehead and Russell's system) it was necessary to have a logic which included sets which had sets as members. (Numbers were defined as sets of sets.) Sets, particularly those with many or an infinite number of members, are usually identified by definition, i.e. the criterion for membership, e.g. 'having red hair,' is the criterion for being a member of the set of all people who have red hair. Whitehead and Russell discovered a most curious set when they considered the following criterion for set membership: a set made up of all of those sets which lack themselves as members. Let's call that set LR (in honor of Lord Russell). All the sets we have mentioned so far lack themselves as members (they are not in themselves). Hence they would all be members of LR. Intuitively it would seem that most if not all sets would lack themselves as members. No problem there. But, we must ask, is LR – a set, and thereby eligible on that count – a member of LR? The answer is paradoxical. Because if LR is, in fact, a member then by definition it lacks itself as a member and, therefore, is not a member. But if

LR is not a member then it lacks itself as a member and is, therefore, by definition, a member.

The discovery of this paradox shook the world of mathematics and logic and led to further mathematical research in the area of proof theory (the study of what it means to prove something in mathematics). Most Marxists paid little or no attention to these extraordinary discoveries. But the most creative and astute Quinean pragmatists recognized that these breakthroughs in the formal sciences might be usable to justify and/or further develop their already pragmatically overdetermined studies of subjectivity and human communication. As Watzlawick, Beavin and Jackson put it (to pragmatic use):

> all interaction may be definable in terms of the game analogy, that is, as a sequence of 'moves' strictly governed by rules of which it is immaterial whether they are within or outside the awareness of the communicants, but about which meaningful metacommunicational statements can be made. This would mean that . . . there exists an as yet uninterpreted calculus of the pragmatics of human communication whose rules are observed in successful, and broken in disturbed, communication.
>
> (1967, pp. 42–3)

And of meaning, they say:

> If someone has his toes stepped on by another, it makes a great deal of difference to him whether the other's behavior was deliberate or unintentional. This view, however, is based on *his* evaluation of the other person's motives and, therefore, on assumptions about what goes on inside the other's head. And, of course, if he were to ask the other about his motives, he could still not be certain, for the other individual might claim his behavior was unconscious when he had meant it to be deliberate, or even claim it was deliberate when in fact it was accidental. All this brings us back to the attribution of 'meaning,' a notion that is essential for the subjective experience of communicating with others, but which we have found to be objectively undecidable for the purposes of research in human communication.
>
> (p. 44)

On their and Quine's account, pragmatics determines logic. For Vygotsky and Marx practice determines everything, including logic. We have taken great pains to show that practice is not to be confused with pragmatics. While a practical-critical historical approach to thinking and speaking led Vygotsky to a practical logic of completion which shapes the radical unity of thinking and speaking in the practice of his life-as-lived, Watzlawick and his colleagues developed a formal logic of separation that effectively eliminates thought in favor of communication (primarily verbal communication). For Marx, Vygotsky and ourselves, the practice of method includes a practice of logic. For Watzlawick and other systems therapists, the pragmatic interpretation of logic rules the day. Thus, in their ongoing effort to 'eliminate' thought, meaning, etc. – nasty old mental acts which did not easily (or did not at all) conform to rule-governed characterizations – these communications theorists found in work being done by the mathematician Gödel and others in foundations of mathematics and logic a way of including the paradoxicality of human life activity without (so they thought) letting in the metaphysicality of mental activity. This twentieth-century pragmatic version of (metaphysical) realism found in foundations of mathematics, logic, cybernetics, decision theory and game theory a 'verifiable' way of understanding human communication by 'applying' (using) these new fields to construct meta-analytic systems therapy. Watzlawick, Beavin and Jackson speak of Gödel's (1962) significance in this manner:

> Two events, it appears, subsequently brought proof theory into the focus of attention. One was the publication, in 1931, of Gödel's epochal paper on formally undecidable propositions, a paper described by the faculty of Harvard University as the most important advance in mathematical logic in a quarter century. The other is the almost explosive emergence of the computer since the end of World War II . . . the question arose whether computers could be designed that would not only carry out a program, but would at the same time be able to effect changes in their program.
>
> (1967, p. 268)

What is raised by Gödel's extraordinary logical analysis and by the theoretical (recursive functions theory) and the practical (mechanical engineering) development of the computer in the last half century is the question of exactly what is decidable. What are the limits in mathematical systems, computer systems and human systems to what can be proved, or even decided? And what, if anything, can be done about these limitations? Let us return to the paradox discovered by Whitehead and Russell. Years before Gödel, they introduced into their logical system an *ad hoc* stipulation (the Theory of Logical Types) which essentially forbade asking the questions that generated the paradox in the first place. They justified this move by pointing out that many systems – language systems, mathematical systems, human systems – have within themselves the potential for self-reference, i.e. of structuring formulae, sentences, actions, which effectively attribute to themselves what they (the formulae, sentences, actions) characteristically attribute to other elements of the system of another type or level. For example, in English it is both grammatically and semantically sound to ask if the book is red. But the question 'Is red red?' seemingly grammatical in our natural language system, should be disallowed semantically because it violates the Theory of Logical Types. You can ask of an object A (of level 1) whether it is red but you cannot ask that of redness (of level 2). Whitehead and Russell view the question about whether the set LR is a member of the set LR as similarly violating the logic of types within their system. Systems, if they are to remain healthy (non-contradictory), must go outside of themselves (to other systems called meta-systems) to ask these kinds of meta-questions or else they will remain 'sick' trying to answer them inside of themselves. Gödel, going even further, recognized that Whitehead and Russell's *ad hoc* solution was not a solution at all. He proved that if their Theory of Logical Types was in the system then the paradox remained (no matter how often the theory of types was 'used' to eliminate a 'sick' self-referential, another could be generated) – and if it wasn't, then, of course, the paradox remained. Watzlawick, Beavin and Jackson put it this way:

> Gödel was able to show that in this [Whitehead and Russell's system] or an equivalent system it is possible to construct a sentence, G, which (1) is provable from the premises and axioms of the system, but which (2) proclaims of itself to be unprovable. This means that if G be provable in the system, its unprovability (which is what it says of itself) would also be provable. But if both provability and unprovability can be derived from the axioms of the system, and the axioms themselves are consistent (which is part of Gödel's proof), then G is undecidable in terms of the system.

> (1967, p. 269)

What began as an attempt to show the absolute *a priori*-ness of logic, and, thereby, of mathematics, in fact exposed the profound limitations of all systems, including logic and mathematics. But the deepened understanding of these very limits opened up the possibility of theoretical and practical discoveries in the fields of cybernetics and computer sciences which in the opinion of many have radically transformed human life itself. Many in the human sciences have used the 'computer revolution' in varied ways. Moreover, the computer as a paradigm for the human mind has influenced all of us (for better or for worse). Watzlawick and his colleagues have most intelligently and directly applied the mathematical and systems analysis discoveries to psychology – in particular, to clinical psychology and human communication. A brief study of their work will reveal a most sophisticated clinical application of neo-Quinean pragmatism and in the process will expose most clearly some of the qualitative differences between Vygotskian psychology-in-the-making and post-modern pragmatic psychology.

The system is the problem

In the 1950s and '60s Watzlawick and his colleagues at the Mental Research Institute in Palo Alto, California, were the chief developers and popularizers of meta-analytic systems therapy (Watzlawick, Beavin and Jackson, 1967; Watzlawick, Weakland and Fisch, 1974), according to which individuals do not suffer psychopathology; it is the system that is pathological. Explanations of emotional pain, schizophrenia, psychosis and neurosis are to be located not in the individual but in the systems of which the individual is a part, the most common pathological system being the family. In its early years, the family systems approach was considered progressive relative to Freudian psychoanalysis because it challenged the 'natural' hierarchy of the family. For example, in systems therapy the father's role is not seen as derived from God or biology, but simply as a particular rule-governed role in a homeostatic system. More generally the approach seemed to 'blame the system' and not the individual, which went well with the liberal politics of the '60s. One characteristic of systems, originally formulated in mathematics and cybernetics and then applied to social systems, is that they continuously 'strive' for a state of equilibrium, called homeostasis – they 'seek to eliminate' contradictions. It is claimed that human beings develop ways of behaving and communicating that maintain homeostasis. All too often these ways are pathological, as, for example, when emotional distance between partners is maintained by the pattern of communication in which one partner tries to establish greater contact and this is followed by the withdrawal of the other partner (Watzlawick, Weakland and Fisch, 1974, p. 16).

The psychological problem – the psychopathology – can be eliminated, according to Watzlawick and his colleagues, by eliminating the pathological communication. Here is where meta-analysis (derived from Whitehead and Russell's Theory of Logical Types and Gödel's advancement of the concept) comes in. In order to eliminate the pathological communication, claim Watzlawick, Weakland and Fisch (1974), one must teach people to meta-communicate, i.e. to communicate about communication:

> What we can observe in virtually all those cases of pathological communication is that they are vicious circles that cannot be broken unless and until communication itself becomes the subject of communication, in other words, until the communicants are able to meta-communicate.
>
> (p. 95)

What is taken as pathology is the paradox engendered by people communicating (or attempting to) at different levels of discourse, not the social origins or substance of the communication; what a couple or parent and child are arguing about or how their pathological communication and interaction developed is considered irrelevant. The therapeutic process involves teaching people to meta-communicate, i.e. to talk about what they are talking about. In a certain sense, it is teaching people another language so that they can communicate at the meta-level about what is going on at the object level. This enables them to see the patterns and paradoxes in their discourse and thereby, presumably, to be in a better position to resolve them.

Watzlawick, Weakland and Fisch (1974) combine the Theory of Logical Types with the Theory of Groups (set theory) to create another meta-analytic technique for conflict resolution which they refer to as change. Using meta-analysis, they make the 'discovery' that people often attempt solutions to problems and/or conflicts at the wrong 'level' of change. For example, a person or persons might apply a first-order change (stepping on the gas pedal with more force) in a situation where a second-order change (shifting gears) is necessary. This 'mixing of levels' (trying to change at one level when a change at the next higher logical level is required) produces 'more of the same' (paradoxes, pathological patterns, emotional pain, being stuck). Watzlawick and his co-authors give several examples, including the pattern common to many marriages of the wife wanting her husband to be more open and the husband, thinking she is being intrusive, withholding more and more information from her. Their analysis is as follows:

> The less information he gives her, the more persistently she will seek it, and the more she seeks it, the less he will give her. By the time they see a psychiatrist, it will be tempting to diagnose her behavior as pathological jealousy – provided that no attention is paid to their pattern of interaction and their attempted solutions, which are the problem.
>
> (Watzlawick, Weakland and Fisch, 1974, p. 36)

This kind of analysis, of course, omits the social-historical-cultural production of the patterns of interaction and attempted solutions in favor of the meta-analytic explanation: 'The attempt to effect a first order change under these conditions either greatly contributes to the problem which it is supposed to solve, or actually is the problem' (p. 38). Note that in the spirit of reform it also eliminates the substance (the sexist, family-preserving bias) of the hypothetical 'traditional' psychiatrist's diagnosis – which takes the wife as having/creating the problem! The intervention in cases such as this one is to prescribe a second-order change, i.e. a behavior that changes the system (the interaction and communication). Frequently, their practical interventions are themselves paradoxical and seemingly 'unreasonable,' such as instructing the husband to talk incessantly to his wife about every detail of his life (Watzlawick, Weakland and Fisch, 1974, p. 36).

What, in Vygotsky's language, is Watzlawick et al.'s 'philosophy of the fact'? Like all pragmatists, they deny truth in favor of 'efficaciousness.' (Following Marx and Vygotsky, we deny truth in favor of history.) 'What works' is what one should do. And this meta-analytic therapeutic approach 'works' – it can, at times, be very effective. People do 'get better'; they can be helped to stop doing destructive things.

What's the problem?

The introduction of meta-level systems analysis to human emotionality (subjectivity) effects behavioral change. If the behavior it changes is destructive and hurtful, that is a worthwhile reform. If the computer is used toward a good end, who would deny its value? But the danger of the systems approach is located in its thoroughgoing distortion of the human activity, of revolutionary activity, of the human capacity to reorganize the determining totality. Family systems therapy cleverly adapts people to the societal system – eliminating the developmental contradictoriness that is life in history/society by eliminating history. The very nature of language and communication is its organized contradictoriness and its dialectical relationship to thought and meaning which it completes. Watzlawick *et al.* view this fact (actually, the primary source of human development in practice – not in the abstract) as a problem to be resolved: 'Unfortunately, natural language often makes a clear distinction between member and class difficult' (1974, p. 8) and 'Logical levels [including subjective and objective] must be kept strictly apart to prevent paradox and confusion' (p. 9).

In their noble attempt to eliminate the metaphysically-and-dualistically-divided-from-society 'mind-in-itself' (which is ontologically required in the Freudian theory they critique) and the pseudo-science that it leads to/is, Watzlawick and his colleagues have not only introduced other metaphysical conceptions – communication patterns and homeostatic systems – which eliminate the dialectical speaking/thinking environment of everyday human performance through a redescription that is both the 'cure' and the analysis. They are forced by 'logical' necessity (and this poses an even greater dilemma) to posit communication communicating itself, in just the same way that, as Vygotsky so clearly pointed out, Piaget was forced by logical necessity to posit 'thoughts thinking themselves' (see Chapter 6). If the systematic redescription is both cure and analysis, then how can the meta-analytic approach – if it is to be consistent with itself – ever explain anything? If communication is all there is (or all that is knowable) and pathology is viewed solely in terms of communication patterns, then what is the basis for any claim of cure – or even changes in behavior? The meta-analytic approach cannot claim, for example, that the children stopped fighting, or the husband stopped drinking, or the couple began to have sex again, or the son stopped being suicidal, because it does not accept non-communication (such things as events, actions, activities) as real. All it can point to is that the communication patterns changed. (The husband and wife are now saying to each other that the sex is better.) Empiricism and logical positivism, systems theory's metaphysical predecessors, failed, in part, because they could not even pass the tests of empiricism or logical positivism. Meta-analytic systems theory, which has no capacity to explain its effectiveness other than its own criterion (pragmatics), cannot even evaluate whether or not it passes the test of pragmatics. There is no way to get from the systematic redescription to what people are doing in their actual, practical-critical lives, because what people are doing in their lives is not real (it is too infected with subjectivity) – only communicating is.

Unlike Freudian theory, for example, that posits a mind and a therapeutic process and discourse which have a specific causal effect on the mind, here there is only therapeutic discourse – no object (e.g. mind) to be changed. The dualism of cause and effect, mind and society, form and content, and fact and theory are eliminated, to be sure. That, in part, accounts for why social therapy and meta-analytic systems analysis 'look alike.' The approach is monistic – radically so – but, more importantly, ahistorically and nihilistically so. This practice and form of psychological analysis denies the fundamentality of history and the dialectic that is history/society – the form and substance of the life space of everyday human performance – in favor of systems and their logical limitations. The self-reflexive activity, the tool-and-result of communication as practiced, is transformed into the most vulgar of tools for result. Instead of a Marxian-Vygotskian dialectical unity of method and result of method, analysis and object of analysis, they have thrown out both the result and the object.

It is likely that Watzlawick and his colleagues would regard our criticism – especially our insistence on explanatory power – as irrelevant, indeed, perhaps, metaphysical! So be it! Yet we feel compelled to attempt an accounting for their (instrumental and coercive) effectiveness in dealing with psychopathology. Vygotsky's understanding of learning leading development in the ZPD, coupled with our specification of the self-reflexivity of human learning, are, together, a useful tool (-and-result). As we have discussed at length in Chapters 6 and 7, the dialectical speaking/thinking environment of early childhood is expressive of the self-reflexive, triadic characteristic of learning – in learning any particular thing, one learns: (1) the particular thing; (2) how to learn; and (3) that one is a learner. Contemporary socialization/societization, where adaptation to post-modern society is so encompassing, eliminates (3), and occasionally even (2), through the overdetermination of thought by language and the subordination of language as activity to language use. The interjection of meta-level discourse – teaching people to communicate about communication – reintroduces (to a very small but nevertheless significant extent) the dialectic, self-reflexive component of the learning process and of language as activity. The capacity to step back and see how we actively learn is ever so slightly reinitiated. The meta-analytic solution – a self-conscious, if pseudo-scientific, attempt to resolve organized contradictoriness – 'works' because and to the extent that it actually reintroduces (allows for the relearning/experiencing of) this very contradictoriness, nearly eliminated through the alienating process of socialization/societization. We are adapted to (immunized against) super-alienation by being exposed in a controlled fashion to paradox and contradiction ('viruses') without sufficient attention being paid to the effects of all this on the immune system, i.e. the total human being.

To our understanding, this meta-analytic form of 'conflict resolution' – attempting to remove the contradiction between history and society (reality), and the dialectical relationship between language, thought and history – not only accepts alienation, but valorizes it. Just as Whitehead and Russell's Theory of Logical Types was a technique for preserving that which is presupposed, i.e. rule-governedness, the therapeutic use of meta-analysis is a technique to make communication conform to a concept of rule-governedness that is presupposed. What underlies the presupposition that natural language and communication are rule-governed is an uncritical acceptance of alienation – the separation of what is produced (speaking, thinking, communicating) from the process which produced it. In fact, both the process and product of human communication are contradictory, paradoxical and self-referential. Denying this – and teaching people techniques which adapt them to increasing alienation from their own capacity for learning and development – at best produces human beings who are societally 'better' (i.e. less dysfunctionally adapted to society) and historically 'sicker' (i.e. more dysfunctionally adapted to history/society). It in no way helps people develop.

Seemingly the opposite of meta-analytic systems approaches, ethnography is more accurately another form of the method of pragmatics. The ecological validity project discussed at length in Chapter 2, instrumental in initiating the Vygotsky revival, is an excellent example. Like meta-analysis, it claims to be anti-interpretive. Radical description – not a meta-level analysis but an 'objective,' surface-level analysis – is the method ethnography employs in its attempt to avoid interpretive analysis. A picture of human interaction is taken (typically on film or video-tape) and a description of what can be seen in the picture is written. It is assumed that if one describes with the utmost accuracy everything that is observable (how people sit, move, talk and walk) then one will have captured activity in its natural environment, free of the biases of the science of the dominant culture. But it is not free of the fundamental scientific bias embedded in objective description, for description is itself an interpretation. Ethnography never engages its commitment to such 'truths' as reality and objectivity and to resolving contradictoriness (the dialectic history/society). Human activity must be performed. It cannot be 'expressed'; it cannot be 'captured' any more than, in alienated society, it can be 'found' in its product. Any attempt to do so distorts what it is. At best, what is captured by ethnography is a distorted portion of human *use* through the tool for result of technologically advanced empiricism.[1]

Unlike some neo-Vygotskians (including some ethnographers), who view life as an endless series of scenes (in which social, but nevertheless eternal, children and adults participate in constructing environments to act on in the world), we, following the historical Vygotsky, view life as seamless performance. Ironically, in order to experience/live life as seamless performance (in these times) one must perform scenes. This is because in the current learning-biased organization/institutionalization of the individual-in-society where alienated knowledge dominates and threatens to destroy permanently (learning-leading-)development, creating ZPDs – reorganizing elements of the societal environment (scenes) to create new meaning and a learning that leads development – requires that we self-consciously put together these elements in ways which make it possible to see and show history because and as we make it. Performing a scene gives expression to this essential activity of human beings (making tools-and-results). In contrast, taking a picture (photographically or ethnographically) depicts ecologically valid reality – human beings as tool (for result) users. Yet the performance of scenes cannot be mere imitation. For such scenes will not reinitiate development. To do that, our performances must take place within the ZPD. But to create a ZPD and/or ZPD-creating environments in these reactionary, ahistorical times, we must imitate that most basic of human activities, revolutionary activity.

Vygotsky's logic of completion (following Marx) is a complete rejection of the method of interpretation, the denial of any attempt to represent human life activity as a rule-governed, premise-filled system (with or without the limitations introduced by Whitehead and Russell, Gödel and the cyberneticists). Vygotsky's discovery of the ZPD and his discovery of language as the completion of thinking is the psychological equal of Gödel's extraordinary discovery. Indeed, Gödel's discovery and what Watzlawick and his colleagues did are related, but not in the vulgarly pragmatic fashion they suggest. What Gödel shows is the limitation of systems. It does not follow that we should therefore create analyses which are systematic but limited. The arbitrariness (*ad hoc*-ness) of rules, the undecidability of calculi, the unprovability of all propositions, in effect constitute an argument that supports Marx's anti-interpretive, practical-critical methodology the premises of which are real people. The logic of the excluded middle (AvÃ) and its equivalent, the logic of non-contradiction ~(A&Ã), shows itself in this century to be severely limited (even in the physical sciences). Quine's righteous dictum (see Chapter 3) suggests that a discovery of the magnitude of Gödel's would have impelled a revolutionary restructuring of the entire scientific world view. The pragmatists (even those who follow Quine) did not undertake such a restructuring. Rather, like Watzlawick, they worked to maintain the rule-governed, interpretive presuppositions of the current scientific world view. Why? It was pragmatically efficacious to do so – proving, if you will, that nothing will lead pragmatists to give up pragmatism; proving, if you will, that pragmatism fails its own test.

Vygotsky (whom we have no reason to believe knew of Gödel's work) recognized that the scientific world view must be revolutionized if we are to continue the Marxian revolution and create a science of human activity. His practical empirical recognition that development requires activity which goes beyond oneself (imitation in the ZPD), and that language is not a systematic representation of thought but a practical-critical completion of thought, affirmed, in practice, a logic of becoming which urges that everything is both what it is and what it isn't (A/Ã). Non-contradiction ~(A&Ã) may be a moral standard for representations; it is not such for a human science of life-as-lived.

Ironically, Watzlawick (with his usual intelligent instincts – and pragmatic morality) turns to Wittgenstein to explicate in philosophical terms the paradox of human existence he finds in Gödel's work. But it is the earlier Wittgenstein of the *Tractatus* – a Wittgenstein who had yet to discover activity and the philosophical significance of life-as-lived. Watzlawick, Beavin and Jackson introduce Wittgenstein's early scientific/mystical thoughts:

> Wittgenstein shows that we could only know something about the world in its totality if we could step outside it; but if this were possible, this world would no longer be the *whole* world. However, our logic knows of nothing outside it:

>> Logic fills the world: the limits of the world are also its limits. We cannot therefore say in logic: This and this there is in the world, that there is not. For that would apparently presuppose that we exclude certain possibilities, and this cannot be the case since otherwise logic must get outside the limits of the world: that is, if it could consider these limits from the other side also.
>> What we cannot think, we cannot think: we cannot therefore say what we cannot think.

>> (Wittgenstein, pp. 149–51; quoted in Watzlawick, Beavin and Jackson, 1967, p. 270)

Wittgenstein's mystical logicality (if 'our logic knows of nothing outside it,' we say: so much the worse for such logic – and so much the better for 'our Vygotsky') remains at bottom Kantian and dualistic. Watzlawick *et al.* quote the compelling conclusion to the *Tractatus*:

> For an answer which cannot be expressed the question too cannot be expressed. *The riddle* does not exist...
> We feel that even if *all possible* scientific questions be answered, the problems of life have still not been touched at all. Of course there is then no question left, and just this is the answer.

The solution of the problem of life is seen in the vanishing of this problem. (Is not this the reason why men to whom after long doubting the sense of life became clear, could not then say wherein this sense consisted?)

There is indeed the inexpressible. This *shows* itself; it is the mystical...

Whereof one cannot speak, thereof one must be silent.

(Wittgenstein, pp. 187–9; quoted in Watzlawick, Beavin and Jackson, 1967, p. 271)

But the later Wittgenstein of the *Philosophical Investigations*, the activity theorist, joins Marx and Vygotsky in the recognition of the developmental paradox and contradiction that is human life in practice. And so we must reformulate with rigor the ending of Wittgenstein's conclusion: whereof one cannot speak, thereof one has not thought.

SOCIAL THERAPY

Our paraphrase of Wittgenstein leads us to speak of social therapy. The social therapy group, the basic cell (in the biological, not the Stalinist, sense) of our self-defining community, is the activity of people collectively creating an environment for making a tool/which is the making of a tool specifically designed and shaped to 'redefine' – in practice – human subjectivity. Using the definitions of subjectivity, emotions, normality, pathology and madness which have societized us (the hardware store tools of named emotions, e.g. anger, joy, sadness; of the DSM–III categories of psychopathology, e.g. schizophrenia, post-traumatic stress disorder, manic-depression; of understandings of what emotions are, e.g. internal states, having causes, excitation of the nerve tissue) produces societal behavior (when it 'works' it produces the societal behavior of 'feeling better'). But it does not produce revolutionary activity (development which produces development...). To do that – to reshape our emotional practice, to decide for ourselves what it is we want to do with anger, joy, humiliation and the rest of our incredibly complex subjectivity which is nameless, and with the emotions newly created through/in the activity of building community that redefines subjectivity (there are more emotions in heaven and earth than are dreamt of in bourgeois psychology!) – we must make the tool which makes this possible. In this ordinary though fantastical process, we must, of course, redefine even what redefine means!

Marx's 'theirness' is the revolutionary activity of human beings organizing and reorganizing the production of their 'actual life process.' It is, in the case of subjectivity, for example, redefining the meaning/experience/understanding/practice of emotions in such a way that the theirness of emotions (their socialness, their historicalness, their process of production) is simultaneously the process and product of consciousness.

The thatness of what's being said

Traditional psychotherapy, psychotherapeutic discourse and ana-lyses of such discourse as a tool for diagnosis and treatment either do not understand or choose to ignore the activity/use, history/ society dialectic and focus instead on the societal use of language. When people talk in traditional group therapy, the psychothera-pist(s) and others in the group typically respond to what is being said. Following Wittgenstein, however, utterances are not to be analyzed at all; the language game strips away the mental mist so as to bring into prominence 'the fact that the *speaking* of language is part of an activity, or of a form of life' (Wittgenstein, 1953, p. 11, quoted in Chapter 6, p. 129). Vygotsky's brilliant discovery that thought is completed (not expressed) in the word admonishes us not to transform the activity of speaking into its use (not to associ-ate its meaning with the expression of dualistically-divided-from-speaking thought or emotion).

Building emotional ZPDs – the practice of social therapy – is non-interpretive in this Wittgensteinian sense and dialectic in this Vygotskian sense. The collective (the therapy group) plays lan-guage games, i.e. uses language (the primary thing society has to offer us with which to communicate) but makes meaning (its activity is not determined by its use). The clinical practice is an investigation of 'emotional muddles' – the emotional trouble people get into that is due at least in part to the societally deter-mined ways of understanding emotions. The language game strips away some of the excesses of reified emotional language, abstrac-tion and interpretation so as to show/discover the activity of speaking/discourse. When someone says something, what is im-portant – what is radically accepted by the social therapist – is *that* it was said (the activity of it being said) and not *what* was said (the 'what' being the assumed, often erroneously so, shared internalized denotative and connotative meaning). Thus people talk about their problems but it is what is done with that dialogue that is critical to cure (which, on our view, is the reinitiation of emotional development, i.e. the unity {meaning-making/learning-leading-development}), so as to be in a different relationship to one's pathology and/or the pain of society.

Social therapy is a specific confrontation between the private and the social; it challenges, for example, psychology's myth of the inner and outer. The language game/history game makes it possible to see and show the dialectic nature of the life space (the organized contradictoriness of history/society) as it is the activity of relating to human beings in a manner which denies the *a priori* 'authority of their individuality.' The therapists relate to human beings in social therapy as historical adults, 'as revolutionaries' (F. Newman, 1991a). Societally determined individuation (what traditional psychology calls development) locates emotions as possessions – my pain, my anger, my anxiety, my depression – or inner states rising or failing to rise, as the case may be, to the surface and 'getting expressed.' The socialization/societization process which produces such a metaphysical and commodified understanding/experience/expression of emotionality transforms emotional learning that leads development into societal emotional behavior (responses) and stops further emotional development.

The social therapeutic process is an attempt to 'free' emotions from their societally overdetermined location inside an egocentric, individuated individual-in-society so they can be used as tool-and-result by individuals-in-society-in-history. For emotions and subjectivity must be social activity in order for emotional development to occur.

How is this done? What does the social therapeutic process look like? The joint activity in the emotional ZPD (the social therapy group) is the building of the group as a 'place' where the members of the group can get help with their societally determined emotional problems. This is the explicit task and it is in the 'thatness' of that first bit of therapeutic discourse (the beginning of the language game/history game) that the confrontation between the private and the social begins. Lawfully, people seek therapy to get help with their own problems. Yet the joint activity of social therapy is building the group, using the members' problems as building materials, not getting help with one's problems! For the social therapy group is a tool-and-result; the activity of building the group is what is curative (F. Newman, 1983; 1989b). People come to therapy seeking hardware store tools to use; they are offered the chance to be toolmakers, to take the predetermining elements of their life space and create something entirely new out of it, to define collectively for themselves what and how their (in the Marxian sense) emotions are to be.

This revolutionary activity is the Vygotskian unity (meaning-making/learning-leading-development). Following Vygotsky, in creating emotional ZPDs the focus must be on what is only partially developed; if the focus is on the fully developed (so-called), then no learning-leading-development will occur.

As we have already said, Vygotskians have misunderstood Vygotsky's focus on the partially developed and missed its implications for continuous development. Our completion of Vygotsky includes a radical therapeutic practice which often makes the least emotionally developed person the focus of the social therapy group. For, to our understanding, being emotionally un- or underdeveloped includes the experience of not being related to by oneself and others as someone who can be emotional and create emotions; it is lacking that critical third component of the learning-leading-development process that occurs in the ZPD. Being emotionally developed in contemporary alienated society includes the experience of having one's revolutionary activity of creating emotions (inseparable from being related to as capable of creating emotions) transformed into the societal behavior of having/expressing the emotions that are available. Those who are 'good' by societal standards at being emotional, who are capable of expressing particular emotions, e.g. of being angry, happy, sad, depressed, have learned so well how to be emotional that learning substitutes for development and they are related to as not needing to develop further. In the social therapy group, the process of collectively creating a ZPD for emotional development develops everyone; the process of the well or overdeveloped members using their societal skills to help the less developed member(s) simultaneously exposes the limitations of their own emotional development by virtue of their having been such good societal learners. Therefore, and since, the unit of growth/study/change in social therapy is not the individual but the group, the collective focus of the group on the emotional proximality of its least developed members develops everyone in the group.

But none of this would be possible without the unnatural activity of performing (revolutionary imitating). The 'realistic' thing to do – if social therapy attempted to replicate (rather than be part of) the real world, as most therapies do – is to relate to people in their societal roles in relation to each other, i.e. as patients or clients seeking help from the experts who are the therapists and even occasionally the most emotionally advanced members of a group. The social therapy group/emotional ZPD is radically unrealistic; it does not attempt to (re-)create a real life situation but to create something new out of what there is – a performance of living which, in our view, is very unlike real life. The social therapist cannot relate to human beings in therapy as patients, for that is what they are societally; to relate to them as such is surely not 'in advance of their development.' To create an emotional ZPD one must relate to human beings as other than who they are (societally) and they must perform as other than who they are (societally). The social therapist relates to human beings in therapy as revolutionaries, i.e. as who they are (historically) (F. Newman, 1991a). In a society and culture where subjectivity (produced by/in history/society) is so thoroughly overdetermined by society, and where revolutionary activity is so thoroughly repressed, we must *perform* the activity of changing the determining totality of our societally produced subjectivity. We must imitate revolutionary activity.

Perhaps we can clarify the non-interpretive nature of the social therapeutic approach – and its Vygotskianism – through an illustration of our work in creating/practicing a Vygotskian pedagogy at the Barbara Taylor School. This multi-racial, independent, community-supported elementary school (an anti-institution) in Harlem began to be transformed into a laboratory in Vygotskian methodology in September 1991.[2] Traditional schools are not ZPDs; they teach children and adults alike to devalue and even destroy ZPDs. In the typical classroom children are taught to view the major activities in the ZPD – working together, imitating that produces something other than mere repetition, collectively changing the total determining environment into something that is not predetermined, reshaping the existing tools of language and play into new meanings and discovery – as illegitimate. In contrast, the Barbara Taylor School is understood as an activity and organized as a performance of building a learning community (a ZPD/ZPD factory). The staff's task is to lead the children in creating an environment where everyone can learn and develop – in the language of social therapy, building the group; in the language of 'our Vygotsky,' making a tool-and-result. They relate to children as mathematicians, writers, readers, artists, scientists and historians – not as knowers and/or non-knowers – even, and especially, when children do not yet know, societally, how to do math, write, read or draw. Children and staff are encouraged and taught to 'cheat' – that is, to create ZPDs. The program itself is called CHEAT (Children Helping to Educate Another Training).

On a certain day, two 10-year-old boys got into a physical fight. The teacher present at the time broke it up and told one of them, John, that his mother would be called and he would be sent home. John cursed, screamed and kicked things off and on for about fifteen minutes. He said, among other things, that the teacher was a liar, that she should be fired, that it wasn't fair that the other boy could stay, that he hated this school and that his mother shouldn't pay all this money for teachers who couldn't teach, that the other boy took his paper and that's why he hit him, that he was here to learn and he couldn't learn if other kids took his things. In those moments when John was calm enough to hear something, the director talked with him. Most of the things she said challenged his way of seeing and his desire to have someone fix things up – in his favor, of course. For example, 'What should we do about people taking other people's things?' 'If you're here to learn and you can't, what do we need to do so you can?' 'You think Susan [the teacher] lied – what should we do about that?' 'You know her well enough to know that if you call her a f–ing bitch she won't hear anything you say. So you need to do something different if you're serious about talking with her.' 'Being angry doesn't explain why you broke the trash can or why you're cursing. There's lots of people in this school who do anger differently. You can do something different too.' The teacher was adamant that John should leave the school, not only because of the fight but because of his disrespect and abuse. When John's mother came to pick him up, she said that she hoped we were documenting what had happened because she needed records of such outbursts by John for her court case. She said that John wouldn't do things like this if only he would talk about the terrible thing that had happened to him the previous summer. In her opinion, he was 'acting out' because he was repressing his feelings; it had nothing to do with anything going on now.

In subsequent discussions, the staff and children were challenged about their need to see this incident as something that interfered with building the learning community/learning, as a problem that needed to be solved so learning could continue. Situations like this – in which two people feel wronged and hurt and are intent on finding out who is right and who is wrong so just punishment can be meted out – occur many times in a typical day. It would be extremely valuable to engage it directly. In fact, from the social-therapeutic perspective, far from being a disruption of the learning process, this incident presented an excellent opportunity for learning-leading-development. The group – the school community – was given the task of deciding what to do with what it had, which included anger, hurt, frustration, moral indignation, interpretations and explanations, along with caring, intimacy, a commitment to each other and the process we were going through. Could the existing conditions be transformed? Did children and teachers and mothers have to act out their societally determined roles of victims? Did everyone have to stick to their part in a predetermined script of telling 'my side of the story' to find out who was 'right'? Did John's and the teacher's actions have to be interpreted; did we have to find the root cause? Did we have to punish the perpetrators? Carrying out this very difficult task of reshaping or transforming what is societally given into something new of necessity involves performing. The 10-year-old boy, the teacher, and everyone else have to engage how they talk and how they feel and what they believe – to engage that from the *historical* perspective of changing the totality that is determining them – in order to create an emotional and learning ZPD.

The social-therapeutic, Vygotskian activity of building the group, of creating ZPDs, of engaging in revolutionary activity, is the dialectical opposite of interpretive analysis, whether psychoanalytic (exemplified so clearly by John's mother), meta-analytic or ethnographic. We did not interpret John's behavior as 'acting out,' or John's and Susan's communication as paradoxical, or describe (replicate) how this incident was mutually constructed by the participants, all of which relate to John and Susan interpretively. Instead, we work to eliminate interpretation, to strip it away so that, in the creating-the-ZPD-activity, in the activist task of playing history games – 'This is what we have, what should/can we do and/or make with it?' – we can come to a deeper understanding, i.e. a revolutionary activist understanding, of the activity itself.[3]

NOT AN ENDING

When we began this book our challenge was to present Vygotsky to you in a manner which we believed was true to 'our Vygotsky' – whom we have called Lev Vygotsky, revolutionary scientist. Our effort has been to show how Vygotsky's science was permeated with revolution; far from being confined to literary citations and quotations from Marx, Lenin and Engels, his revolutionariness both influenced and was influenced by his intellectual rigor. Those who separate Vygotsky the revolutionary from Vygotsky the scientist (or deny the revolutionary altogether) do a great disservice not only to the historical Vygotsky but also to science.

In attempting to meet this challenge, we have discovered/learned-and-developed much about Vygotsky's life-as-lived and ours; about psychology, methodology and ideology; about the life space in which human beings – individuals-in-society-in-history – live (what we call the dialectic history/society); about the paradoxical and contradictory process of human development, whereby in contemporary alienated society the revolutionary activity necessary for development transforms into societal behavior which represses revolutionary activity; and about the revolutionary science activity needed to reinitiate revolutionary activity and thereby human development.

Vygotsky, Marx (who was one of his most important mentors) and Wittgenstein (who, as we have tried to show, turns out to be a necessary tool-and-result for completing Vygotsky) were not unique in recognizing that human activity embodies its own paradox. What is unique to Vygotsky, however, and uniquely practical-critical, i.e. revolutionary, i.e. non-instrumentally usable, is the specification of that paradox as 'activity that goes beyond itself' and the historical/societal location of such activity as the ZPD. The human capacity to make meaning, to change the determining totality, to create something new out of whatever exists, to make tools-and-results by the activity of creating the environments which make such toolmaking possible, to build the unity ZPD factory/ZPDs (or self-defining community), to build anti-institutions to intersect with and actively (practically-critically) deconstruct total institutions, to alter in practice the pragmatically organized activity/use dialectic so as to employ the societally fixed tools of speaking and thinking to make meaning (to see and show language as activity) and thereby create a new learning that leads development and revolutionary activity that produces revolutionary activity, to imitate as revolutionary activity in early childhood and then, in adulthood, to imitate revolutionary activity itself (perform) – these activities that go beyond themselves (formulations of our going-beyond-itself activity) are both ordinary and extraordinary.

Vygotsky affirms the philosophical and political power of the ontological socialness of human beings. He offers us something rare in this post-modern epoch – possibility. For pragmatism – the dominant ideology/methodology/religion – determines even our dreams and hopes. By and large the current human understanding of what is possible is dualistically limited to and by what is actual; it does not 'go beyond itself.' Vygotsky's radically monistic historical methodology, produced by and productive of his life-as-lived – including his investigations and discoveries of the mechanisms of human speaking, thinking, learning, playing, development, socialization and societization – not only teaches us the difference between the eternal child and the historical child. It affords us the possibility of becoming historical adults – of making history at a time when history seems not makeable, of reorganizing the determining and destructive totality of the human life space to produce revolutionary activity that produces revolutionary activity, development that produces development, community that produces community, the ZPD factory/ZPD, a changing which is changing... Only in this is his life-as-lived 'learning worthy of the name' and only in this can it be completed.

Notes

1 VYGOTSKY AND PSYCHOLOGY

1 There is not one Soviet psychology but several. In modern terms, Vygotsky is identified closely with two related but not identical Soviet psychological traditions – activity theory and socio-historical or socio-cultural psychology. Information on Soviet psychology is plentiful. In addition to the original works of those of the activity theory and/or socio-cultural schools – Vygotsky, Luria, Leont'ev and Davydov (see Bibliography) – the journal *Soviet Psychology* is a useful source of translations of contemporary research of these and other psychological approaches. Histories of Soviet psychology include Corson (1976); Joravsky (1989); Kozulin (1984); Petrovsky (1990); and Yaroshevsky (1990). See also Levitan (1982) and Wertsch (1981).

2 In our view, the traditional distinction between dialectical materialism (Marxism applied to nature) and historical materialism (Marxism applied to social structures and institutions) dualistically distorts the Marxian method. We prefer the synthesized term, dialectical historical materialism.

3 For a useful discussion of changes in the social sciences, see Bernstein (1978).

4 Some of the thinkers whose work was examined during this period were Brentano, Brunswik, Dilthey, Lewin and, notably, Hegel. Among the many sources of discussion of their role in the history of psychology are Apfelbaum (1986); Cole, Hood and McDermott (1978); and Polkinghorne (1983). Interestingly, Marx's writings were not subject to the same kind of intense re-examination.

5 See Broughton (1989) for a thorough history and assessment of the conflicts within developmental psychology concerning social relevance and social change. Also Cole, Hood and McDermott are clear about their belief that an ecologically valid psychology can contribute to greater educational equality (1978).

6 These include Joravsky (1989), Kozulin (1990), Moll (1990), D. Newman, Griffin and Cole (1989), Tharp and Gallimore (1988), Valsiner (1988), and Van der Veer and Valsiner (1991).

7 Schreiber (1987) and *American Educator* (1989).

8 See, for example, Cole and Cole (1989); Moshman, Glover and Bruning (1987); Thomas (1992); and Vasta, Haith and Miller (1992).

9 An informative dialogue on these matters is Holzman (1990), an interview with an international group of scholars concerning the Vygotsky revival and debate.

10 Kuhn's conception of paradigm, as put forth in his 1962 book *The Structure of Scientific Revolutions*, has become part of the conventional wisdom regarding how science develops and how scientific discoveries are made. A paradigm is a way of looking at things, a general model which covers a particular segment of the physical or mental world. Examples of paradigms in science are: regarding the sun as the center of our planetary system; regarding blood as circulating; regarding the mind as heavily influenced by unconscious forces.

11 Some of the more comprehensive and influential discussions can be found in P. Brown (1973); Deleuze and Guattari (1977); Fanon (1963; 1967); Freire (1972); Gilligan (1982); Gornick and Moran (1972); Habermas (1971); Ingleby (1974, 1987); Laing (1983); Marcuse (1962); Merleau-Ponty (1964); Riegel (1979); Szasz (1961); and Walkerdine (1984; 1988).

12 Feyerabend (1978) was one of the first to challenge the paradigmist view of science, coining the term 'anti-paradigm.' In our view, the anti-paradigm is a non-interpretive, non-dualistic method which does not impose a 'model of reality' on the object of study, but is simultaneously a tool for investigating the world and a result (its transformation). In other words, the anti-paradigm is a practical-critical *activity*. See Holzman and Newman (1985) and F. Newman (1978) for extensive discussions of the anti-paradigm.

13 Wertsch (1985) notes that during the 1980s there was an ongoing debate in the Soviet Union concerning whether an 'activity-based' psychology distorts Vygotsky. Vygotsky himself did not formulate his psychology in these terms, although the concept of activity (including his frequent use of the term) permeates his writings. It was his followers, in particular Leont'ev, who used the term 'activity theory' to describe their Marxist-based psychology. According to Kozulin (1990), the German linguist Humboldt defined language as an activity in a work published in 1836.

14 The phrase 'the revolt against dualism' stems from the 1930 compilation of lectures by the American philosopher Arthur Lovejoy in a book by that name (1960). Lovejoy reviews and evaluates American and British philosophy during the first quarter of the twentieth century as 'The Age of the Great Revolt Against Dualism' (including theology and cosmology).

15 Metaphysics – an approach to understanding the world by going 'beyond' it to the realm of 'first principles,' 'causes' and abstract, universal propositions – dominated philosophy until the eighteenth century. With the establishment of modern science in the eighteenth, nineteenth and twentieth centuries, metaphysics came more and more to be a pejorative term, referring to so-called truths – metaphysical truths – which are unverifiable by any objective means.

16 For example, Piaget's voluminous body of work on the origins and development of intelligence is based on Kant's *a priori* synthetic categories. The traditional view of Piaget is that he is not a Kantian because he discovered how the categories of knowledge are constructed. However, the categories Piaget chooses to investigate are Kantian. What the child constructs is a perception and understanding of laws of motion, speed, temporality and causality that are taken by Piaget to be how the world is, independent of our construction of it. A random selection of passages from *The Essential Piaget* (Gruber and Voneche, 1977) yields statements such as the following:

> Every notion, whether it be scientific or merely a matter of common sense, presupposes a set of principles of conservation, either explicit or implicit... In the field of perception, the schema of the permanent object presupposes the elaboration of what is no doubt the most primitive of all these principles of conservation.
>
> (p. 300)

> Is our intuitive grasp of time primitive or derived? Is it identical with our intuitive grasp of velocity?
>
> (p. 548)

> Topological space is wholly inherent to the object and consists of operations worked out step by step. It therefore corresponds to no more than a series of possible perceptions capable of being juxtaposed, and the main task of such operations is to assemble the data of this space into one coherent whole.
>
> (pp. 625–6)

> Thus the perspective system which the child builds up in the course of the four substages we have identified is not perceptual but conceptual in character. It is the psychological counterpart of a projective space.
>
> (p. 626)

Finally, note Piaget's attempt to conceive of a non-Kantian world. To the extent that he can describe it, it is chaotic and totally individualistic (like, he says, the world of the very young child). Yet note that ultimately he fails even to conceptualize such a universe:

> A universe without objects would not present the character of spatial homogeneity and of coherence in displacements that marks our universe... From the point of view of causality it is a world in which the connections between things are masked by the relations between the action and its desired results; hence the subject's activity is conceived as being the primary and almost the sole motive power.
>
> (p. 250)

From our vantage point, Piaget is far more Kantian than most of the traditional literature suggests while Kant is more proto-constructionist than most of the literature suggests. Our reading of Kant is similar to that of the twentieth-century pragmatist-Kantian C. I. Lewis (1990). In the writings of this modern pragmatist-constructionist, e.g. *Mind and the World Order*, one can see more clearly the proto-constructivism implicit in Kant.

2   THE LABORATORY AS METHODOLOGY

1 Cognitive science refers to an interdisciplinary approach to the study of human cognition, including problem-solving, thinking, perception and language. In the course of their investigations into how the mind processes and stores information, cognitive scientists – who work in the fields of artificial intelligence, neuropsychology and psycholinguistics as well as psychology – have come to rely on the computer as the model for the human mind. While most psychological paradigms are inter-actionist, i.e. models of development and behavior which presume some kind of interaction between organism and environment, we are referring here to approaches which take this relationship to be explan-atory.

3   PRACTICE

1 The phrase 'method of practice' focuses on method, while the phrase 'practice of method' focuses on practice. The practice of method, there-fore, emphasizes doing something different relative to practice, rather than reifying a different method. The specific application of Marx's method discussed in Chapter 8, what we call the practice of method, is the reinitiation of practical-critical, revolutionary activity (Holzman and Newman, 1979). The practice of method is not a new method to be practiced, but a method which is a practice (in Vygotsky's words, 'a tool and a result').

2 Founded in the 1920s in Vienna, logical positivism was a self-conscious attempt to synthesize idealism and empiricism that was highly influ-enced by developments in science and mathematics, especially logic. The logical positivists attempted to construct a universal methodolog-ical criterion of verifiability which would serve as a contemporary scientific first principle to answer our most basic questions about the world and how we understand it, and resolve our most puzzling meta-scientific riddles. But logical positivism failed on its own terms (e.g. its verification principle could not be verified) and with the rise of Nazism its proponents – many of them Jewish and/or progressive – left Vienna and scattered to British and American universities.

3 No less a political personage than Francis Fukuyama, an advisor to the Bush administration, has written that we are now living through the end of history (1989). This is the ultimate victory of pragmatism.

4 While there are significant differences between and among causal models and functional models, it can be argued that, generally speak-ing, the functional is the historical outgrowth of the causal. Our justification for not examining this causal–functional distinction-for-itself is that we hope to show the whole causal–functional nexus to be

a thoroughly unsuitable paradigm for delineating the essential human method necessary to comprehend essentially human activity.

5 For an excellent discussion of Galileo's discoveries and their social-political-scientific impact, see Butterfield (1962).

6 Here and in the rest of the text we use the slash (/) to express a dialectical relationship.

7 Newman (1987) continues:

> The 'me-ness' of American culture goes beyond any single generation... The question Reich raised in Germany in the 1930s was how was it possible to transform the ideological responses, values and attitudes of a mass of people in so short a period of time. How could that have happened? How could German fascism have happened? That is an important question for us, for obvious socio-political reasons. It is also profoundly relevant to personal depression, because one of the factors of personal depression that must be engaged if we hope to help anybody with it is: how could this have happened 'just like that'? How does someone go, in the face of a serious loss, from being a relatively stable 'coper' to someone who is essentially disembodied? How does this radical breakdown occur? . . . What I believe, and what we've come to see in our social therapeutic work, is that our *normal* social interaction is so profoundly alienated and lacking a sense of *historical connectedness* that relatively minor changes in the actual process by which information is communicated and disseminated can create total transformation overnight. The absence of a sense of history leaves us extremely vulnerable.
>
> (pp. 20–2)

8 A commodity is therefore a mysterious thing, simply because in it the social character of men's labour appears to them as an objective character stamped on the product of that labour . . . [with commodities] the existence of the things *qua* commodities, and the value-relation between the products of labour which stamps them as commodities, have absolutely no connexion with their physical properties and with the material relations arising therefrom. There it is a definite social relation between men, that assumes, in their eyes, the fantastic form of a relation between things. In order, therefore, to find an analogy, we must have recourse to the mist-enveloped regions of the religious world. In that world the productions of the human brain appear as independent beings endowed with life, and entering into relation both with one another and with the products of men's hands. This I call the Fetishism which attaches itself to the products of labour, so soon as they are produced as commodities, and which is therefore inseparable from the production of commodities.

(Marx, 1967, p. 72)

9 Hood, Fiess and Aron present a radical Vygotskian critique of Piaget and Piagetian research into the development of 'causality' (1982).

Another critic of Piaget's ahistorical bias is Buck-Morss (1975). See also Chapter 1, note 16, pp. 202–3.

10   One is capable of historical transformation as an individual only insofar as one is *involved in* (more accurately, *is*) the activity of changing society in a self-conscious manner. This should not be taken to mean that one must be a revolutionary in order to change; being a revolutionary is working to change society in a very particular way. But, while being involved in the activity of self-consciously changing society is not identifiable with being a revolutionary, it is identifiable with having revolutionary consciousness, or with revolutionary, practical-critical activity in the sense Marx explicates in the theses on Feuerbach.

(Holzman and Newman, 1979, pp. 22–3)

Revolutionary activity is not to be equated with 'the activity of making a revolution.' Obviously making the revolution is a revolutionary activity (albeit a very special historical/societal one) even though not all revolutionary activity is making the revolution. Less obvious but even more important is that in the absence of the ongoing *historical* activity of *making the revolution* the societally-located, practical-critical revolutionary activity will eventually be transformed into reform. Studying twentieth century revolution makes this plain.

(F. Newman, 1989a, p. 6)

11 There has been more than two decades of opposition to Kuhn's paradigmatic position on paradigms, as first laid out in Feyerabend's book on anti-paradigms (1978).

12 For example, Cole and his colleagues, editors of *Mind in Society*, open this second publication of Vygotsky's writings in English (1978) with this very quotation. Wertsch is also subject to this error, as can be seen in the following:

Whereas Marx clearly emphasized the emergence of socially organized labor and production as the key to distinguishing humans from animals, Vygotsky considered the emergence of speech to be equally important. In this connection he made his most important and unique contributions but also departed in significant ways from the ideas of Marx and even Engels.

(1985, p. 29; see also p. 32)

Wertsch's choice of words is important; after all, given that Vygotsky was investigating the developmental relationship between speech and thinking, it would make sense that he would emphasize semiotics and communication. But Wertsch sees this stress as a deviation, not merely a placement of emphasis. In this he reveals a position on language and communication that is, to our understanding, in opposition to Vygotsky's Marxian analysis.

In setting up the opposition between 'socially organized labor and production' and 'the emergence of speech,' Wertsch appears to be following in the tradition of Western philosophy, psychology and linguistics, which treat language and communication as outside the realm of socially organized labor. That tradition takes the ontogenetic and phylogenetic emergence of language as occurring in some interplay with social production, not *as* social production. But for both Marx and Vygotsky, language is a product of socially organized labor. Over and over Vygotsky insists that signs, speech and meaning (the host of meaning and communication concepts) are material – not metaphorical – tools, meaning that they have been produced by human labor. This critical fact is often lost in discussions of Vygotsky's claim that signs are psychological tools; they are wrenched from their history of social production and appear as if from the air, all ready to be used. But human beings are not just tool users; they are toolmakers.

It is worth noting that to the extent that Vygotsky 'deviated' from Marx, it was in not accompanying Marx down the functionalist path. Indeed, Vygotsky identifies 'labor as the fundamental means of relating humans to nature' (1978, p. 19) rather than as a way of distinguishing humans from animals. In so doing, Vygotsky is free to view thinking/speaking as the 'fundamental means of relating humans to humans.' The unifying principle connecting Vygotsky's correct formulation about labor and his recognition of the fundamentality of thinking/speaking is, of course, revolutionary activity, which relates humans to humans to nature. It is for this reason that we reject the traditional distinction between 'dialectical materialism' and 'historical materialism' in favor of dialectical historical materialism (Chapter 1, see note 2).

13 Human development did not and does not begin propositionally. The concept of proposition comes out of human life. Taking propositions as fundamental to human life biases one's analysis of human life in favor of the propositional. It was this overly cognitive – and logical as opposed to active and practical – world view that Marx challenged.

14 Those, like Lichtman (1977), who argue that Marx's conception of humankind denies any essence at all are both right and wrong. For the absence of any essence in the Platonic or Aristotelian sense is, seemingly contradictorily, itself the distinctly human essence. The continuous creation of essence by revolutionary activity is the essence/non-essence of our species. Human beings are essence-makers, toolmakers, revolution-makers, meaning-makers.

15 Almost from the beginnings of the first socialist state and the beginnings of psychology, there have been attempts to synthesize Marx and Freud. Most of these begin with the assumption that there are deep internal contradictions in the works of both Marx and Freud, and that parts of the one can be 'synthesized' with parts of the other. Some of the more notable (influential and/or interesting) discussions are those by Vygotsky's student and colleague Luria (1978), the Soviet philosopher Volosinov (1987), those of the Frankfurt School (e.g. Adorno, 1951; Fromm, 1973; Habermas, 1971), various psychologists, philosophers and social critics (e.g. P. Brown, 1973; Jacoby, 1975; Lichtman, 1977), and of course Reich (1970).

4   THE ZONE OF PROXIMAL DEVELOPMENT

1 Vygotsky used the Russian word 'obuchenie,' which refers to both teaching and learning. Since Vygotsky (1978), the Cole *et al.* translation, it is conventional to refer to the relationship between learning and development, rather than instruction and development.

2 Critiques of IQ tests and other diagnostic methods and materials for assessing development and learning proliferated in the 1960s and '70s. Most, however, left untouched the fundamental bias inherent in the view that learning depends on development. For example, attempts to develop culture-free and/or culture-fair IQ tests addressed the more obvious political and social biases inherent in testing (race, class and gender biases, in particular), but they did not question the scientific invalidity of testing itself and its basis in the separatist perspective on learning and development. As we have said elsewhere (Holzman and Newman, 1985),

> culture-free IQ tests accept the possibility of 'pure' intellect and, by extension, 'pure' development. Even the more progressive move-ment toward culture-*fair* tests still holds to a separation of development and learning; for one thing, it assumes that the domi-nant culture has not permeated every aspect of all of our lives, including those who are 'culturally deprived,' 'culturally different,' and so on. However, this is obviously false, for if it were not, IQ tests (unfair, culture-fair, or culture-free), themselves a product of the dominant culture, would not be used at all!
>
> (p. 60)

3 Knowledge about infancy was not available during Vygotsky's life. Recent findings of the complex psychological functioning of infants (e.g. Bruner, 1975; Kaye, 1982; Lock, 1978; Newson, 1978; and Ratner and Bruner, 1978) has led to speculation concerning Vygotsky's empha-sis on speech, school instruction and the ZPD. For example, to Van der Veer and IJzendoorn (1985) Vygotsky's 'neglect' of infant development reinforces the belief that he took pre-verbal psychological processes to be passive and 'natural.' In our view, Vygotsky's extended discussion of the development of language is a refutation of this position. Wertsch (1985) sees findings from infancy research as compatible with Vygotsky's work but suggests that it might bear more on the precursors of the ZPD than on the zone itself. We think findings that infants' psychological functioning occurs through joint activity is evidence *for* the ZPD, and in fact such a position was anticipated by Vygotsky himself, e.g. in his discussion of the development of pointing (1978, p. 56). See Holzman (1985) for a critique of the pragmatist interpretations given to much of this research.

4 In his commentary on Vygotsky's work, Piaget (in Vygotsky, 1962) defends himself against Vygotsky's charges in a way that even more clearly reveals his separatist position on learning and development and his reductionistic, psychologistic (while biologically biased)

methodology. For example, as part of his argument that lack of awareness is a 'residue of egocentrism,' Piaget argues that

> a subject whose perspective is determined by his actions has no reason for becoming aware of anything except its results; decentering, on the other hand, i.e., shifting one's focus and comparing one action with other possible ones, particularly with the actions of other people, leads to an awareness of 'how' and to true operations.

> (p. 13)

Moreover, while Piaget says he is in agreement with Vygotsky that spontaneous and scientific concepts start at different points and later meet, he clearly has no dialectical understanding of 'starting' or 'meeting' (or development):

> [We are] in complete accord, if he means that a true meeting takes place between the sociogenesis of scientific notions (in the history of science and in the transmission of knowledge from one generation to the next) and the psychogenesis of 'spontaneous' structures (influenced, to be sure, by interaction with the social, familial, scholastic, etc. milieu), and not simply that psychogenesis is entirely determined by the historical and the ambient culture.

> (p. 12)

5 In accordance with conventional usage, we use such brackets ({}) to indicate that what is contained within them is a unity.
6 D. Newman, Griffin and Cole understand Leont'ev's concept of appropriation to be a replacement of Piaget's biologically oriented metaphor with a socio-historical one. Through active involvement in culturally organized activities children 'appropriate' cultural tools (1989, pp. 62–5).
7 Kozulin (1990) cites an article Vygotsky wrote called 'The Collective as a Factor in the Development of a Disabled Child.'
8 Chapter 3, see note 3.
9 Bakhurst (1988) makes an even stronger point. He claims that it is *a priori* impossible for the child to mean what the adult means. This interesting argument arises in Bakhurst's critique of some of Vygotsky's critics. According to Bakhurst, Vygotsky has been criticized for employing a 'third-person perspective' relative to how the child internalizes meaning, which causes him to ignore the fact that 'how the child is able to see his own actions as meaningful must surely be expressed in the relation between the child and the contents of his mind' (p. 104).

Bakhurst points out that such an argument rests on the assumption that a necessary condition for any account of internalization is that it must make sense from the child's point of view. But this cannot be the case for a child first acquiring concepts:

> We have no idea how to imagine what it is like to develop the ability to imagine, to think about what it is like to come to be able to think, to hope, to want, to believe. And we have no such idea not through lack of imagination, but because there is no idea to have. There is no

first-person perspective on the acquisition of those abilities for, prior to their acquisition, the child has no perspective. Thus, the qualitative leap from a stage of primitive problem-solving activity to fully developed consciousness mediated by language cannot be retrospectively bridged by an act of imagination.

(1988, pp. 104–5)

Bakhurst also notes that this argument takes facts about meaning to be subjective; meaning is understood as a special relation between an individual and the contents of her/his mental world. On this account, if we want to explain how a certain meaning is acquired we have to look into the mind of the person who is 'making' the meaning. Bakhurst, appealing to Wittgenstein (1953), notes the difficulties inherent in this position. If we treat ideas as 'mental pictures,' some interpretation on the part of the child will be needed in order to explain how she/he makes the correct association between a particular sign and a particular idea or mental picture. But such interpretation requires capacities, such as memory and abstraction, which both Wittgenstein and Vygotsky claim have language acquisition as a prerequisite! We cannot assign such capacities to the child first learning language.

It thus seems that the empiricist's only option is to hold that the ideas before the child's mind require no interpretation; they are intrinsic representational mental objects. But this is a counsel of despair, for at best the invocation of such objects is just a metaphysically laden way of saying that interpretation must end *somewhere*, and at worst it is the incantation of the very philosophical prejudice Vygotsky is challenging; that meaning can only be understood as a special property of mental objects.

(Bakhurst, 1988, p. 106)

10 See Harding and Hintikka (1983), *Discovering Reality: Feminist Perspectives on Epistemology, Metaphysics, Methodology and Philosophy of Science*, particularly the articles by Addelson, Keller and Grontkowski, and Moulton.
11 See Vickers (1991) for a philosophically traditional but clear and succinct history of cognition as the dominant paradigm of human identity.

5 PLAYING IN/WITH THE ZPD

1 Ethnographic and observational studies of preschool and primary school classrooms have found that play is an infrequently occurring phenomenon (Adelman, 1976; Eynard and Walkerdine, 1981; Wood, McMahon and Cranstoun, 1980). Adelman, quoting an unpublished PhD thesis by King (1977), makes the further point that when teachers do use play activities they do so to make school work more relevant and interesting; the children redefine such activities as work. Teachers thus turn play into work instead of turning work into play (Adelman, 1987, p. 27).

2 While a thorough examination of theories of play is well beyond the scope of this book, we would be remiss if we did not mention the influence of Piaget (1962), for whom play is essentially an assimilation of reality to the self, and Erikson (1977), for whom play is a critical means of 'working through' emotional conflicts. The work of even the most social of social constructionists shows the influence of Piaget's and Freud's dualistic and instrumentalist understanding of play. For example, Sutton-Smith, one of the leading play researchers in the United States, emphasizes that children's play provides evidence that they can take the role of the other (1976); Bruner, Jolly and Sylva (1976) introduce their impressive collection of numerous authors' work on the role of play in development and evolution by noting that one of the important things about play is that it is 'the first carrier of rule systems through which a world of cultural restraint is substituted for the operation of impulse' (p. 20). See Adelman (1987) for a review of nineteenth-century views of play among those now identified as important philosophers of education (e.g. Froebel and Rousseau).

3 For example, Goffman treats human beings and their interactions with social structures, institutions and relationships as dramas. As one example, consider the 'burdens sustained by normal appearances' when people need to keep an individual from suspecting something out of the ordinary is taking place. According to Goffman, they have 'two dramaturgical tasks': 'to play out roles that are alien to them, as when a policeman acts like a graduate student in order to penetrate a radical organization,' and to 'act natural' so as to conceal their concern about giving themselves away (1971, p. 268). See Gouldner (1970) for a critique of Goffman's dramaturgical metaphor.

4 See the series of studies by McNamee and her colleagues (Harris-Schmidt and McNamee, 1986; McNamee, 1987; McNamee, McLane, Cooper and Kerwin, 1985; McLane and McNamee, 1990).

5 It is interesting but not surprising that much Vygotskian and neo-Vygotskian research outside of school settings sets up play situations (e.g. Wertsch's puzzle copying) but does not utilize Vygotsky's analysis of play. The everyday life settings set up by the researchers involved in the Vygotskian-inspired Rockefeller University ecological validity project discussed in Chapter 2 (such as cooking clubs and 'IQ bees') were in fact play situations, yet they were approached as cognitive problem-solving situations. The researchers approached play not historically (as revolutionary activity) but experimentally (as an experimental setting). In this, they strayed from Vygotsky's goal (a psychology of human, i.e. historical, beings) and his revolutionary practice.

6 THE STUDY OF THINKING AND SPEECH

1 Vygotsky makes the distinction between meaning and sense in his discussion of inner speech. He says,

> A word's sense is the aggregate of all the psychological facts that arise in our consciousness as a result of the word . . . a dynamic, fluid

and complex formation which has several zones that vary in their stability. Meaning is only one of those zones of the sense that the word acquires in the context of speech... Meaning is nothing more than a potential that can only be realized in living speech, and in living speech meaning is only a cornerstone in the edifice of sense.

(1987, pp. 275–6)

Bakhurst notes that

while analytic philosophers may deride the primitive distinction between sense and meaning on which his account rests, Vygotsky, in turn, would have scorned the analytic philosopher's propensity to tie the primary meaning of expressions to rigid 'assertability' or 'truth' conditions, and to consign issues of 'imagery' and 'metaphor' to the outer regions of the theory of meaning.

(1988, p. 111)

2 Many activity theorists incorporate the work of Vygotsky's student and colleague Leont'ev in their research. Leont'ev (1978) proposed that in a theory of activity there were distinct but interrelated levels of analysis and a specific unit of analysis associated with each level. He distinguished three levels: activity (associated with motives); action (associated with goals); and operation (associated with conditions). Besides Wertsch, those especially influenced by Leont'ev are the Soviets Davydov and Zinchenko, who also take 'tool-mediated action' to be the critically important unit of analysis. Even granting the taxonomic validity of this account, however, the problem we are addressing is not eliminated, for the unmediated nature of activity is still denied.

3 Vygotsky (1962) includes an appendix in which Piaget responds to Vygotsky's criticisms of his work. We find his responses unconvincing. For example, with reference to the point made here, Piaget says that his subsequent work shows that he did not separate thought from action. Rather than addressing directly the methodological and philosophically factual differences between himself and Vygotsky, Piaget merely defends himself against Vygotsky's charges.

4 While some contemporary psychologists and linguists have taken Piaget to task for this logical–methodological error (cf. Donaldson, 1978, for a critique of Piaget's assumptive methodology in general; Hood, 1977, and Hood, Fiess and Aron, 1982, with regard to Piaget's assumptions concerning the development of causal reasoning and talk about causality), many more have uncritically perpetuated this dualistic and mechanistic understanding of the relationship between thinking and speaking, even while adding a social-constructionist facade to what remains basically a Piagetian metaphysical superstructure (e.g. Bickerton, 1981; Bruner, 1983; Slobin, 1973). Language development research is an area where the impact of the method of pragmatics is clear – in how the field has been shaped along Piagetian lines and in its misguided use of Vygotsky to critique structuralist approaches.

5 In Chapter 3 we stated that while animals may communicate they don't make meaning, and that what distinguishes human beings from ani-

mals is not the ability to communicate but the ability to make meaning. It might seem that there is a disagreement between us and Vygotsky on the issue of whether other species do or do not communicate. But what Vygotsky means by saying that other animals do not communicate is, of course, precisely what we mean by saying that they may communicate; like him, we are pointing out that other species do not make meaning.

6 Kant distinguished between 'occasion' and 'cause.' *A priori* synthetic categories are both grounded in experience and themselves the condition for, or occasion of, experience. For Kant, then, as for Marx and Vygotsky, there is no causal predecessor.

7 See Chapter 3, note 3.

8 Bruner is referring to the influential work in the philosophy of science by Popper.

9 These quotations contain, in addition to the main point we are making, statements whose implications are questionable, to say the least: 'The development of language, then, involves two people negotiating.' Can Bruner really mean to reduce the complexity of language development to dyadic negotiation 'without a sufficient sample of instances'? Clearly, if there is insufficient data for an inductive leap, it is Bruner – not the child learning language – who is making it.

10 In contrast to recent attempts to formulate sharper and more sophisticated rules, our enterprise is to understand language without introducing the conceptual tool or intervening variable of rules.

7 COMPLETING THE HISTORICAL VYGOTSKY

1 What we find problematic is the level of dualism introduced by representationalism. Just as we do not deny empirics but question the (pseudo-)method of empiricism, we do not deny that one thing can represent another, but do question the general theory that dualistically posits things and their representation.

2 It might strike readers as contradictory that we are saying learning is not ahead of development, given that Vygotsky says it is. Our point is that the language used – 'ahead of' – connotes linearity or temporality, and, more generally, instrumentation. Some scholars have addressed the ambiguity of linguistic connotation in terms of the inadequacy of translation from one language to another. For example, Cole makes the important point that readings of Vygotsky's work are dependent on the interpretations we give to particular Russian words. He cites two examples: in the 1962 *Thought and Language*, *razvitie* is often translated as 'evolution,' while in the 1987 version it is translated as 'development'; '*obuchenie* . . . although often translated . . . as "teaching" in fact can be used for both the activities of students and teachers, implicating a double sided process of teaching/learning, a mutual transformation of teacher and student' (quoted in Moll, 1990, pp. 23–4). We in no way deny the legitimacy of this concern; our point is about logic and methodology, not Russian and English. Our concern can be

understood in relation to *and* and *for*, to the distinction we have been making throughout this book between tool for result and tool-and-result. By arguing that learning is not ahead of development we mean to emphasize that learning is not an instrumentation.

3 Since the 1970s an empirical debate has been conducted among researchers concerning whether imitation is 'progressive.' Messer (1991), in a review of Speidel and Nelson's (1989) volume on the role of imitation in language learning, points out the long-standing difference between the common sense view – ask the person on the street or a parent how children learn language and they will answer 'By imitating' – and the academic theorizing which, until recently, was adamant in its position that imitation could not possibly be how children learn. The contemporary debate is focused on the learning of language particulars, such as syntax, morphology, phonology or vocabulary in order to determine whether imitation facilitates cognitive processes assumed necessary for learning how to speak, such as encoding information, matching referent with linguistic structure, and remembering. As an example, Bloom, Hood and Lightbown (1974) hypothesized that 'Imitating the model utterance provides experience in encoding the relevant aspects of the situation to which the utterance refers, consolidating the mapping or coding relation between form and content' (p. 418). Whatever active role the child is said to play in her/his learning, the only thing that is transformational in this account is perhaps the grammar, not learning or development.

4 Empirical studies by psycholinguists have found variation in the extent to which children learning to speak imitate the language they hear (e.g. Bloom, Hood and Lightbown, 1974; Moerk, 1977; Speidel and Nelson, 1989). None, however, disputes the fact that all children imitate some of the time. In our view, the significance of individual variation in imitative behaviors among children is significant only if one is concerned with behavior and not activity.

5 For example, Joravsky refers to 'the legendary aura that radiates from Vygotsky' (1989, p. 255) and, in an earlier article (1987), argues that Vygotsky was deified.

6 Vygotsky's family name was Vygodsky. Believing the name derived from the town Vygotovo where his family originated, when he was in his twenties Lev changed his own name to reflect this (Blanck, 1990, p. 33).

7 This speech, entitled 'The Methodology of Reflexologic and Psychological Investigations,' was delivered at the Second Neurological Congress in Leningrad; it marked Vygotsky's first public appearance before the Russian psychological community.

8 The relationship between psychology and ideology – particularly the ways in which psychology serves capitalism – has been written about extensively. Foucault (1978) and others, for example, provide sophisticated historical analyses of the complex ways psychology and psychologists have wielded power; their work challenges simplistic functionalist and mechanistic accounts of psychology's role in oppres-

sion and exploitation and points out some of the positive, humane effects of psychology.

Others, such as Ratner (1991), take the view that psychology and social practices are reified and intertwined to such a degree that a new psychology is not possible:

> If political viewpoints truly underlie the conceptualizing and acceptance of psychological doctrines, then it follows that sociohistorical psychology will become increasingly acceptable as social change becomes politically more palatable.
>
> (p. 320)

We think these views reject both Vygotsky as revolutionary scientist and the science of revolution. Vygotsky's search for method was neither a pragmatic tool for improving the existing psychology (a liberal god is a god nevertheless), nor an idealist result of 'social change.' Rather, his critique of psychology – and ours – is the practical-critical activity of discarding psychology as adaptation to society in favor of revolution.

9 The collapse of the Soviet Union has helped to mask the profound crisis in which the contemporary world capitalist economy finds itself. Nevertheless, it is widely acknowledged – by economists and commentators of various persuasions in the United States, Western Europe and Japan – that the US-dominated world economy is in very serious trouble.

Under what turns out to have been the bogus pretext of a Soviet threat, for forty years the US manufacturing base – along with the transportation and communication infrastructures that support it – were allowed to deteriorate while the country's resources were largely diverted to military production. A small number of people made enormous profits, relatively quickly, from the militarization of the US economy. But military production, being non-productive, dead-end production, has resulted not in development, or even growth, but in the atrophying of the United States' productive capacity, which had been, for much of the twentieth century, the planet's industrial dynamo.

The relatively short lived post-World War II Bretton Woods Agreement – which made the US dollar the standard currency of the world capitalist market – created the conditions for massive non-productive speculation by US (and other) financiers. Like military production, the trade in paper has also been enormously profitable for a handful of people, but has similarly contributed nothing to economic development. Given the moribund condition of the US economy, it would take trillions of dollars sunk into the manufacturing base to revive it. However, those with the capital to invest continue to keep it where it can turn the fastest and easiest profit – in military production and speculation.

While the capitalist economic crisis is most apparent among the industrialized nations, in the United States (and Britain, where the decay of the industrial base has been even more rapid), evidence of its universal nature is growing, e.g. the recent drop in Japan's forty-year economic boom. Even more revealing of the limitations facing world capitalism is the inability of US, Western European or Japanese capital to invest in any significant way in the capitalist development of Eastern Europe and the former Soviet Union.

Hand-in-glove with the decay of the industrial base of the nations of the Northern Hemisphere is the debt crisis facing the impoverished nations of the Southern Hemisphere. The astronomical debt owed by the non-industrialized nations of the South to the financial institutions based in the industrialized nations of the North has created an untenable financial stalemate for both. The billions lent have resulted not in development, but in the futher dependence of the impoverished South on the more wealthy North (and the South's continued underdevelopment). Thus the debt can *never* be repaid. The ability of the North to continue to squeeze debt repayments from the South is limited (you can't get blood from a stone). The North's continued pressure (in the form of International Monetary Fund and World Bank demands to cut back even further the living standards of an already starving population) cannot but result in continued political instability and the emergence of revolutionary movements in the poor nations, despite the death of European communism. The South's inability to repay the debt cannot but lead to a financial collapse of unprecedented proportions in the North. The move to put Eastern Europe and the former Soviet Union into the loop of debt and underdevelopment, while it will result in some quick profits for Western financiers, can only intensify the crisis and accelerate the decay of world productive capabilities and living standards.

10 Green and Newman argue that American ideology is an 'exceptionalist' capitalist ideology, a form of bourgeois ideology arising from the European social contract philosophers (of both the empiricist and rationalistic variety), which transformed an ideology of progress into an ideology of destiny. They note,

> The essence of American ideology is this contradiction: The importation of the ideology of progress from Europe (where it had evolved out of what was a progressive class struggle) and the use of that ideology to justify a no-contest fight with Native Americans and the enslavement of African people.

> (1986, p. 21)

They continue,

> In the framing of the United States Constitution, the contractual and conservative liberalism of Locke predominated over the more transcendent and absolute notion of the 'rights of man' of the Continental tradition, reflecting the propertied and slave-holder status of its ratifiers. However, this imported liberalism . . . was not organic to the American experience, and it assumed the pragmatic and commercial cast of the Founding Fathers from the outset.

> (pp. 23–4)

11 Rosa Luxemburg was a Jewish-Polish Marxist economist and revolutionary. Exiled from her native Poland, she became a leader in the

German Social Democratic Party, was jailed for her opposition to World War II and became a founder of the German Communist Party in 1919. She was assassinated for her leadership of the aborted Spartacist (communist) uprising in Germany that same year.

Her major contributions to Marxist theorical development are to be found in two books, *The Accumulation of Capital* (1968) and *An Anti-Critique* (1972), in which she challenged Marx's analysis of capitalism in *Das Kapital* as a closed (self-contained) economic system. Luxemburg demonstrated that capitalism was, in fact, dependent for its growth on the penetration and transformation of pre-capitalist economies. Her theories were rejected by the orthodox Marxists of her time, but have begun to enjoy wider influence as an explanation of the seemingly permanent decline of the world capitalist economy in the last decades of the twentieth century.

12 Manifestations of this terminal illness are new emotional maladies such as panic disorders and addictions of all kinds, which are inseparable from their categorization and location as individual pathology. Examples of coercive psychological practices that are fairly recent developments include: the manufacture and widespread use of new drugs to control symptoms of panic disorder, obsessive compulsive behavior, depression and schizophrenia; the return of electroshock therapy; new technologies such as MRI (Magnetic Resonance Imaging), scanning and PET (Positron Emission Tomography) scanning to delineate structural abnormalities of mental disorders; and behavior modification therapies such as 'tough love' (Neff, 1984) originally derived from family therapy (Haley, 1984) in which parents are directed to lock their 'uncontrollable' children out of the house and make their bed-wetting children bury their wet sheets in the backyard.

13 Feminism, for example, has attempted to deal with sexism by giving women a heightened awareness of their oppression, showing them how the social institutions reproduce that oppression, and teaching men (those who are willing to learn) that – regardless of their intentions – they participate in the institutionalized oppression of women. But the women's movement has failed to build the environment necessary to do battle with those institutions; its battlefield is in fact determined by the institutions because it has not organized outside of them. Similarly, the black liberation movement, the peace movement and the environmentalist movement have generated awareness of, but no independent organized opposition to, institutionalized racism, militarism and the corporate depredation of the environment.

14 Ratner (1991) contains one of the few discussions of a Vygotskian approach to psychopathology. He devotes seventy pages to 'testing' the applicability of sociohistorical psychology (the work of Vygotsky and his followers) to extreme psychosis, saying little about less debilitating neuroses. He states his purpose this way: 'If sociohistorical psychology can render madness intelligible, then the case is strengthened for contending that sociohistorical psychology is an adequate paradigm for explaining all psychological activity' (Ratner, 1991, p. 243).

Ratner delineates the asocial and coercive character of traditional psychology and psychiatry; he also points out the failure of humanistic psychology to engage in social analysis and shows the positivistic roots it shares with behavior modification and biomedical treatment. What is most interesting for our purposes – exploring the relationship between politics and psychology – however, is his failure to see in sociohistorical psychology the possibility of a practice, i.e. to see Vygotsky's method. Ratner believes that since current social conditions are not conducive to such a humane, progressive psychology one cannot be created. He concludes:

> Psychotherapy can only be successful in a humane social system which complements rather than contradicts therapeutic care. Ironically, a more humane society will need less psychiatry and psychotherapy because people will be more at ease. In other words, the most effective psychiatry is that which occurs in a humane society which reduces the need for psychiatry. Conversely, a malevolent society that creates psychological problems and creates a massive need for psychiatry is one where psychiatry cannot solve those overwhelming problems.
>
> (Ratner, 1991, p. 305)

This perspective is an expression of orthodox Marxism similar to that of the progressives of whom Reich was so critical. The emergence of a new psychology, one that could engage the pain, repression and oppression people experience and that keeps them from participating in making social change, is regarded as being impossible until social change occurs. Moreover, once that happens, there will be no need for it. Ratner's conclusion seems to us erroneous empirically and methodologically. Not only is there no empirical evidence that people are more at ease under more humane and/or socialist systems (it is likely that socialism and/or communism would produce as many or more emotional conflicts), to envision a utopia is in opposition to Marx's and Vygotsky's dialectical historical materialism. Completing Vygotsky, as opposed to applying him, involves creating a progressive psychology in the service of progressive politics, not the other way around.

15 The anti-institutions which comprise the independent political movement built over the past twenty years include (in addition to the East Side Center for Social Therapy and affiliated centers across the United States where social therapy is practiced, the East Side Institute for Short Term Psychotherapy, and the Barbara Taylor School, the Vygotskian elementary school in Harlem, New York): the community-supported and artist-run Castillo Cultural Center; the All Stars Talent Show Network, a 10,000-member youth organization produced by Castillo; the New Alliance Party, the fourth largest electoral party in the United States; the 150,000-member Rainbow Lobby, the Washington, DC-based citizens lobby that advocates for democracy in the United States and abroad; and the International Peoples' Law Institution.

16 In his influential book *Asylums*, Goffman (1962) coined the term 'total institution' to characterize mental institutions, hospitals, prisons, etc.,

whose 'official' purpose (curing illness, rehabilitation, etc.) becomes displaced by another priority, which is to perpetuate their own existence.

17 One example of an anti-institution in the mainstream is the Somerset Community Action Program (SCAP) in New Jersey. Community Action Programs were initiated in the United States in the late 1960s as part of the 'War on Poverty.' They are government-funded institutions providing educational, legal and other services to poor communities (and as such are traditional institutions in the mainstream). Central to these programs is community control, i.e. the community's (consumers') right to determine the kind of services they receive. In the late 1980s, SCAP was involved in a battle with the federal government over the right of the community to control it. SCAP's Head Start program (government-funded comprehensive education, health and mental health services for preschoolers from low-income families – 90 per cent live below the official poverty line) had initiated a radically progressive educational practice developed initially at the Barbara Taylor School and employing social therapists from the East Side Institute for Short Term Psychotherapy to train their staff. The federal agency controlling Head Start monies accused SCAP of violating Head Start regulations by 'bringing politics' into Head Start and threatened to cut off its funding. A prolonged court case was settled in SCAP's favor, largely due to SCAP's attorneys' successful argument that this was an issue of academic freedom and community control, and to the support of the SCAP community and professionals who attested to the high professional level and success of the Head Start program. SCAP has continued to advance its social therapeutic work within its own agency and to train Head Start staffs across the country.

18 The distinction between undevelopment, or nondevelopment, and underdevelopment is useful for understanding the contemporary crisis of psychology. We borrow the term underdevelopment from economics. Most provocatively used by the Guyanese revolutionary Walter Rodney in his book *How Europe Underdeveloped Africa*, the term underdevelopment is applied to countries in Asia, Africa and Latin America that were once colonies. Colonization resulted in the systematic stripping of the colony's natural resources by which it maintained self-sufficiency, albeit being undeveloped, and turning these resources into a source of capitalist expansion and, thereby, turning the country/culture into one dependent on the world market. According to Rodney (1974), the economic backwardness and underdevelopment of these now neo-colonies are the symptoms, not the causes, of their problems. Speaking psychologically, the importation of drugs into poor communities underdevelops these communities and the individuals who comprise them: the sub-economy of drug-dealing, often the only means of livelihood in impoverished inner-city communities, dramatically and tragically underdevelops men, women and children; indeed, it too often kills them. A more subtle, but no less vicious, example is the pervasive educational approach to poor urban children known as remediation. As long as what it means to be developed is defined by

those in power, those not in power will remain un-and underdeveloped; an approach that presumes to help them 'catch up' only serves to underdevelop them. (See Holzman and Newman, 1985; Strickland and Holzman, 1988.)

19 As we have said before, Vygotsky did not fully adhere to Marx's conception of revolutionary activity. His practice was therefore not fully historical, but an historico-experimental activity.

8   LOGIC AND PSYCHOTHERAPY

1 In a personal account of the ecological validity project and its demise as a scientific movement, Holzman (1986) identifies validity as a bourgeois conception ultimately constrained by the implicit definition of science as a description of alienated reality:

> No matter how progressive one's intentions, no matter how sensitive one is to the fact of the social organization of human activity, no matter how critical one's stance is toward biased traditional psychology, the search for scientific validity based on the acceptance of alienation is still oriented toward maintenance of the social order, not its transformation.

(p. 134)

2 For discussions about the early years of the Barbara Taylor School, see Biesta and Miedema (1989), Holzman (1987), LaCerva (1992) and Strickland and Holzman (1988).

3 Holzman (1992) discusses further the ongoing development of this radical Vygotskian pedagogy as an advance over consciousness-raising methods of dealing with sexism and homophobia in the classroom.

Bibliography

Addelson, K.P. (1983). The man of professional wisdom. In S. Harding and M.B. Hintikka (Eds), *Discovering reality: feminist perspectives on epistemology, metaphysics, methodology, and philosophy of science*. Dordrecht: D. Reidel Publishing Company, pp. 165–86.

Adelman, C. (1976). *The use of objects in the education of 3 to 5 year old children*. London: Final Report to the Social Science Research Council.

Adelman, C. (1987). Self-activity and research into theories of play. *Evaluation and research in education, 1(3)*, 113–29.

Adorno, T.W. (1951). Freudian theory and the pattern of fascist propoganda. In G. Roheim (Ed.), *Psychoanalysis and culture*. New York: International University Press.

American Educator. (1989).

Apfelbaum, E. (1986). Prolegomena for a history of social psychology: some hypotheses concerning its emergence in the 20th century and its raison d'être. In K.S. Larsen (Ed.), *Dialectics and ideology in psychology*. Norwood, NJ: Ablex Publishing Corporation, pp. 3–13.

Austin, J. (1962). *How to do things with words*. Oxford: Oxford University Press.

Bacon, F. (1960). *New organon*. New York: The Liberal Arts Press.

Bakhurst, D.J. (1986). Thought, speech and the genesis of meaning: on the 50th anniversary of Vygotsky's '*Myshlenie i rech*'. *Studies in soviet thought, 31*, 103–29.

Bakhurst, D.J. (1988). E.V. Ilyenkov and contemporary Soviet philosophy. Unpublished D. Phil. dissertation, Exeter College, Oxford.

Barker, R.G. (1968). *Ecological psychology*. Stanford, CA: Stanford University Press.

Bateson, G. (1942). Social planning and the concept of deutero-learning. In Conference of Science, Philosophy and Religion (Ed.), *Science, philosophy and religion: second symposium*. New York, pp. 81–97. Reprinted in G. Bateson (1972), *Steps to an ecology of mind*. New York: Ballantine Books, pp. 159–76.

Bernstein, R.J. (1978). *The restructuring of social and political theory*. Philadelphia, PA: University of Pennsylvania Press.

Bickerton, D. (1981). *Roots of language*. Ann Arbor, MI: Karoma Publishers.

Biesta, G. and Miedema, S. (1989). Vygotskij in Harlem: de Barbara Taylor School. *Jeugd en samenleving, 9,* 547–62.

Blanck, G. (1990). Vygotsky: the man and his cause. In L. Moll (Ed.), *Vygotsky and education.* Cambridge: Cambridge University Press, pp. 31–58.

Bloom, L. (1970). *Language development: form and function in emerging grammars.* Cambridge, MA: MIT Press.

Bloom, L. (1973). *One word at a time: the use of single-word utterances before syntax.* The Hague: Mouton.

Bloom, L. *et al.* (1991). *Language development from two to three.* Cambridge: Cambridge University Press.

Bloom, L., Hood, L. and Lightbown, P. (1974). Imitation in language development: if, when and why. *Cognitive psychology, 6,* 380–420. Reprinted in L. Bloom *et al.* (1991), *Language development from two to three.* Cambridge: Cambridge University Press, pp. 399–433.

Brenner, E. (1992). Theater of the unorganized: the radical independence of the Castillo Cultural Center. *The drama review, 36(3),* 28–60.

Bronfenbrenner, U. (1977). Toward an experimental ecology of human development. *American psychologist, 32,* 513–31.

Broughton, J.M. (1987). An introduction to critical developmental psychology. In J.M. Broughton (Ed.), *Critical theories of psychological development.* New York: Plenum, pp. 1–30.

Brown, A.L. and Ferrara, R.A. (1985). Diagnosing zones of proximal development. In J.V. Wertsch (Ed.), *Culture, communication and cognition: Vygotskian perspectives.* Cambridge: Cambridge University Press, pp. 273–305.

Brown, A.L. and French, L.A. (1979). The zone of potential development: implications for intelligence testing in the year 2000. *Intelligence, 3,* 255–77.

Brown, P. (Ed.), (1973). *Radical psychology.* New York: Harper Colophon Books.

Bruner, J.S. (1975). The ontogenesis of speech acts. *Journal of child language, 2(1),* 1–19.

Bruner, J.S. (1983). *Child's talk: learning to use language.* New York: W.W. Norton & Co.

Bruner, J.S. (1985). Vygotsky: a historical and conceptual perspective. In J.V. Wertsch (Ed.), *Culture, communication and cognition: Vygotskian perspectives.* Cambridge: Cambridge University Press, pp. 21–34.

Bruner, J.S. (1987). Prologue to the English edition. In L.S. Vygotsky, *The collected works of L.S. Vygotsky. Vol. 1.* New York: Plenum, pp. 1–16.

Bruner, J.S., Jolly, A. and Sylva, K. (Eds), (1976). *Play: its role in development and evolution.* New York: Basic Books.

Brunswik, E. (1943). Organismic achievement and environmental probability. *Psychological review, 50,* 255–72.

Buck-Morss, S. (1975). Socio-economic bias in Piaget's theory and its implications for cross-cultural studies. *Human development, 18,* 35–49.

Bulhan, H.A. (1985). *Frantz Fanon and the psychology of oppression.* New York: Plenum.

Butterfield, H. (1962). *Origins of modern science.* New York: Collier Books.

Campione, J.C., Brown, A.L., Ferrara, R.A. and Bryant, N.R. (1984). The zone of proximal development: implications for individual differences and learning. In B. Rogoff and J.V. Wertsch (Eds), Children's learning in the 'zone of proximal development.' *New directions for child development*, no. 23. San Francisco: Jossey-Bass.

Chomsky, N. (1957). *Syntactic structures*. The Hague: Mouton.

Chomsky, N. (1965). *Aspects of the theory of syntax*. Cambridge, MA: MIT Press.

Clay, M.M. and Cazdan, C.B. (1990). A Vygotskian interpretation of Reading Recovery. In L. Moll (Ed.), *Vygotsky and education*. Cambridge: Cambridge University Press, pp. 206–22.

Cole, M. (1979). Epilogue: a portrait of Luria. In A.R. Luria, *The making of mind: a personal account of Soviet psychology*. Cambridge, MA: Harvard University Press, pp. 189–225.

Cole, M. (1990a). Cultural psychology: a once and future discipline? In J.J. Berman (Ed.), *Nebraska symposium on motivation: cross-cultural perspectives*. Lincoln, NE: University of Nebraska Press.

Cole, M. (1990b). Cultural psychology: some general principles and a concrete example. Paper presented at the Second International Congress of Activity Theory. Lahti, Finland.

Cole, M. and Cole, S. (1989). *The development of children*. New York: Scientific American Books.

Cole, M., Hood, L. and McDermott, R.P. (1978). *Ecological niche-picking: ecological invalidity as an axiom of experimental, cognitive psychology*. Working paper of the Laboratory of Comparative Human Cognition. New York: Rockefeller University.

Cole, M., Hood, L. and McDermott, R.P. (1979). *Ecological niche-picking: ecological invalidity as an axiom of experimental, cognitive psychology*. Working paper of the Laboratory of Comparative Human Cognition. New York, Rockefeller University, unpublished manuscript.

Corson, S.A. (1976). *Psychiatry and psychology in the Soviet Union*. New York: Plenum.

Davydov, V.V. and Markova, A. (1983). A concept of educational activity for children. *Soviet psychology, 21*, 50–76.

Davydov, V.V. and Radzikhovskii, L.A. (1985). Vygotsky's theory and the activity-oriented approach in psychology. In J. V. Wertsch (Ed.), *Culture, communication and cognition: Vygotskian perspectives*. Cambridge: Cambridge University Press, pp. 35–65.

Deleuze, G. and Guattari, F. (1977). *Anti-Oedipus: capitalism and schizophrenia*. New York: Viking Press.

Donaldson, M. (1978). *Children's minds*. New York: W.W. Norton & Co.

Engestrom, Y., Hakkarainen, P. and Hedegaard, M. (1984). On the methodological basis of research in teaching and learning. In M. Hedegaard, P. Hakkarainen and Y. Engestrom (Eds), *Learning and teaching on a scientific basis*. Aarhus, Denmark: Aarhus University, pp. 119–89.

Erikson, E. (1977). *Toys and reasons: stages in the ritualization of experience*. New York: W. W. Norton & Co.

Eynard, R. and Walkerdine, V. (1981). *The practice of reason: investigations into the teaching and learning of mathematics in the early years of schooling*.

Vol. 2: Girls and mathematics. London: Thomas Coram Research Unit and the Leverhulme Trust.

Fanon, F. (1963). *The wretched of the earth.* New York: Grove Press.

Fanon, F. (1967). *Black skin, white masks.* New York: Grove Press.

Feyerabend, P. (1978). *Against method: outline of an anarchistic theory of knowledge.* London: Verso.

Forman, E. and McPhail, J. (1989). Positive benefits of peer interaction – a Vygotskian critique. Paper presented at American Educational Research Association Conference, San Francisco.

Foucault, M. (1978). *The history of sexuality. Vol. 1: an introduction.* New York: Pantheon.

Freire, P. (1972). *Pedagogy of the oppressed.* New York: Herder and Herder.

Fromm, E. (1973). *The crisis of psychoanalysis.* Harmondsworth: Penguin.

Fukuyama, F. (1989, Summer). The end of history? *The national interest, 16,* 3–18.

Fulani, L. (1988). Poor women of color do great therapy. In L. Fulani (Ed.), *The psychopathology of everyday racism and sexism.* New York: Harrington Park Press, pp. 111–20.

Gilligan, C. (1982). *In a different voice: psychological theory and women's development.* Cambridge, MA: Harvard University Press.

Gödel, K. (1962). *On formally undecidable propositions of Principia Mathematica and related systems.* London: Oliver and Boyd.

Goffman, E. (1962). *Asylums.* Chicago, IL: Adline Publishing Co.

Goffman, E. (1971). *Relations in public.* New York: Harper Colophon Books.

Goodman, Y.M. and Goodman, K.S. (1990). Vygotsky in a whole-language perspective. In L. Moll (Ed.), *Vygotsky and education.* Cambridge: Cambridge University Press, pp. 223–50.

Gornick, V. and Moran, B.K. (1972). *Woman in sexist society.* New York: NAL-Dutton.

Gouldner, A.W. (1970). *The coming crisis in Western sociology.* New York: Basic Books.

Green, D. and Newman, F. (1986). The divine right of white Americans: Eurocentric ideology in the United States. *Practice: The journal of politics, economics, psychology, sociology and culture, 4*(2), 8–26. Reprinted in L. Holzman and H. Polk (Eds), (1988), *History is the cure: a social therapy reader.* New York: Practice Press, pp. 103–25.

Greenfield, P.M. (1978). Structural parallels between language and action in development. In A. Lock (Ed.), *Action, gesture and symbol: the emergence of language.* New York: Academic Press.

Greenfield, P.M. (1984). A theory of the teacher in the learning activities of everyday life. In B. Rogoff and J. Lave (Eds), *Everyday cognition: its development in social context.* Cambridge, MA: Harvard University Press, pp. 117–38.

Gruber, H.E. and Voneche, J.J. (1977). *The essential Piaget.* New York: Basic Books.

Habermas, J. (1971). *Knowledge and human interests.* Boston, MA: Beacon Press.

Haley, J. (1984). *Ordeal therapy: unusual ways to change behavior.* San Francisco: Jossey-Bass.

Harding, S. and Hintikka, M.B. (Eds), (1983). *Discovering reality: feminist perspectives on epistemology, metaphysics, methodology, and philosophy of science.* Dordrecht: D. Reidel Publishing Company.

Harris-Schmidt, G. and McNamee, G.D. (1986). Children as authors and actors: literacy development through basic activity. *Child language, teaching and therapy, 2(1)*, 63–73.

Hedegaard, M. (1990). The zone of proximal development as basis for instruction. In L. Moll (Ed.), *Vygotsky and education.* Cambridge: Cambridge University Press, pp. 349–71.

Holzman, L. (1985). Pragmatism and dialectical materialism in language development. In K.E. Nelson (Ed.), *Children's language, Vol. 5*, pp. 345–67.

Holzman, L. (1986). Ecological validity revisited. *Practice: the journal of politics, economics, psychology, sociology and culture, 4(1)*, 95–135.

Holzman, L. (1987). Humanism and Soviet psychology: friends or foes? *Practice: the journal of politics, economics, psychology, sociology and culture, 5(2)*, 6–28. Reprinted in L. Holzman and H. Polk (Eds), (1988), *History is the cure: a social therapy reader.* New York: Practice Press, pp. 103–25.

Holzman, L. (1989). Vygotsky in Harlem, Somerset and on Capitol Hill. *Newsletter of the Association of Progressive Helping Professionals, 1*, 1–3.

Holzman, L. (1990). Lev and let Lev: a dialogue on the life and work of renowned psychologist/methodologist Lev Vygotsky. *Practice: the magazine of psychology and political economy, 7*, 11–23.

Holzman, L. (1992). When learning leads development: building a humane learning environment. *The community psychologist, 25(3)*, 9–11.

Holzman, L. and Newman, F. (1979). *The practice of method: an introduction to the foundations of social therapy.* New York: Practice Press.

Holzman, L. and Newman, F. (1985). History as an anti-paradigm: work in progress toward a developmental and clinical psychology. *Practice: the journal of politics, economics, psychology, sociology and culture, 3(3)*, 60–72. Reprinted in L. Holzman and H. Polk (Eds), (1988), *History is the cure: a social therapy reader.* New York: Practice Press, pp. 55–67.

Holzman, L. and Newman, F. (1987). Language and thought about history. In M. Hickmann (Ed.), *Social and functional approaches to language and thought.* London: Academic Press, pp. 109–21.

Holzman, L. and Polk, H. (Eds), (1988). *History is the cure: a social therapy reader.* New York: Practice Press.

Hood, L. (1977). A longitudinal study of the development of the expression of causal relations in complex sentences. Unpublished PhD dissertation, Columbia University.

Hood, L. and Bloom, L. (1979). What, when and how about why: a longitudinal study of early expressions of causality. *Monographs of the Society for Research in Child Development, 44*. Reprinted in L. Bloom *et al.* (1991), *Language development from two to three.* Cambridge: Cambridge University Press, pp. 335–73.

Hood, L., Fiess, K. and Aron, J. (1982). Growing up explained: Vygotskians look at the language of causality. In C. Brainerd and M. Pressley (Eds), *Verbal processes in children.* New York: Springer-Verlag, pp. 265–85.

Reprinted in *Practice: the journal of politics, economics, psychology, sociology and culture*, (1983), *1(2–3)*, 231–52.

Hood, L., McDermott, R.P. and Cole, M. (1980). 'Let's try to make it a nice day' – Some not so simple ways. *Discourse processes, 3*, 155–68. Reprinted in *Practice: the journal of politics, economics, psychology, sociology and culture*, (1986), *4(1)*, 103–16.

Ingleby, D. (1974). The psychology of child psychology. In M.P.M. Richards (Ed.), *The integration of a child into a social world*. Cambridge: Cambridge University Press, pp. 295–308.

Ingleby, D. (1987). Psychoanalysis and ideology. In J.M. Broughton (Ed.), *Critical theories of psychological development*. New York: Plenum, pp. 177–210.

Jacoby, R. (1975). *Social amnesia*. Boston, MA: Beacon Press.

James, W. (1916). *Pragmatism: a new name for some old ways of thinking*. New York: Longsmans, Green.

Joravsky, D. (1987). L.S. Vygotskii: The muffled deity of Soviet psychology. In M.G. Ash and W.R. Woodward (Eds). *Psychology in twentieth-century thought and society*. Cambridge, Cambridge University Press, pp. 189–211.

Joravsky, D. (1989). *Russian psychology: a critical history*. Oxford: Basil Blackwell.

Kant, I. (1929). *Critique of pure reason*. New York: St Martin's Press.

Kaye, K. (1982). *The mental and social life of babies*. Chicago, IL: University of Chicago Press.

Keller, E.F. and Grontkowski, C.R. (1983). The mind's eye. In S. Harding and M.B. Hintikka (Eds), *Discovering reality: feminist perspectives on epistemology, metaphysics, methodology, and philosophy of science*. Dordrecht: D. Reidel Publishing Company, pp. 207–24.

King, N. (1977). The hidden curriculum and the socialization of the kindergarten school. Unpublished PhD dissertation, University of Wisconsin.

Kozulin, A. (1984). *Psychology in utopia: toward a social history of Soviet psychology*. Cambridge, MA: MIT Press.

Kozulin, A. (1986a). The concept of activity in Soviet psychology. *American psychologist, 41(3)*, 264–74.

Kozulin, A. (1986b). Vygotsky in context. In L.S. Vygotsky, *Thought and language*. Cambridge, MA: MIT Press, pp. xi–lvi.

Kozulin, A. (1990). *Vygotsky's psychology: a biography of ideas*. Cambridge, MA: Harvard University Press.

Kuhn, T. (1962). *The structure of scientific revolutions*. Chicago, IL: University of Chicago Press.

Labov, W. (1972). *Language in the inner city*. Philadelphia, PA: University of Pennsylvania Press.

LaCerva, C. (1992). Talking about talking about sex: the organization of possibilities. In J. T. Sears (Ed.), *Sexuality and the curriculum: the politics and practices of sexuality education*. New York: Teachers College Press, pp. 124–38.

Laing, R.D. (1983). *The politics of experience*. New York: Pantheon.

Lasch, C. (1976). The family as a haven in a heartless world. *Salmagundi*, *35*.

Leont'ev, A.N. (1978). *Activity, consciousness, and personality*. Englewood Cliffs, NJ: Prentice Hall.

Levitan, K. (1982). *One is not born a personality: profiles of Soviet education psychologists*. Moscow: Progress Publishers.

Lewin, K. (1943). Defining the 'field at a given time.' *Psychological review*, *50*, 292–310.

Lewis, C.I. (1990) *Mind and the world order: outline of a theory of knowledge*. New York: Dover.

Lichtman, R. (1977). Marx and Freud, part three: Marx's theory of human nature. *Socialist revolution*, *7(6)*, 37–78.

Lock, A. (Ed.), (1978). *Action, gesture and symbol: the emergence of language*. New York: Academic Press.

Lovejoy, A.O. (1960). *The revolt against dualism: an inquiry concerning the existence of ideas*. Second edition. LaSalle, IL: The Open Court Publishing Co.

Luria, A.R. (1978). Psychoanalysis as a system of monistic psychology. *Soviet psychology*, *16*, 7–45. Reprinted in M. Cole (Ed.), (1978), *The selected writings of A.R. Luria*. White Plains, NY: Sharpe.

Luria, A.R. (1979). *The making of mind: a personal account of Soviet psychology*. Cambridge, MA: Harvard University Press.

Luxemburg, R. (1968). *The accumulation of capital*. New York: Monthly Review Press.

Luxemburg, R. (1972). *The accumulation of capital – an anti-critique*. New York: Monthly Review Press.

Lyons, J. (1981). *Language and linguistics: an introduction*. Cambridge: Cambridge University Press.

McDermott, R.P. (1976). Kids make sense: an ethnographic account of the interactional management of success and failure in one first-grade classroom. Unpublished PhD dissertation, Department of Anthropology, Stanford University.

McDermott, R.P. (1987). The acquisition of a child by a learning disability. Unpublished manuscript, Stanford University.

McLane, J.B. (1990). Writing as a social process. In L. Moll (Ed.), *Vygotsky and education*. Cambridge: Cambridge University Press, pp. 304–18.

McLane, J.B. and McNamee, G.D. (1990). *Early literacy*. Cambridge, MA: Harvard University Press.

McNamee, G.D. (1987). The social origins of narrative skills. In M. Hickmann (Ed.), *Social and functional approaches to language and thought*. New York: Academic Press, pp. 287–304.

McNamee, G.D. (1990). Learning to read and write in an inner-city setting: a longitudinal study of community change. In L. Moll (Ed.), *Vygotsky and education*. Cambridge: Cambridge University Press, pp. 287–303.

McNamee, G.D., McLane, J.B,. Cooper, P.M. and Kerwin, S.M. (1985). Cognition and affect in early literacy development. *Early childhood development and cure*, *20*, 229–44.

Marcuse, H. (1962). *Eros and civilization*. Boston, MA: Beacon Press.

Marx, K. (1964). *Economic and philosophical manuscripts of 1844*. New York: International Publishers.

Marx, K. (1967). *Capital. Vol. 1*. New York: International Publishers.

Marx, K. (1971). *Grundrisse: foundations of the critique of political economy*. New York: Harper & Row.

Marx, K. (1973). Theses on Feuerbach. In K. Marx and F. Engels, *The German ideology*. New York: International Publishers, pp. 121–3.

Marx K. and Engels, F. (1973). *The German ideology*. New York: International Publishers.

Merleau-Ponty, M. (1964). *Sense and non-sense*. Evanston, IL: Northwestern University Press.

Messer, D. (1991). Review of *The many faces of imitation in language learning*. *Journal of child language, 18*, 227–9.

Minick, N. (1987). The development of Vygotsky's thought: an introduction. In L.S. Vygotsky, *The collected works of L.S. Vygotsky. Vol. 1*. New York: Plenum, pp. 17–36.

Moerk, E.L. (1977). Processes and products of imitation: Additional evidence that imitation is progressive. *Journal of psycholinguistic research, 6*, 187–202.

Moll, L. (Ed.), (1990). *Vygotsky and education: instructional implications and applications of socio-cultural psychology*. Cambridge: Cambridge University Press.

Moll, L. and Greenberg, J. (1990). Creating zones of possibilities: combining social contexts for instruction. In L. Moll (Ed.), *Vygotsky and education*. Cambridge: Cambridge University Press, pp. 319–48.

Moshman, D., Glover, J.A. and Bruning, R.H. (1987). *Developmental psychology: a topical approach*. Boston, MA: Little, Brown & Co.

Moulton, J. (1983). A paradigm of philosophy: the adversary method. In S. Harding and M.B. Hintikka (Eds), *Discovering reality: feminist perspectives on epistemology, metaphysics, methodology, and philosophy of science*. Dordrecht: D. Reidel Publishing Company, pp. 149–64.

Neff, P. (1984). *Tough love: how parents can deal with drug abuse*. Nashville, TN: Abingdon.

Newman, D., Griffin, P. and Cole, M. (1984). Social constraints in laboratory and classrooom tasks. In B. Rogoff and J. Lave (Eds), *Everyday cognition: its development in social context*. Cambridge, MA: Harvard University Press, pp. 171–93.

Newman, D., Griffin, P. and Cole, M. (1989). *The construction zone: working for cognitive change in school*. Cambridge: Cambridge University Press.

Newman, F. (1978). *Practical-critical activities*. New York: Institute for Social Therapy and Research. Reprinted in *Practice: the journal of politics, economics, psychology, sociology and culture* (1983), *1(2–3)*, 52–101.

Newman, F. (1983). Talkin transference. *Practice: the journal of politics, economics, psychology, sociology and culture, 1(1)*, 10–31. Reprinted in F. Newman (1991), *The myth of psychology*. New York: Castillo International, pp. 16–44.

Newman, F. (1987). Crisis normalization and depression: a new approach to a growing epidemic. *Practice: the journal of politics, economics, psychology, sociology and culture*, 5(3), 14–32. Reprinted in F. Newman (1991), *The myth of psychology*. New York: Castillo International, pp. 79–96.

Newman, F. (1989a). Seven theses on revolutionary art. *Stono*, 1(1), 7.

Newman, F. (1989b). Panic in America. *Practice: the journal of politics, economics, psychology, sociology and culture*, 6(3), 43–67. Reprinted in F. Newman (1991), *The myth of psychology*. New York: Castillo International, pp. 97–110.

Newman, F. (1991a). The patient as revolutionary. In F. Newman, *The myth of psychology*. New York: Castillo International, pp. 3–15.

Newman, F. (1991b). Community as a heart in a havenless world. In F. Newman, *The myth of psychology*. New York: Castillo International, pp. 140–57.

Newman, F. (1992). Surely Castillo is left – but is it right or wrong? Nobdy knows. *The drama review*, 36(3), 24–7.

Newson, J. (1978). Dialogue and development. In A. Lock (Ed.), *Action, gesture and symbol: the emergence of language*. New York: Academic Press, pp. 31–42.

Paley, V. (1984). *Wally's stories*. Cambridge, MA: Harvard University Press.

Papert, S. (1980). *Mindstorms: children, computers and powerful ideas*. New York: Basic Books.

Peirce, C.S. (1957). *Essays in the philosophy of science*. New York: The Liberal Arts Press.

Petrovsky, A. (1990). *Psychology in the Soviet Union: a historical outline*. Moscow: Progress Publishers.

Piaget, J. (1929). *The child's conception of the world*. London: Kegan Paul.

Piaget, J. (1955). *The language and thought of the child*. London: Kegan Paul.

Piaget, J. (1962). *Play, dreams and imitation in childhood*. New York: W. W. Norton & Co.

Piaget, J. (1968). *Judgement and reasoning in the child*. Totowa, NJ: Littlefield, Adams.

Polkinghorne, D. (1983). *Methodology for the human sciences*. Albany, NY: State University of New York Press.

Prigogine, I. (1984). *Order out of chaos: man's new dialogue with nature*. Toronto: Bantam. [First published in French under the title *La nouvelle alliance*.]

Quine, W.V.O. (1961). Two dogmas of empiricism. In W.V.O. Quine, *From a logical point of view*. Second edition. New York: Harper & Row, pp. 20–46.

Ratner, C. (1991). *Vygotsky's sociohistorical psychology and its contemporary applications*. New York: Plenum.

Ratner, N. and Bruner, J.S. (1978). Games, social exchange and the acquisition of language. *Journal of child language*, 5, 391–401.

Reich, W. (1970). *The mass psychology of fascism*. New York: Farrar, Straus & Giroux.

Riegel, K.F. (1979). *Foundations of dialectical psychology*. New York: Academic Press.

Rodney, W. (1974). *How Europe underdeveloped Africa*. Washington, DC: Howard University Press.

Rogoff, B. (1990). *Apprenticeship in thinking: cognitive development in social context*. New York: Oxford University Press.

Rogoff, B. and Gardner, W. (1984). Guidance in cognitive development: an examination of mother–child instruction. In B. Rogoff and J. Lave (Eds), *Everyday cognition: its development in social context*. Cambridge, MA: Harvard University Press, pp. 95–116.

Rogoff, B. and Lave, J. (Eds), (1984). *Everyday cognition: its development in social context*. Cambridge, MA: Harvard University Press.

Rosa, A. and Montero, I. (1990). The historical context of Vygotsky's work: a sociohistorical approach. In L. Moll (Ed.), *Vygotsky and education*. Cambridge: Cambridge University Press, pp. 59–88.

Russell, B. (1912). *The problems of philosophy*. London: Oxford University Press.

Sacks, H. (1974). An analysis of the course of a joke's telling in conversation. In R. Bauman and J. Sherzer (Eds), *Explorations in the ethnography of speaking*. New York: Cambridge University Press, pp. 337–53.

Schreiber, L.L. (1987). Vygotsky and Montessori: the process of learning in the preschooler. *American Montessori Society*, 5–11.

Seve, L. (1978). *Man in Marxist theory and the psychology of personality*. Brighton: Harvester Press.

Slavin, R.E. (1983). *Cooperative learning*. New York: Longman.

Slobin, D. (1973). Cognitive prerequisites for the development of grammar. In C. Ferguson and D. Slobin (Eds), *Studies of child language development*. New York: Holt, Rinehart & Winston, pp. 175–208.

Speidel, G.E. and Nelson, K.E. (1989). *The many faces of imitation in language learning*. New York: Springer-Verlag.

Strickland, G. and Holzman, L. (1988). Developing poor and minority children as learners with the Barbara Taylor School Educational Model. *Journal of negro education*, *58(3)*, 383–98.

Sutton-Smith, B. (1976). *The psychology of play*. Salem, NH: Ayer Co. Publishers.

Szasz, T. (1961). *The myth of mental illness: foundations of a theory of personal conduct*. New York: Harper & Row.

Tharp, R.G. and Gallimore, R. (1988). *Rousing minds to life: teaching, learning and schooling in social context*. Cambridge: Cambridge University Press.

Thomas, R.M. (1992). *Comparing theories of child development*. Third edition. Belmont, CA: Wadsworth Publishing Co.

Travarthan, C. and Hubley, P. (1978). Secondary intersubjectivity: confidence, confiding and acts of meaning in the first year. In A. Lock (Ed.), *Action, gesture and symbol: the emergence of language*. New York: Academic Press, pp. 183–229.

Tudge, J. (1990). Vygotsky, the zone of proximal development, and peer collaboration: implications for classroom practice. In L. Moll (Ed.), *Vygotsky and education*. Cambridge: Cambridge University Press, pp. 155–72.

Valsiner, J. (1988). *Developmental psychology in the Soviet Union*. Bloomington, IN: Indiana University Press.

Van der Veer, R. and Valsiner, J. (1991). *Understanding Vygotsky: a quest for synthesis*. Oxford: Basil Blackwell.

Van der Veer, R. and Van IJzendoorn, M.H. (1985). Vygotsky's theory of the higher psychological processes: some criticisms. *Human development*, *28*, 1–9.

Vasta, R., Haith, M.M. and Miller, S.A. (1992). *Child psychology: the modern science*. New York: John Wiley & Sons.

Vickers, J.M. (1991). Objectivity and ideology in the human sciences. *Topoi*, *10(2)*, 175–86.

Volosinov, V.N. (1987). *Freudianism: a critical sketch*. Bloomington, IN: Indiana University Press.

Vygotsky, L.S. (1962). *Thought and language*. Cambridge, MA: MIT Press.

Vygotsky, L.S. (1978). *Mind in society*. Cambridge, MA: Harvard University Press.

Vygotsky, L.S. (1982). The historical meaning of the crisis in psychology. In A.R. Luria and M.G. Iaroshevski (Eds), *L.S. Vygotsky: collected works. Vol I*. Moscow: Pedagogika. [In Russian.]

Vygotsky, L.S. (1986). *Thought and language*. Newly revised. Cambridge, MA: MIT Press.

Vygotsky, L.S. (1987). *The collected works of L.S. Vygotsky. Vol. 1*. New York: Plenum.

Vygotsky, L.S. (in press). *Problems of abnormal psychology and learning disabilities: the fundamentals of defectology*. New York: Plenum.

Walkerdine, V. (1984). Developmental psychology and the child-centered pedagogy: the insertion of Piaget into early education. In J. Henriques, W. Hollway, C. Urwin, C. Venn and V. Walkerdine, *Changing the subject: psychology, social regulation and subjectivity*. London: Methuen, pp. 153–202.

Walkerdine, V. (1988). *The mastery of reason: cognitive development and the production of rationality*. London: Routledge.

Watzlawick, P., Beavin, J. and Jackson, D. (1967). *Pragmatics of human communication: a study of interactional patterns, pathologies and paradoxes*. New York: W. W. Norton & Co.

Watzlawick, P., Weakland, J. and Fisch, R. (1974). *Change: principles of problem formation and problem resolution*. New York: W. W. Norton & Co.

Wertsch, J.V. (Ed.), (1981). *The concept of activity in Soviet psychology*. Armonk, NY: M.E. Sharpe.

Wertsch, J.V. (1985). *Vygotsky and the social formation of mind*. Cambridge, MA: Harvard University Press.

Wertsch, J.V. (1991). *Voices of the mind: a sociocultural approach to mediated action*. Cambridge, MA: Harvard University Press.

Whitehead, A.N. and Russell, B. (1962). *Principia mathematica*. Cambridge: Cambridge University Press.

Wittgenstein, L. (1953). *Philosophical investigations*. Oxford: Basil Blackwell.

Wittgenstein, L. (1961). *Tractatus logico-philosophicus*. London: Routledge.

Wittgenstein, L. (1965). *The blue and brown books*. New York: Harper Torchbooks.

Wood, D., Bruner, J. and Ross, G. (1976). The role of tutoring in problem-solving. *Journal of child psychology and psychiatry*, *17*, 89–100.

Wood, D., McMahon, L. and Cranstoun, Y. (1980). *Working with under fives*. London: Grant McIntyre.

Yaroshevsky, M. (1989). *Lev Vygotsky*. Moscow: Progress Publishers.

Yaroshevsky, M. (1990). *A history of psychology*. Moscow: Progress Publishers.

Name index

Subject index